THE RAGHUVANSA

THE RAGHUVANSA

SIVANATH SHASTRI

GYAN

Published by

Gyan Publishing House
5, Ansari Road
Daryaganj, New Delhi-110002
Phone: 011-47034999, 9811692060
E-mail: books@gyanbooks.com

Distribution Network
gyanbooks.com
India, USA, Canada, UK, Australia

ISBN: 978-93-7225-282-8 (PB)

First Published, 1888

2nd Impression 2025

Printed at: Gyan Press, Delhi.

THE RAGHUVANSA
Author: SIVANATH SHASTRI

THE

RAGHUVANSA

BY

KALIDASA

(FIRST FOUR CANTOS)

WITH COPIOUS NOTES, EXPLANATORY GRAMMATICAL & CRITICAL AND ENGLISH & BENGALI TRANSLATIONS.

BY

SIVANATH SASTRI M. A.

PROFESSOR OF SANSKRIT, LOGIC & PHILOSOPHY, CITY COLLEGE.

CALCUTTA:

S. K. LAHIRI & Co.

PUBLISHERS & BOOKSELLERS.

1888.

INTRODUCTION

THE present edition of the first four cantos of Raghuvansa, is intended for students preparing for the First Examination in Arts of the Calcutta University. Hence the reader will find in it many things which are useless to more advanced readers.

The commentary of Mallinath is too well known to need any commendation. Specially his commentary on Raghuvansa has this great recommendation in its favour, that it is brief, yet sufficiently illustrative. I have made it still more intelligible to the student reader, whose knowledge of Sanskrit is limited, by lopping off as it were, almost all the paranthetical sentences, where Mallinath explains points of grammar. In some cases I have placed these separate explanations in the foot-notes under his name, but as a general rule I have omitted them altogether, to give both the students and their teachers a little work, in finding out their grammatical constructions for themselves. A clever teacher can teach almost all the rules of Sanskrit grammar orally as he goes on explaining verse after verse of the text book, and grammar thus taught is taught more effectively than by making the student get by heart, at considerable trouble to his memory, all the dry niceties of those rules, taught apart from actual applications. No good Sanskrit teacher should neglect to avail of every opportunity of explaining a new point of grammar, as it arises during the course of a lesson. Thus the student will be equipped with a workable stock of grammatical knowledge, during these two years, which will be really valuable to him in subsequent years.

In the additional notes I have taken care not to make them redundant. To try to improve upon points, noticed and explained by Mallinatha is sheer pedantry. I have tried to explain passages, left unexplained by that commentator. These additional explanations, again, I have taken care not to make too many; for I strongly object to the practice of modern key-makers of doing every thing for the student, and leaving him no intellectual work to be done. This practice I fear, is doing material injury to the cause of successful and sound education. When the student finds everything ready made to his hand, he has little or no incentive to work. So the power of penetrating into a subject is not developed in him; and he becomes an intellectual looser. While trying to make the key quite complete in itself and making it really useful gloss for the student of Raghuvansa, I have tried, as much as I could, to avoid thiss ystem, and have left some thing for the student himself to solve or to have explained by his teacher. This is a novel practice to some extent; and the dullards amongst them will most likely pass these over, never caring to bother their teacher; but the industrious and intelligent amongst them will find themselves more than amply repaid for the little trouble.

As to the translations, I have tried to make them brief and expressive. The student will perhaps notice slight differences of expressions between the Bengali and English renderings, as if they come from two different persons. The reason is that they have been made at two different times. In undertaking the English translation I have been convinced of the real difficulty that lies in the way of rendering the thoughts of an old and now defunct race of writers into the language of another race, so unlike in their traditions, usages, and modes of life. The English rendering as it is, is perhaps, unintelligible in many parts, to an English reader. The reason is to be found in the difference of national habits and associations. I have tried my best, with the aid of dictionaries, to make the English rendering a good one, but owing to the poverty of my knowledge of English have not entirely succeeded. The critical reader will notice many defects, which, I hope, he will judge indulgently.

It was a part of my original intention to write a short dissertation on Kalidasa, and the times and on his place in Sanskrit literature, simply to help in creating in the student a taste for the literary and poetic beauty of the work appointed for his study. For unless such a taste is created in him, it is in vain that one of the grandest achievements, of the poetical genius of our greatest poet, has been placed in his hands. Many a reader will, perhaps, be startled to hear the Raghuvansa described as one of the grandest achievements of Kalidasas' genius ; for general current of opinion amongst Indian scholars, ascribes to अभिज्ञानशकुन्तलं the first place amongst his productions. There is a current Sanskrit saying :

कालिदासस्य सर्व्वस्वमभिज्ञानशकुन्तलम् ।
तत्रापि च चतुर्थोऽङ्को यत्र याति शकुन्तला ॥

Which means :—अभिज्ञानशकुन्तलं is Kalidasa's greatest treasure, his all in all ; and in it again that portion in the 4th Act, where Saukuntala is being "sent away." The critic who composed that couplet must have had a nice discriminating eye for moral beauty. Indeed we have seldom met within the whole range of Sanskrit literature, with lovelier scenes than those that take place at the time of Sakuntala's going. They show, what marvellous beauty can a master-painter produce out of the common every day materials of human life. Let the reader who has read अभिज्ञानशकुन्तलं but transfer himself in imagination to that quiet river bank, the favourite haunt of large-eyed deer, and the loved retreat of Saukuntala and her maiden friends, during the declining hours of the day, and what scene does he find there. He finds the solitary Rishi Kanwa, standing alone, and wondering that there was so much love in that old heart of his. He makes a new discovery that he loves Saukuntala, though not his own daughter and only a foundling picked up in the forest. Let him take his stand on that solitary river-bank and listen to what old Kanwa says :—

यास्यत्यद्य शकुन्तलेति हृदयं संस्पृष्टमुत्कण्ठया
अन्तर्बाष्पभरोपरोधि गदितं चिन्ताजडं दर्शनम् ।
वैक्लव्यं मम तावदीदृशमपि स्नेहादरण्यौकसः
पीड्यन्ते गृहिणः कथं नु तनयाविश्लेषदुःखैर्नवैः ॥

Has not that a sort of moral beauty ennobling to to our hearts. However this is a digression. Whilst not disputing the claims of Saukuntala to be regarded as the first amongst the productions of the poet's genius, the Raghuvansa can be ranked as the next best. There are special considerations in its favour. In his other works the poet confines himself to a single or a few incidents of history ; and accordingly has room enough for the play of his imagination. But in Raghuvansa, he attempts a rapid sketch of the history of an illustrious line of princes. It partly resembles a historical synopsis in its character ; such works are calculated to be dull and tedious full of rapid narration of facts and events. But that facts and events manupulated by a master charmer have assumed quite another shape. Within the restricted limits he has prescribed to himself, he has found room enough for the play of his imagination. The student need not go through the whole book ; within these four cantos he will find enough to illustrate what I have said above. The description of Dilip, and his manly and regal virtues for instance, of his visit to Basista's forest and his vows and austerities how life-like and real, how morally elevating to heart and soul! But I have no time to carry out my original intention of writing a dissertation. Having had to leave the country rather unexpectedly, I must postpone the execution of that intention to some other time.

On board *SS. Mirzapore.*
The 17*th April* 1888.

S. N. Sastri.

रघुवंशम् ।

प्रथमः सर्गः ।

वागर्थाविव * सम्पृक्तौ वागर्थप्रतिपत्तये ।
जगतः † पितरौ वन्दे पार्वतीपरमेश्वरौ ॥१॥

वागर्थाविति । वागर्थौ इव, शब्दार्थौ इव, सम्पृक्तौ नित्यसम्बद्धौ, जगतः लोकस्य, पितरौ, माता च पिता च पितरौ, पार्वती च परमेश्वरश्च पार्वतीपरमेश्वरौ, वागर्थप्रतिपत्तये शब्दार्थयोः सम्यग्ज्ञानार्थं, वन्दे अभिवादये ॥ १ ॥

বাক্য এবং অর্থ যেমন পরস্পরের সহিত চিরসম্বদ্ধ, সেইরূপ যাঁহারা পরস্পরের সহিত অভিন্নভাবে মিলিত, সেই জগতের জনক-জননী হর-পার্ব্বতীকে, বাক্যার্থের সম্যক্ জ্ঞান লাভের উদ্দেশে, বন্দনা করি ॥ ১ ॥

---

1. For the proper comprehension of words, and their meanings, I bow down to Parvati, and Siva—the greatest of the gods—the divine pair, who are the parents of creation and the union between whom is as close as the one subsisting between a word and its meaning.

---

* सम्पृक्तौ—सं+पृच्—क्तौ, यदा, आत्मनेपदी ।—indicating relationship, formed by क्तः ।

† पितरौ—माता च पिता च—पितरौ, एकशेषो द्वन्द्वः, according to पिता मात्रा ।१।२।७०।—*Panini.*

क्व सूर्य्यप्रभवो वंशः क्व चाल्पविषया मतिः।
*तितीर्षुर्दुस्तरं मोहादुडुपेनास्मि सागरम् ॥२॥
† मन्दः कवियशःप्रार्थी गमिष्याम्युपहास्यताम्।

सम्प्रति कविः स्वाहङ्कारं परिहरति क्व सूर्य्येत्यादिश्लोकद्वयेन, क्वेति। प्रभवति अस्मात् इति प्रभवः, कारणम्, सूर्य्यः प्रभवो यस्य सः सूर्य्यप्रभवः वंशः क्व, अल्पः विषयः ज्ञेयोऽर्थो यस्याः सा मे मतिः प्रज्ञा च क्व? (द्वौ क्वशब्दौ महदन्तरं सूचयतः) सूर्य्यवंशमाकलयितुं न शक्नोमीत्यर्थः। तथाहि दुस्तरं सागरं, मोहात् अज्ञानात्, उडुपेन प्लवेन, तितीर्षुः तरीतुम् इच्छुः, अस्मि भवामि ॥ २ ॥

मन्द इति। किन्तु मन्दः मूढः, तथापि कवियशःप्रार्थी कवीनां यशः काव्यनिर्माणेन जातं तत्प्रार्थनाशीलः, अहं प्रांशुना उन्नतपुरुषेण,

সূর্য্যসম্ভূত বংশই বা কোথায়, আর আমার স্বল্প পরিমিত জ্ঞানই বা কোথায়? আমি যেন অজ্ঞতাবশতঃ সামান্য ভেলার সাহায্যে সাগর উত্তীর্ণ হইবার ইচ্ছা করিতেছি ॥ ২ ॥

যে ফল দীর্ঘাকৃতি পুরুষেরই হস্তগ্রাহ্য, লোভবশতঃ তাহা পাড়িবার নিমিত্ত উর্দ্ধবাহু হইয়া বামন যেমন হাস্যাস্পদ হয়, মূঢ়মতি

How great is the dynasty of the princes, who trace their origin to the sun, and how little my intellect, with its limited range of subjects! Methinks! from sheer ignorance I am bent upon crossing the ocean with a raft.

3. I am wanting in intelligence; yet I am covetous of the

* (1) तितीर्षुः—Desiderative form of तॄ with उः according to सनाशंस भिक्ष उः (३।२।१६८)—*Panini*.

† मन्दः—Here it means stupid or slow in understanding, compare it with another sense in which it has been used in

प्रांशुलभ्ये फले लोभात्* उद्बाहुरिव वामनः ॥३॥
अथवा कृतवाग्द्वारे वंशेऽस्मिन् पूर्वसूरिभिः ।
मणौ † वज्रसमुत्कीर्णे सूत्रस्येवास्ति मे गतिः ॥४॥

—लभ्ये प्राप्ये, फले फलविषये, लोभात् उद्बाहुः फलग्रहणाय उच्छ्रित-हस्तः, वामनः खर्व्वः इव, उपहास्यताम् उपहासविषयताम्, गमिष्यामि प्राप्स्यामि ॥ २ ॥

अथवेति । अथवा पूर्वैः सूरिभिः कविभिः वाल्मीकादिभिः, कृतवाग्द्वारे कृतं रामायणादिप्रबन्धरूपा या वाक् सैव द्वारं प्रवेशो यस्य तस्मिन्, अस्मिन् सूर्य्यप्रभवे वंशे कुले, वज्रेण अयोवेधकसूची-विशेषेण, समुत्कीर्णे विद्धे, मणौ रत्ने सूत्रस्य इव मे मम गतिः सञ्चारः अस्ति ॥ ४ ॥

আমি তেমনি কবি-প্রাপ্য যশের কামনা করিয়া উপহাস-ভাজন হইব ॥ ৩ ॥

অথবা হীরক খণ্ডের দ্বারা কৃতছিদ্র কাচখণ্ডে সূত্র যেমন অনায়াসে প্রবিষ্ট হয়, সেইরূপ পূর্ব্ব কবিগণ যে বংশে বর্ণনার দ্বার খুলিয়া দিয়া গিয়াছেন, তাহাতে আমারও প্রবেশের পথ আছে ॥ ৪ ॥

fame of a poet ; by reason of which I shall make myself as ridiculous as a dwarf, who stretches up his little arm to pluck fruits, attainable only by tall men.

4. Or rather in this royal line, where the door for poetical description has been opened by preceding poets, there is also a way for me to enter ; just as there is a passage for the

---

the passage—दिशि मन्दायते तेजः दक्षिणस्यां रवेरपि—Verse 49 Canto IV.

* उद्बाहुः—उत्, उद्गतः बाहुः यस्य,—one whose arm has been lifted up.

† वज्रसमुत्कीर्णे—सम्+उत्+कॄ+क्तः, वेधनं—that which has been

सोऽहमाजन्मशुद्धानामाफलोदयकर्मणाम् ।
आसमुद्रक्षितीशानामानाकरथवर्त्मनाम् ॥ ५ ॥
यथाविधिहुताग्नीनां यथाकामार्चितार्थिनाम् ।
यथापराधदण्डानां यथाकालप्रबोधिनाम् ॥ ६ ॥

सोऽहमिति । सः अहं रघूणाम् अन्वयं वक्ष्ये इत्युत्तरेण सम्बन्धः । किंविधानां रघूणाम्? इत्यत उत्तराणि विशेषणानि योज्यानि । आजन्मनः जन्म आरभ्येत्यर्थः शुद्धानाम् आजन्मशुद्धानां, निषेकादिसर्वसंस्कारसम्पन्नानामित्यर्थः, आफलोदयम् आफलसिद्धेः कर्म येषां ते तथोक्ताः तेषां प्रारब्धान्तगामिनामित्यर्थः, आसमुद्रं क्षितेः ईशानां सार्वभौमानामित्यर्थः, आनाकं रथवर्त्म येषां ते तेषाम् इन्द्रसहचारिणामित्यर्थः ॥ ५ ॥

यथाविधीति । विधिम् अनतिक्रम्य यथाविधि, यथाविधि हुताः

অতএব যদিও আমার বাক্শক্তি অতি সামান্য, তথাপি রঘুবংশীয় রাজগণের গুণাবলী শ্রবণ করিয়া আমার চিত্ত চঞ্চল হইতেছে, সুতরাং রঘুদিগের বংশাবলী একবার বর্ণন করিব ;—যে বংশের রাজগণ আজন্ম বিশুদ্ধচরিত্র ছিলেন; যাঁহারা ফল প্রাপ্তি পর্য্যন্ত কোন সৎকার্য্য হইতে বিরত হইতেন না ; যাঁহাদের প্রভুত্বের সীমা সমুদ্র পর্য্যন্ত সমুদায় ক্ষিতিতলে ব্যাপ্ত হইয়াছিল ; যাঁহাদের রথমার্গ স্বর্গ পর্য্যন্ত বিস্তৃত

(tiniest piece of) thread, in the (hardest) piece of precious stone, previously bored by diamond.

5. The great virtues of the princes of the dynasty of the Raghus, coming to my ears, make it difficult for me to hold my peace, and I, though wanting in poetical powers, will yet describe their line -- a line of monarchs, who maintained the

---

bored, वज्र means a peice of diamond, मणि a precious stone.

त्यागाय सम्भृतार्थानां सत्याय * मितभाषिणाम् ।
यशसे विजिगीषूणां प्रजायै गृहमेधिनाम् ॥ ७ ॥

अग्नयो यैः तेषां, यथाकामम् अभिलाषम् अनतिक्रम्य अर्चितार्थिनां, यथापराधम् अपराधम् अनतिक्रम्य दण्डो येषां तेषां, यथाकालं कालम् अनतिक्रम्य प्रबोधिनां प्रबोधनशीलानाम् । षड्भिर्विशेषणैः देवताराधनातिथिसत्कारदण्डधरत्वप्रजापालनसमयज्ञत्वादीनि विवक्षितानि ॥ ६ ॥

त्यागायेति । त्यागाय सत्पात्रे विनियोगः त्यागः तस्मै, सम्भृतार्थानां न तु दुर्व्ययाय, सत्याय मितभाषिणां मितभाषणशीलानां न तु पराभवाय, यशसे कीर्त्तये, विजिगीषूणां विजेतुम् इच्छूनां न तु अर्थसंग्रहाय, प्रजायै सन्तानाय गृहमेधिनां न तु कामोपभोगाय, गृहैः दारैः मेधन्ते सङ्गच्छन्ते इति गृहमेधिनः । मेधृ सङ्गमे इति धातोर्णिनिः । एभिर्विशेषणैः परोपकारित्वं सत्यवचनत्वं यशःपरत्वं पितृणां शुद्धत्वञ्च विवक्षितानि ॥ ७ ॥

হইয়াছিল ; যাঁহারা শাস্ত্রোক্ত বিধির অনুসারে হোমাদি সম্পন্ন করিতেন ; প্রার্থিগণের সকল কামনা পূর্ণ করিতেন ; যাঁহারা অপরাধের অনুরূপ দণ্ড দান করিতেন ; যথা সময়ে শয্যা হইতে গাত্রোত্থান

purity of their lives from their birth ; whose undertakings were never given up till they were crowned with success ; who held sway over the whole earth bounded by the ocean ; whose chariot-wheels furrowed all the way from earth to heaven ; who were punctual in the performance of *home* in the fire ; who granted the prayers of all who sought their help ; whose punishments were proportionate to the crimes ;

---

* मितभाषिणां—मितं परिमितं स्वल्पमित्यर्थः भाषन्ते ये ते मितभाषिणः तेषां, स्वल्पभाषणशीलानां ;—men of few words.

शैशवेऽभ्यस्तविद्यानां यौवने विषयैषिणाम् ।
वार्द्धके मुनिवृत्तीनां * योगेनान्ते तनुत्यजाम् ॥८॥

शैशव इति। शिशोर्भावः शैशवं बाल्यम्, तस्मिन् वयसि अभ्यस्त-विद्यानाम् (एतेन ब्रह्मचर्याश्रमो विवक्षितः) यूनो भावः यौवनं तारुण्यम्, तस्मिन् वयसि विषयैषिणां भोगाभिलाषिणाम् (एतेन गृहस्थाश्रमो विवक्षितः) वृद्धस्य भावः वार्द्धकं वृद्धत्वम्, तस्मिन् वार्द्धके वयसि मुनीनां वृत्तिः इव वृत्तिः येषां तेषाम् (एतेन वानप्रस्थाश्रमो विवक्षितः।) अन्ते शरीरत्यागकाले योगेन परमात्मध्यानेन, तनुं देहं त्यजन्ति इति तनुत्यजां देहत्यागिनाम्। (एतेन भिक्षाश्रमो विवक्षितः ॥ ८ ॥

করিতেন; দানের নিমিত্তই অর্থ সঞ্চয় করিতেন; সত্য-প্রিয়তার জন্যই মিতভাষী হইতেন; যশের জন্যই দিগ্বিজয়ে বহির্গত হইতেন; এবং সন্তান লাভার্থই দারপরিগ্রহ করিতেন; যাঁহারা শৈশবে বিদ্যাভ্যাস,

with whom it was a habit to rise early from their beds; who collected their revenues only for acts of charity; regulated their speech only through love of truth; led their armies into battle only for glory; and took wives to themselves only for issue;—who devoted their childhood to education, their youth to the enjoyment of temperal power and

---

* योगेनान्ते तनुत्यजां—योग, is a state of perfect self-concentration, योगश्चित्तवृत्तिनिरोधः—*Patanjali*. It is genarally belived in this country that great sages, by the practice of *yoga*, acquire mastery over life and death. योग has another meaning;—संयोगो योग इत्युक्तो जीवात्म-परमात्मनोः; Trans—The union between God and the human soul is *yoga*, hence a state of communion with God.

रघूणामन्वयं वक्ष्ये * तनुवाग्विभवोऽपि सन् ।
तद्गुणैः कर्णमागत्य चापलाय प्रचोदितः ॥९॥
तं सन्तः श्रोतुमर्हन्ति † सदसद्व्यक्तिहेतवः ।
हेम्नः संलक्ष्यते ह्यग्नौ विशुद्धिः श्यामिकापि वा ॥१०॥

रघूणामिति । सः अहं अल्पप्रज्ञः तनुवाग्विभवः अपि अल्पवाणी-प्रचारः अपि सन्, तेषां गुणैः तद्गुणैः आजन्मशुद्धत्वादिभिः कर्तृभिः कर्णं मम श्रोत्रम् आगत्य चापलाय चापलं अयथाकर्म अविमृश्यकरण-रूपं कर्तुं, प्रचोदितः प्रेरितः सन् रघूणाम् अन्वयं तद्विषयप्रबन्धं वक्ष्ये । कुलकम् ॥ ९ ॥

तमिति । तं रघुवंशाख्यं प्रबन्धं सदसतोः गुणदोषयोः व्यक्तेः हेतवः कर्तारः सन्तः श्रोतुम् अर्हन्ति; तथाहि हेम्नः विशुद्धिः निर्दोषस्वरूपं श्यामिका अपि लोहान्तरसंसर्गात्मको दोषः अपि वा अग्नौ संलक्ष्यते न अन्यत्र, तद्वत् अत्रापि सन्त एव गुणदोषविवेकाधि-कारिणो न अन्ये इति भावः ॥ १० ॥

যৌবনে বিষয়-সেবা, এবং বার্দ্ধকে বনবাস করিতেন, এবং অবশেষে যোগপরায়ণ হইয়া কলেবর পরিত্যাগ করিতেন। ৯ ।

সদসৎবিচারক্ষম সজ্জন সকলে সেই বংশের কথা তবে শ্রবণ করুন,

their declining years to a residence in the forest, finally closing their worthy lives in a state of rapt communion.

10. Hear that description of mine, all ye good men,—for

---

* तनुवाग्विभवः—वाचां वाक्यानां काव्यात्मकानामित्यर्थः विभवः सम्पत्तिः वाग्विभवः, तनुः क्षुद्रः वाग्विभवो यस्य,—one gifted with limited powers of speech ;—hence one lacking poetical genius.

† सदसद्व्यक्तिहेतवः—वि+अनज्+क्ति—व्यक्तिः । अञ्जि, ञु, संरक्षै-

বৈবস্বতো মনুর্নাম মাননীয়ো মনীষিণাম্।
আসীন্মহীক্ষিতামাদ্যঃ প্রণবশ্ছন্দসামিব ॥১১॥

তদন্বয়ে শুদ্ধিমতি প্রসূতঃ শুদ্ধিমত্তরঃ।
দিলীপ ইতি রাজেন্দুরিন্দুঃ ক্ষীরনিধাবিব ॥১২॥

বৈবস্বত ইতি। মনসঃ ঈষিণঃ মনীষিণঃ, ধীরাঃ বিদ্বাংসঃ ইতি যাবৎ, তেষাং মাননীয়ঃ পূজ্যঃ, ছন্দসাং বেদানাম্ প্রণবঃ ওঁকারঃ ইব, মহীং ক্ষিয়ন্তি ঈশতে ইতি মহীক্ষিতঃ ক্ষিতীশ্বরাঃ তেষাম্, আদ্যঃ আদিভূতঃ, বিবস্বতঃ সূর্য্যস্য অপত্যং পুমান্ বৈবস্বতঃ, নাম বৈবস্বতঃ ইতি প্রসিদ্ধঃ, মনুঃ আসীৎ ॥ ১১ ॥

তদন্বয়ে ইতি। শুদ্ধিঃ অস্য অস্তীতি শুদ্ধিমান্ তস্মিন্ শুদ্ধিমতি, তদন্বয়ে তস্য মনোঃ অন্বয়ে বংশে, অতিশয়েন শুদ্ধিমান্ শুদ্ধিমত্তরঃ, দিলীপঃ

সুবর্ণ বিশুদ্ধ কি খাদ-মিশ্রিত তাহা অগ্নিতেই পরীক্ষিত হয় ॥ ১০ ॥

ওঁকার যেমন সকল বেদের আদি, সেইরূপ সমুদয় রাজকুলের আদিপুরুষ, মনীষীদিগের সমাদৃত মনুনামক সূর্য্যের পুত্র ছিলেন ॥ ১১ ॥

ক্ষীরোদসাগর হইতে চন্দ্র যেমন সমুৎপন্ন হইয়াছিলেন সেইরূপ সেই মনুর পবিত্র বংশ হইতে পবিত্রচেতা রাজ-শ্রেষ্ঠ দিলীপ অভ্যুত্থিত হইয়াছিলেন ॥১২॥

ye alone can discriminate between good and bad; it is fire alone that can test the purity or the impurity of gold.

11. As the letter "Om" is the first word of the *Vedas*, so Manu the son of the Sun, was the esteemed progenitor of all the princes

12. From his pure line sprang a prince of purer fame,—the

সদী। দীপ্তিঃ।—literally the sources of the distinction between right and wrong.

* व्यूढोरस्को वृषस्कन्धः शालप्रांशुर्महाभुजः।
† आत्मकर्मक्षमं देहं क्षात्रो धर्म इवाश्रितः ॥१३॥

इति प्रसिद्धः राजा इन्दुः इव राजेन्दुः राजश्रेष्ठः, क्षीरनिधौ इन्दुः इव प्रसूतः जातः ॥ १२ ॥

व्यूढेति। व्यूढेत्यादिभिस्त्रिभिः श्लोकैर्दिलीपं विशिनष्टि। व्यूढं विपुलम् उरः यस्य सः व्यूढोरस्कः, वृषस्य स्कन्धः इव स्कन्धः यस्य सः तथा, शालः वृक्षः इव प्रांशुः उन्नतः शालप्रांशुः, महाभुजः महाबाहुः, आत्मकर्म्मक्षमं स्वव्यापारानुरूपं देहम् आश्रितः प्राप्तः क्षात्रः क्षात्रसम्बन्धी धर्म्मः इव स्थितः, मूर्त्तिमान् पराक्रम इव स्थितः, इत्युत्प्रेक्षा ॥ १२ ॥

ঐ দিলীপ রাজার বক্ষ বিশাল, স্কন্ধদ্বয় বৃষস্কন্ধের ন্যায় স্থূল, দেহ শাল বৃক্ষ সম দীর্ঘাকার, এবং ভুজদ্বয় সুদূরলম্বিত ছিল; দেখিলে বোধ হইত ক্ষত্রিয়োচিত বীরধর্ম্মই যেন নিজ-কর্ম্মানুরূপ দেহ ধারণ করিয়া রহিয়াছে ॥ ১৩ ॥

great Dileep—the best of the princes,—who resembled the moon which sprang from the milky ocean.

13. His chest was broad and full, his shoulders like those of a bull, his height like that of a *sal* tree, and his arms were long; so that he looked like the martial spirit of a Kshattriya in flesh and blood.

* व्यूढोरस्कः—वि+ऊह+क्तः—व्यूढं वि+ऊह, means here व्यूढ means well formed or full, व्यूढं उरः वक्षःस्थलं यस्य सः having a well-formed and full chest.

† आत्मकर्म्मक्षमं—आत्मनः (क्षात्रधर्म्मस्य) कर्म्म युद्धादिकं राज्यपालनादि-

सर्वातिरिक्तसारेण सर्वतेजोऽभिभाविना।
स्थितः सर्वोन्नतेनोर्वीं क्रान्त्वा मेरुरिवात्मना ॥१४॥

सर्वातिरिक्तेति। सर्वातिरिक्तसारेण सर्वेभ्यः भूतेभ्यः अधिकबलेन, सर्वाणि भूतानि तेजसा अभिभवति इति सर्वतेजोऽभिभावी तेन, सर्वेभ्यः उन्नतेन, आत्मना शरीरेण, मेरुः इव उर्वीं क्रान्त्वा आक्रम्य स्थितः। "अष्टाभिश्च सुरेन्द्राणां मात्राभिर्निर्मितो नृपः। तस्मादभिभवत्येष सर्वभूतानि तेजसा॥" इति मनुवचनात् राज्ञः सर्वतेजोऽभिभावित्वं ज्ञेयम्॥ १४ ॥

মেরু যেমন নিজের সমুন্নত দেহের দ্বারা ধরণীকে আক্রমণ করিয়া আছে, সেই রূপ দিলীপও সারবত্তা বিষয়ে সর্ব্বশ্রেষ্ঠ ও সকল প্রকার তেজের প্রশমনকারী নিজ দেহের দ্বারা জগৎকে অধিকার করিয়াছিলেন ॥ ১৪ ॥

14. As the mount *Meru,* with its wieghty mass, has firmly established itself upon the earth, so did king Dileep, with his tall and muscular frame, which surpassed all others in its substance, and vanquished all by its strength, gain mastery over the world.

क्षमं आत्मकर्म्मक्षमं, आत्मकर्म्मणि क्षमं समर्थम्।—fit for the onerous duties pertaining to the office of a king.

Manu describes the duties of a king to be the following—

प्रजानां रक्षणं दानमिज्याध्ययनमेव च।
विषयेष्वप्रसक्तिश्च क्षत्रियस्य समासतः॥

Trans.—The duties of a Kshattrya are brieflythese—the protection of the people, charity, sacrificial ceremonies, study, and want of inordinate attachment to temporal things.

* आकारसदृशप्रज्ञः प्रज्ञया सदृशागमः ।
आगमैः सदृशारम्भः आरम्भसदृशोदयः ॥ १५ ॥
† भीमकान्तैर्नृपगुणैः स बभूवोपजीविनाम् ।
अधृष्यश्चाभिगम्यश्च यादोरत्नैरिवार्णवः ॥ १६ ॥

आकारेति। आकारेण मूर्त्त्या सदृशी प्रज्ञा यस्य सः, प्रज्ञया सदृशागमः प्रज्ञानुरूपशास्त्रपरिश्रमः, आगमैः सदृशः आरम्भः कर्म्म यस्य सः तथोक्तः, आरभ्यते इति आरम्भः कर्म्म तत्सदृशः उदयः फलसिद्धिः यस्य सः तथोक्तः ॥ १५ ॥

भीमेति। भीमैः कान्तैश्च नृपगुणैः राजगुणैः तेजः-प्रतापादिभिः कुलशीलदाक्षिण्यादिभिश्च, सः दिलीपः उपजीविनाम् आश्रितानां

তাঁহার আকৃতি যেমন পুরুষোচিত, ধীশক্তি তেমনি প্রখর ছিল; ধীশক্তি যেমন প্রখর, শাস্ত্রে তেমনি নিপুণতা ছিল; শাস্ত্রজ্ঞানে যেমন পটুতা, সদনুষ্ঠানে তেমনি উৎসাহ ছিল; এবং যেমন সদনুষ্ঠান তেমনি কৃতকার্যতা ছিল॥ ১৫ ॥

সমুদ্রে নক্র মকরাদি হিংস্র জন্তু আছে, এবং মুক্তাপ্রবালাদি রত্ন-

15. His intellect was as powerful as his body was muscular and strong; his learning was as vast as his intellect was powerfull; his actions corresponded to the vastness of his learning; and his successes were also proportionate to the greatness of his undertakings.

16. He was endowed with the softer graces as well as the

---

* आकारसदृशप्रज्ञः—प्र, सम्यक् ज्ञायन्ते पदार्थाः अनया, इति प्रज्ञा बुद्धिः—the faculty of understauding—intelligence.

† भीमकान्तैः—भी+मक्—भीमाः भयोत्पादकाः; कम्+क्तः—कान्ताः

রেখামাত্রমপি * ক্ষুণ্ণাদামনোর্বর্ত্মনঃ পরম্‌।
ন ব্যতীয়ুঃ প্রজাস্তস্য নিয়ন্তুর্নেমিবৃত্তয়ঃ ॥ ১৭ ॥

যাদোভিঃ জলজীবৈঃ, রত্নৈশ্চ অর্ণবঃ ইব অধৃষ্যঃ অনভিভবনীয়শ্চ অভিগম্যঃ আশ্রয়ণীয়শ্চ বভূব ॥ ১৬ ॥

রেখামাত্রমিতি। নিয়ন্তুঃ শিক্ষকস্য সারথেশ্চ তস্য দিলীপস্য সম্বন্ধিন্যঃ নেমীনাং চক্রধারাণাং বৃত্তিঃ ইব বৃত্তিঃ আচারঃ যাসাং তাঃ প্রজাঃ, আ মনোঃ মনুম্‌ আরভ্য, ক্ষুণ্ণাৎ অভ্যস্তাৎ প্রহতাৎ,

---

রাজিও আছে; এই কারণে সমুদ্র যেমন ভয় ও প্রলোভন উভয়েরই বিষয়, সেইরূপ দিলীপের চরিত্রে রাজোচিত ভয়োদ্দীপক ও কমনীয় উভয়বিধ গুণাবলীর একত্র সমাবেশ হওয়াতে, তিনি অনুচরবর্গের অগ্রহণীয় এবং স্পৃহণীয় উভয়ই হইয়াছিলেন ॥ ১৬ ॥

তাঁহার শাসন গুণে প্রজাকুল মনুপ্রদর্শিত চিরাভ্যস্ত চক্রধারার ন্যায় সুনির্দ্দিষ্ট কর্ত্তব্যপথ হইতে রেখা মাত্রও ভ্রষ্ট হইত না ॥ ১৭ ॥

---

sterner qualities of a high-born prince; accordingly, to all his dependants he was both accessible and inaccessible at the same time; just as the ocean is a thing both courted and dreaded at the same time, on account of its pearls and sea-monsters respectively.

17. When he held sway, his subjects, like wheels under a clever charioteer, never deviated even to a hair's breadth from

---

কমনীয়াঃ স্পৃহণীয়াঃ, ভীমাশ্চ, কান্তাশ্চ, ভীমকান্তাঃ তৈঃ qualities exciting fear and love at the same time.

* ক্ষুণ্ণাৎ—ক্ষুদ্‌- ক্ষুদির্‌ ক, উভয়পদী। মর্দ্দনম্‌। বর্ত,—ক্ষুণত্তি, ক্ষুন্তঃ ক্ষুন্দন্তি। লুঙ্‌-অক্ষুদৎ, অক্ষৌৎসীৎ। নিষ্ঠা-ক্ষুদাৎ ক্ত ক্ষুণ্ণঃ,—beaten or trodden.

प्रजानामेव भूत्यर्थं स ताभ्यो बलिमग्रहीत्।
सहस्रगुणमुत्स्रष्टुमादत्ते हि रसं रविः ॥ १८ ॥
सेना परिच्छदस्तस्य द्वयमेवार्थसाधनम्।
शास्त्रेष्वकुण्ठिता बुद्धि*र्मौर्वी धनुषि चातता ॥ १९ ॥

वर्त्मनः आचारपद्धतेः अध्वनश्च, परम् अधिकम् इत्यर्थः, रेखा प्रमाणम् अस्येति रेखामात्रं रेखाप्रमाणम् ईषदपीत्यर्थः, न व्यतीयुः न अतिक्रान्तवत्यः। कुशलसारथिप्रेरिता रथनेमय इव ताः प्रजाः पूर्वक्षुण्णमार्गं न जहुरिति भावः ॥ १७ ॥

प्रजानामिति। सः राजा प्रजानां भूत्यै अर्थाय भूत्यर्थं वृद्ध्यर्थम्, एव ताभ्यः प्रजाभ्यः, बलिं षष्ठांशरूपं करम्, अग्रहीत्। तथाहि रविः, सहस्रं गुणाः यस्मिन् कर्मणि तत् यथा तथा सहस्रगुणं, सहस्रधा, उत्स्रष्टुं, दातुम्, रसम् अम्बु, आदत्ते गृह्णाति ॥ १८ ॥

सेनेति। तस्य राज्ञः सेना चतुरङ्गबलं, परिच्छाद्यते अनेन इति

রবি যেমন সহস্র গুণ জল বর্ষণের জন্যই এক গুণ জল শোষণ করেন, সেইরূপ তিনিও প্রজাকুলেরই উন্নতি ও কল্যাণের উদ্দেশেই তাহাদিগের নিকট হইতে কর গ্রহণ করিতেন ॥ ১৮ ॥

সৈন্যদল দিলীপের রাজোচিত সম্ভ্রমের উপকরণ মাত্র ছিল, তিনি

the paths of duty laid down by Manu and trodden by thousands ever since.

18. It was for the good of the people alone, that he collected taxes from them. In this he resembled the sun, who draws up watery vapour from the earth only to pour it thousand-fold (in the shape of rain) at some other time.

19. His army was more an ornament of his royal office, than

* मौर्वी—मूर्वा, is a creeper of that name, मौर्वी, made of its

तस्य संवृतमन्त्रस्य गूढाकारेङ्गितस्य च।
फलानुमेयाः प्रारम्भाः*संस्काराः प्राक्तना इव॥२०॥

परिच्छदः उपकरणं, बभूव छत्रचामरादिवस्तुमभूदित्यर्थः; अर्थस्य प्रयोजनस्य तु साधनं द्वयम् एव; शास्त्रेषु अकुण्ठिता(अव्याहता) बुद्धिः (व्याप्तता इत्यपि पाठः।) धनुषि आतता आरोपिता मौर्वी च। नीतिपुरःसरमेव तस्य मौर्व्यमभूदित्यर्थः॥ १९॥

तस्येति। संवृतमन्त्रस्य गुप्तविचारस्य, शोकहर्षादिसूचको भ्रुकुटी-मुखरागादिः आकारः, इङ्गितं चेष्टितं हृदयगतविकारो वा, गूढे

স্বীয় অভীষ্ট সিদ্ধির নিমিত্ত দুইটী পদার্থের উপর প্রধানতঃ নির্ভর করিতেন;—প্রথম, শাস্ত্রে অপ্রতিহত বুদ্ধি; দ্বিতীয় নিজের জ্যাযুক্ত ধনু॥ ১৯॥

পূর্ব্ব জন্মের সংস্কার সকল যেমন পরজন্মের ফলের দ্বারাই ধরিতে

of any practical value to him. For the accomplishment of his purposes he mainly relied upon two things;—first, his great knowledge of the Shastras, and secondly, his well-strung bow-string.

20. The policy of his government as well as his internal

fibres.—It was the ancient custom to make bow-strings out of the fibres of that plant.

* संस्काराः प्राक्तना इव—It is the general belief in this country that every soul upon earth had a former birth, and that the influence of the actions of a previous birth is communicated in some mysterious way to the re-born spirit. The previous experiences are no longer facts of the new man's memory, but the secret influences of those actions called 'संस्काराः' speard to the re-born soul; and we discern them only when we mark their consequences. Similar were all the measures that

जुगोपात्मानमत्रस्तो भेजे धर्ममनातुरः।

आकारेङ्गिते यस्य, स्वभावचापलात् अन्यपरम्परया मुखरागादिलिङ्गैः वा अन्यतीयगामिमन्त्रस्य, तस्य प्रारभ्यन्ते इति प्रारम्भाः सामाद्युपायप्रयोगाः, प्रागित्यव्ययेन पूर्वजन्म उच्यते तत्र भवाः प्राक्तनाः, संस्काराः पूर्वकर्मवासनाः, इव फलेन कार्य्येण अनुमेयाः अनुमातुं योग्याः, आसन्। अत्र याज्ञवल्क्यः, "मन्त्रमूलं यतो राज्यमतो मन्त्रं सुरक्षितम्। कुर्य्यात् यथा तन्न विदुः कर्म्मणामाफलोदयात्" इति॥ २०॥

जुगोपेति। अत्रस्तः अभीतः सन्, त्रासोपाधिमन्तरेणैव त्रिवर्ग-

পারা যায়, সেইরূপ তাঁহার গূঢ় রাজনীতি ও তাঁহার ইঙ্গিত ভাব সকল এরূপ প্রচ্ছন্ন থাকিত, এবং এরূপ গোপনে কার্য্যারম্ভ করিতেন যে ফলের দ্বারা অবশেষে সেই সকলের অনুমান করিতে হইত॥ ২০॥

•তিনি ভয়শূন্য হইয়া আপনাকে রক্ষা করিতেন, দেহকে ক্লেশ না

---

designs, were carefully concealed, so much so that, all his secret purposes were discernible only through the result of his various measures, like unto the influences of the actions of a previous birth.

21. His measures of self-defence were not actuated by

---

this great king initiated; his ulterior motives being discernible only through the working out of his policy. About the transmission of the influences of a previous birth, there is the following well-known saying, in ancient Sanskrit literature;—"पूर्व्वजन्मार्ज्जिता विद्या पूर्व्वजन्मार्ज्जितं धनम्। पूर्व्वजन्मार्ज्जितं पुण्यमग्रे धावति धावति।" Trans.—The learning, and wealth, and the virtue acquired in a previous birth go before the man, as he takes his second birth.

*अगृध्नुराददे सोऽर्थ†मसक्तः सुखमन्वभूत् ॥२१॥

त्रिभेः प्रथमसाधनत्वादेव आत्मानं शरीरं जुगोप रक्षितवान्, अनातुरः अरुग्णः एव धर्मं सुकृतं भेजे अर्जितवान् इत्यर्थः, अगृध्नुः अगर्धनशीलः एव अर्थम् आददे स्वीकृतवान्, असक्तः आसक्तिरहितः एव सुखम् अन्वभूत् ॥ २१ ॥

দিয়া ধর্ম্ম সাধন করিতেন; সম্পূর্ণ রূপে লোভ বিবর্জ্জিত হইয়া কর গ্রহণ করিতেন, এবং অনাসক্ত থাকিয়া সকল প্রকার সুখ ভোগ করিতেন ॥ ২১ ॥

fear of his enemies ; his religious exercises were free from self-inflicted sufferings ; the collection of his revenues was free from avarice, and he enjoyed temporal pleasures without being inordinately attached to them.

* अगृध्नुः—गृधि स्वधि धृषि क्षिपेः क्नुरिति क्नुप्रत्ययः—*Mallinatha.*

† असक्तः सुखमन्वभूत्—सं+सञ्ज+क्त—सक्तः ; षञ्ज, भ्वादि, परस्मैपदी संङ्गार्थकः । असक्तः—सङ्गविरहितः । The secret attachment that is engendered in us by the constant contemplation of objects of the senses, is called सङ्गः ; or आसक्तिः । The भगवद्गीता gives the following definition of सङ्गः—

ध्यायतो विषयान् पुंसः सङ्गस्तेषूपजायते ।

Trans—As a man contemplates the objects of his senses a secret attachment for them is formed.

To be above this attachment is the mark of a perfectly holy life ; and it is also in accordance with the highest teachings of the Hindu *Shastras.—Viz.*

ज्ञाने मौनं क्षमा शक्तौ त्यागे श्लाघाविपर्य्ययः।
गुणा गुणानुबन्धित्वात् तस्य सप्रसवा इव ॥ २२॥

ज्ञाने इति। ज्ञाने परवृत्तान्तज्ञाने सति अपि मौनं वाङ्नियमनम्, शक्तौ प्रतीकारसामर्थ्ये अपि क्षमा अपकारसहनम्, त्यागे वितरणे सति अपि श्लाघायाः विकत्थनस्य विपर्य्ययः अभावः, एवं तस्य गुणाः ज्ञानादयः गुणैः विरुद्धैः मौनादिभिः अनुबन्धित्वात् सहचारित्वात्, सह प्रसवः जन्म येषां ते सप्रसवाः सोदराः इव अभूवन्, विरुद्धा अपि गुणाः तस्मिन् अविरोधेनैव स्थिता इत्यर्थः ॥ २२ ॥

তাঁহার জ্ঞান থাকিয়াও প্রদর্শনেচ্ছা ছিল না; নিগ্রহ-সামর্থ্য সত্ত্বেও বৈরনির্যাতনস্পৃহা ছিল না; প্রভূত দান সত্ত্বেও বিন্দুমাত্র আত্ম-শ্লাঘা ছিল না; এই সকল গুণ তাঁহাতে আশ্চর্য্য ভাবে মিলিত হইয়া সহোদরের ন্যায় একত্র বাস করিত ॥ ২২ ॥

22. In him there was knowledge conjoined to modest silence power graced by forbearance, and charity, free from self-adulation,—in short these contrary qualities so harmonised in him, as if they were twins.

ईशावास्यमिदं सर्व्वं यत् किञ्च जगत्यां जगत्।
तेन त्यक्तेन भुञ्जीथाः मा गृधः कस्यस्विद्धनम् ॥—*Ishopnishad.*

वा।

रागद्वेषवियुक्तैस्तु विषयानिन्द्रियैश्चरन्।
आत्मवश्यैर्विधेयात्मा प्रसादमधिगच्छति ॥—*Gitá.*

Trans—One, whose soul is entirely free from attachment and hatred, and who enjoys all objects, with senses completely under his control, is a man of well-disciplined life and such a one attains to perfection.

अनाकृष्टस्य विषयैः* विद्यानां पारदृश्वनः ।
तस्य धर्मरतेरासीत् वृद्धत्वं जरसा विना ॥ २३ ॥

अनाकृष्टस्येति । विषयैः शब्दादिभिः अनाकृष्टस्य अवशीकृतस्य विद्यानां वेदवेदाङ्गादीनां पारदृश्वनः पारम् अन्तं दृष्टवतः, धर्मे रतिः यस्य तस्य राज्ञः जरसा जरया विना, वृद्धत्वं वार्द्धकम् आसीत् । तस्य यूनोऽपि विषयवैराग्यादिगुणसम्पत्त्या ज्ञानतो वृद्धत्वमासीदित्यर्थः ॥ २३ ॥

বিষয়ে তাঁহাকে আবদ্ধ করিতে পারে নাই; এবং তিনি সকল বিদ্যার পারদর্শী হইয়াছিলেন; এই কারণে এবং ধর্ম্মে তাঁহার একান্ত অনুরাগ থাকাতে তিনি বার্দ্ধক্যপ্রাপ্তি ব্যতিরেকেও প্রবীণত্ব লাভ করিয়াছিলেন ॥ ২৩ ॥

23. Worldliness had no hold on him; and he had mastered all the branches of learning; consequently this virtuous prince had all the wisdom of age without its attendant infirmities.

* विद्यानां पारदृश्वनः—There are fourteen main branches of learning mentioned in ancient Sanskrit literature.

अङ्गानि वेदाश्चत्वारो मीमांसा न्यायविस्तरः ।
धर्मशास्त्रं पुराणञ्च विद्या ह्येताश्चतुर्दश ॥

6 Vedangas, namely शिक्षा, कल्पो व्याकरणं, निरुक्तः, छन्दो, ज्योतिषम् । 4 Vedas namely, ऋक्, यजुः, साम, अथर्व्व; मीमांसा, न्यायः, धर्मशास्त्रं and पुराणम् । दृश्वनः दृष्टः कश्चित्—one who has mastered these fourteen branches of learning.

प्रजानां विनयाधानात् रक्षणात् भरणादपि ।
स पिता पितरस्तासां केवलं जन्महेतवः ॥ २४ ॥
स्थित्यै दण्डयतो दण्ड्यान् परिणेतुः प्रसूतये ।
अप्यर्थकामौ तस्यास्तां धर्म एव मनीषिणः ॥२५॥

प्रजानामिति। प्रजायन्ते इति प्रजाः जनाः, तासां विनयस्य शिक्षायाः, आधानात् करणात्, सन्मार्गप्रवर्त्तनात् इति यावत्, रक्षणात् भयहेतुभ्यः त्राणात् आपन्निवारणात् इति यावत्, भरणात् अन्नपानादिभिः पोषणात् अपि सः राजा पिता अभूत्, तासां पितरस्तु जन्महेतवः जन्ममात्रकर्त्तारः केवलमुत्पादका एवाभूवन्। जननमात्र एव पितॄणां व्यापारः, सदा शिक्षारक्षणादिकन्तु स एव करोतीति तस्मिन् पितृत्वव्यपदेशः ॥ २४ ॥

स्थित्यै इति। दण्डम् अर्हन्तीति दण्ड्याः तान् दण्ड्यान् एव लोकप्रतिष्ठायै दण्डयतः शिक्षयतः, प्रसूतये सन्तानाय एव

তিনি প্রজাদিগকে শিক্ষা দিতেন, রক্ষা করিতেন, এবং পালন করিতেন, সুতরাং, তিনিই তাহাদের প্রকৃত পিতা ছিলেন ; তাহাদের স্বীয় স্বীয় পিতাগণ কেবল জন্মদাতা ছিলেন ॥ ২৪ ॥

তিনি লোকস্থিতি রক্ষার জন্যই দণ্ড দান করিতেন ; (অর্থাৎ ক্রোধের জন্য দণ্ড দিতেন না) এবং সন্তানের জন্যই দার পরিগ্রহ

---

24. For enforcing discipline on his subjects and also for protecting and supporting them, he was truly their father ; whereas their fathers in the flesh, were merely the authors of their birth.

25. He inflicted punishments on criminals only to maintain justice ; and took a wife to himself only for the hope of

दुदोह गां स *यज्ञाय सस्याय मघवा दिवम् ।
सम्पद्विनिमयेनोभौ दधतुर्भुवनद्वयम् ॥ २६ ॥

परिणेतुः दारान् परिगृह्णतः, मनीषिणः विदुषः दिलीपस्य इति यावत् तस्य अर्थकामौ अपि धर्म एव आस्तां जातौ, अर्थकामसाधनयोर्दण्डविवाहयोर्लोकस्थापनप्रजोत्पादनरूपधर्मार्थित्वेन अनुष्ठानात् अर्थकामावपि धर्मशेषतामापादयन् स राजा धर्मोत्तरोऽभूदित्यर्थः ॥ २५ ॥

दुदोहेति । सः राजा यज्ञाय यज्ञं कर्त्तुं गां भुवं दुदोह करग्रहणेन रिक्तां चकार इत्यर्थः, मघवा देवेन्द्रः सस्याय सस्यं वर्द्धयितुं दिवं स्वर्गं दुदोह द्युलोकात् महीलोके वृष्टिमुत्पादयामास इत्यर्थः, एवम् उभौ सम्पदः विनिमयेन परस्परमादानप्रतिदानाभ्यां भुवनद्वयं दधतुः

করিয়াছিলেন (অর্থাৎ রিপু বিশেষের চরিতার্থতার জন্য নহে) ; সুতরাং তাঁহার পক্ষে অর্থ এবং কাম উভয়েই ধর্ম্মের পরিপোষক হইয়াছিল ॥২৫॥

রাজা দিলীপ যজ্ঞ সম্পাদনার্থ করগ্রহণ দ্বারা পৃথিবীকে দোহন করিতেন ; দেবরাজ ইন্দ্র শস্য উৎপাদনের নিমিত্ত জলাভিষেকাদির দ্বারা স্বর্গকে দোহন করিতেন ; এইরূপে তাঁহারা পরস্পরের সম্পত্তির বিনিময়ের দ্বারা ভুবনদ্বয়কে রক্ষা করিতেন ॥ ২৬ ॥

issue ;—thus his temporal power as well as his sensual enjoyment were both conducive to his spiritual growth.

26. He drained the earth of its resources for performing his ceremonies ; Indra drained the heavens for nourishing his crops ; thus by a friendly exchange of their wealth, as it were, they maintained both the worlds.

* यज्ञाय सस्याय—क्रियार्थोपपदस्येत्यादिना चतुर्थ्यौ

Mallinatha.

क्रियार्थोपपदस्य च कर्मणि स्थानिनः । २ । ३ । १४ ।—*Panini.*

न किलानुययुस्तस्य राजानो रक्षितुर्यशः ।
व्यावृत्ता यत् परस्वेभ्यः श्रुतौ तस्करता स्थिता ॥२७

द्वेष्योऽपि सम्मतः शिष्टस्तस्यार्त्तस्य यथौषधम् ।
त्याज्यो दुष्टः प्रियोऽप्यासीदङ्गुलीवोरगक्षता ॥२८

पुपुषतुः। राजा यज्ञैरिन्द्रलोकम्, इन्द्रश्च वृष्ट्या भूर्लोकमपोषयदित्यर्थः। उक्तञ्च दण्डनीतौ, ("राजा त्वर्थान् समाहृत्य कुर्य्यादिन्द्रमहोत्सवम्। प्रीणितो मेघवाहस्तु महतीं वृष्टिमावहेत्" इति ॥ २६ ॥

न किलेति। राजानः अन्ये नृपाः, रक्षितुः भयेभ्यस्त्रातुः, तस्य राज्ञः यशः न अनुययुः किल न अनुचक्रुः खलु, कुतः यत् यस्मात् कारणात् तस्करता चौर्य्यं परस्वेभ्यः परधनेभ्यः स्वविषयभूतेभ्यः व्यावृत्ता सती श्रुतौ वाचकशब्दे स्थिता प्रवृत्ता, अपहार्य्याभावात् तस्करशब्द एव अपहृतः इत्यर्थः, अथवा "अत्यन्तासत्यपि ह्यर्थे ज्ञानं शब्दः करोति हि" इति न्यायेन शब्दे स्थिता स्फुरिता न स्वरूपतोऽस्ति इत्यर्थः ॥ २७ ॥

द्वेष्य इति। शिष्टः जनः द्वेष्यः शत्रुः अपि आर्त्तस्य रोगिणः

রাজকুলের মধ্যে আর কেহই তাঁহার যশের অনুকরণ করিতে পারে নাই ; কারণ তাঁহার রাজত্ব কালে, পরধন হরণ দূরে থাকুক, চৌর্য্য শব্দই ছিল না ॥ ২৭ ॥

ঔষধ (নিতান্ত তিক্ত হইলেও) যেমন রোগীর নিকট আদরণীয়

---

27. No other prince after him could rival his fame in the art of government ; in as much as failing to find its application on other men's riches, theft came to be applied to the term itself.

28. Even an enemy, possessed of estimable qualities was acceptable to him, as is a phial of medicine to a man suffer-

तं वेधा विदधे नूनं महाभूतसमाधिना।
तथाहि सर्वे तस्यासन् परार्थैकफला गुणाः॥२९॥

औषधं यथा औषधम् इव तस्य सम्मतः अनुमतः आसीत्, दुष्टः स्वजनः प्रियः अपि प्रेमास्पदीभूतः अपि उरगक्षता सर्पदष्टा अङ्गुली इव त्याज्यः आसीत्। तस्य शिष्ट एव बन्धुः दुष्ट एव शत्रुः इत्यर्थः॥ २८॥

तस्य परोपकारित्वमाह, तमिति। वेधाः स्रष्टा, तं दिलीपं समाधीयते अनेनेति समाधिः कारणसामग्री महाभूतानां यः समाधिः तेन महाभूतसमाधिना विदधे ससर्ज नूनं ध्रुवम्, इत्युत्प्रेक्षा, तथाहि, तस्य राज्ञः सर्वे गुणाः रूपरसादिमहाभूतगुणवदेव परार्थः परप्रयोजनम् एव एकं मुख्यं फलं येषां ते तथोक्ताः आसन्। महाभूतगुणोपमानेन कारणगुणाः कार्य्ये संक्रामन्तीति न्यायः सूचितः॥ २९॥

হয়, সেইরূপ তাঁহার বিপক্ষ ব্যক্তিও যদি সদ্গুণশালী হইত তাহা হইলে তাঁহার আদরভাজন হইত; অপর দিকে তাঁহার প্রিয় ব্যক্তিও যদি দোষী হইত, তাহা হইলে লোকে সর্পদষ্ট অঙ্গুলিকে যেমন করিয়া কাটিয়া ফেলে সেই রূপে তিনি তাহাকে বর্জ্জন করিতেন॥ ২৮॥

নিশ্চয় বিধাতা তাঁহাকে মহাভূতগণের উপাদান সামগ্রীর দ্বারাই গঠন করিয়াছিলেন; কারণ মহাভূত সকলের গুণাবলীর ন্যায় তাঁহার গুণাবলীও সর্ব্বতোভাবে পরোপকারার্থে নিযুক্ত হইয়াছিল॥ ২৯॥

ing from disease, whilst a bad man, even if bound to him by ties of friendship, he would cut, just as one would amputate a finger bitten by a snake.

29. Surely God formed him with the substance of the five great elements, (earth, water, fire, air, ether) for like unto theirs all his qualities were devoted to the service of others.

स वेलावप्रवलयां परिखीकृतसागराम् ।
अनन्यशासनामुर्वीं शशासैकपुरीमिव ॥ ३० ॥
तस्य दाक्षिण्यरूढेन नाम्ना मगधवंशजा ।
पत्नी सुदक्षिणेत्यासी* दध्वरस्येव दक्षिणा ॥ ३१ ॥

स इति। सः दिलीपः वेलाः समुद्रकूलानि ताः एव वप्रवलयाः प्राकारवेष्टनानि यस्याः ताम्, परितः खातं परिखा, दुर्गवेष्टनं खातम् खनेर्डप्रत्ययः, अपरिखाः परिखाः सम्पद्यमानाः कृताः परिखीकृताः सागराः यस्याः ताम्, अविद्यमानम् अन्यस्य राज्ञः शासनं यस्याः ताम् अनन्यशासनाम् उर्वीम् एकपुरीम् इव शशास अनायासेन शासितवान् इत्यर्थः ॥ ३० ॥

तस्येति। तस्य राज्ञः मगधवंशे जाता मगधवंशजा, (एतेनाभिजात्यमुक्तम्।) दाक्षिण्यं परच्छन्दानुवर्त्तनम्, तेन रूढं प्रसिद्धं तेन

তাঁহার শাসন কালে সাগরতীরবর্ত্তী বালুকাময় বেলাভূমিই দুর্গ-প্রাকার রূপে পরিণত হইয়াছিল ; এবং মহাসিন্ধু দুর্গপার্শ্ববর্ত্তী পরিখার কার্য্য করিত ; সেই সমগ্র ধরাতল মধ্যে অন্য কাহারও শাসনাধিকার ছিল না, তিনিই তাহাকে একখানি নগরের ন্যায় শাসন করিতেন ॥৩০॥

দক্ষিণা যেমন যজ্ঞের চির অনুগতা তেমনি দাক্ষিণ্য গুণের জন্য

---

30. The sea-beach formed the ramparts of his kingdom and the high seas were its moats ; the vast dominions, comprised within these limits, he governed as if they were a single city.

31 He had Sudakshina for his wife,—a princess of the royal line of Magadha, and so called on account of her well-known

* अध्वरस्य—अध्वानं सत्पथं+राति, ददाति यः सः अध्वरः यज्ञः तस्य—

कलत्रवन्तमात्मानम् अवरोधे महत्यपि।
तया मेने मनस्विन्या लक्ष्म्या च वसुधाधिपः ॥३२

नाम्ना अध्वरस्य यज्ञस्य दक्षिणाख्या पत्नी इव सुदक्षिणा इति प्रसिद्धा पत्नी आसीत्। अत्र श्रुतिः "यज्ञो गन्धर्वस्तस्य दक्षिणा अप्सरस इति दक्षिणाया दाक्षिण्यं नाम ऋत्विजो दक्षिणात्वं प्रापकत्वं ते ददन्ते दक्षिणां प्रतिगृह्णन्तीति च" ॥ ३१ ॥

कलत्रवन्तमिति। वसुधाधिपः अवरोधे अन्तःपुरवर्गे महति सति अपि, मनस्विन्या दृढचित्तया, पतिचित्तानुवृत्त्यादिनिर्बन्धक्षमया इत्यर्थः, तया सुदक्षिणया लक्ष्म्या च आत्मानं कलत्रवन्तं भार्यावन्तं मेने, वसुधाधिप इत्यनेन वसुधया नेति गम्यते ॥ ३२ ॥

সুপ্রসিদ্ধা মগধবংশজাতা, সুদক্ষিণা নামে তাঁহার মহিষী ছিলেন ॥৩১॥

রাজ অন্তঃপুরে যদিও বহুসংখ্যক রমণী ছিলেন, তথাপি সেই মনস্বিনী সুদক্ষিণাকে ও রাজলক্ষ্মীকে পাইয়াই তিনি আপনাকে বাস্তবিক সপত্নীক বলিয়া গণনা করিতেন ॥ ৩২ ॥

obliging disposition. She was as constant a companion of the king, as are the concluding fees offered to the officiating priests, of a sacreficial ceremony.

32. Though there was no lack of pretty damsels in his seraglio, it was by reason of his union with this noble princess and also with the goddess of his kingly power, that Dileep regarded himself as truly married.

---

a sacrificial ceremony, so called because it helps people in treading the right path.

तस्यामात्मानुरूपायामात्मजन्मसमुत्सुकः।
विलम्बितफलैः कालं स निनाय मनोरथैः ॥३३॥
सन्तानार्थाय विधये स्वभुजादवतारिता।
तेन धूर्जगतो गुर्वी सचिवेषु निचिक्षिपे ॥३४॥

तस्यामिति। सः राजा आत्मानुरूपायां आत्मनः जन्म यस्य असौ आत्मजन्मा पुत्रः, तस्मिन् समुत्सुकः यद्वा आत्मनः जन्मनि पुत्ररूपेण तत्र असौ समुत्सुकः सन् विलम्बितं फलं पुत्रप्राप्तिरूपं येषां तैः मनोरथैः, कदा मे पुत्रो भवेत् इत्याशाभिः, कालं निनाय यापयामास॥ ३३॥

सन्तानेति। तेन दिलीपेन, सन्तानः अर्थः प्रयोजनं यस्य तस्मै

---

*নিজের অনুরূপ ভার্য্যা সুদক্ষিণার ক্রোড়ে পুত্রের মুখদর্শন করিবার আশাতে রাজা বহুকাল কাটাইলেন, তথাপি আশা পূর্ণ হইল না। ৩৩॥

অবশেষে পুত্রলাভার্থ কোন প্রকার ধর্ম্মানুষ্ঠান করিবার সংকল্প

33. Anxious to see the birth of a son from this most noble queen who was in every respect worthy of himself, the king passed his painful days with hopes long delayed.

34. At last he resolved to hold a ceremony with the pur-

---

* आत्मजन्मसमुत्सुकः—It is a well-known belief often expressed by the old Sanskrit writers, that it is the father who reappears as the son, in his wife; hence is a wife called जाया in Sanskrit; meaning,—she in whom the husband takes his birth. In connection with this there is the following saying, in the institutes of *Manu.*—

पतिर्भार्यां संप्रविश्य गर्भो भूत्वेह जायते।
जायायास्तद्धि जायात्वं यदस्यां जायते पुनः॥

अथाभ्यर्च्य विधातारं प्रयतौ* पुत्रकाम्यया।
तौ † दम्पती वशिष्ठस्य गुरोर्जग्मतुराश्रमम् ॥३५॥
स्निग्धगम्भीरनिर्घोषम् एकं स्यन्दनमास्थितौ।

समानायाय, विधये सन्तानाय, सम्भृतात् आयतात्मिता अवरोपिता, जगतः लोकस्य गुर्वी भूः भारः, सचिवेषु निचिक्षिपे निहिता ॥ ३४ ॥

अथेति। अथ गुरोऽवतारानन्तरं, पुत्रकाम्यया आत्मनः पुत्रेच्छया, तौ दम्पती जायापती, प्रयतौ पूतौ, विधातारं ब्रह्माणम्, अभ्यर्च्य गुरोः कुलगुरोः वशिष्ठस्य, आश्रमं जग्मतुः। पुत्रप्राप्त्युपायापेक्षया इति शेषः ॥ २५ ॥

स्निग्धेति। स्निग्धः मधुरः गम्भीरः निर्घोषः यस्य तम्, एकं स्यन्दनं

করিয়া তিনি নিজস্কন্ধ হইতে রাজ্যভার মন্ত্রিগণের স্কন্ধে অর্পণ করিলেন ॥ ৩৪ ॥

অনন্তর রাজদম্পতী পুত্রেচ্ছাতে সংযতচিত্ত হইয়া বিধাতার অর্চ্চনা পূর্ব্বক কুলগুরু বশিষ্ঠের আশ্রমাভিমুখে প্রস্থান করিলেন ॥ ৩৫ ॥

তাঁহারা উভয়ে মধুর অথচ গম্ভীর ধ্বনিবিশিষ্ট একটী রথে এক

---

pose of getting issue, and took leave from the duties of the state, delegating them to the shoulders of his ministers.

35. After having duly worshipped the creator of the world, self-controlled and purified, the royal couple started for the hermitage of Basista—their venerable spiritual preceptor.

36. They sat side by side on the same chariot,—which

Trans.—The husband enters the womb of his wife and reappears as the son, hence is a wife called जाया.

* पुत्रकाम्यया—काम्यचेति पुत्रशब्दात् काम्यच्प्रत्ययः—Mallinath.

† दम्पती—जाया च पतिश्च जम्पती, दम्पती वा। राजदन्तादिषु परं २।२।३१—*Panini.*

*প্রাবৃষেণ্যং পয়োবাহং বিদ্যুদৈরাবতাবিব ॥ ৩৬ ॥
মা ভূদাশ্রমপীড়েতি পরিমেয়পুরঃসরৌ।
†অনুভাববিশেষাৎ তু সেনাপরিবৃতাবিব ॥ ৩৭ ॥

প্রাবৃষি ভবঃ প্রাবৃষেণ্যঃ তং প্রাবৃষেণ্যং, পয়োবাহং মেঘং বিদ্যুদৈরাবতৌ ইব আস্থিতৌ আরূঢ়ৌ জম্পতী ইতি পূর্ব্বেণ সম্বন্ধঃ। ইরাবান্ সমুদ্রঃ তত্র ভবঃ ঐরাবতঃ অভ্রমাতঙ্গঃ, অতএব মেঘারোহণং বিদ্যুৎসাহচর্য্যঞ্চ ঘটতে। কিন্তু বিদ্যুত ঐরাবতসাহচর্য্যাদেব ঐরা সংজ্ঞা ঐরাবতস্য স্ত্রী ঐরাবতীতি ক্ষীরস্বামী। তস্মাৎ যুক্তং বিদ্যুদৈরাবতাবিবেতি। একরথারোহণোক্ত্যা কার্য্যসিদ্ধিবীজং দম্পত্যোরব্যভিচারিমনস্কং সূচয়তি ॥ ৩৬ ॥

মা ভূদিতি। পুনঃ কিম্ভূতৌ দম্পতী? আশ্রমপীড়া মা ভূৎ মা অস্থিতি হেতোঃ পরিমেয়পুরঃসরৌ পরিমিতপরিচরৌ অনুভাববিশেষাৎ সেনাপরিবৃতৌ ইব স্থিতৌ ॥ ৩৭ ॥

সঙ্গে আরোহণ করিলেন, বর্ষাকালের নবজলধরে বিদ্যুৎ এবং ঐরাবত একসঙ্গে আরোহণ করিলে যেরূপ শোভা হয়, সেইরূপ শোভা হইল ॥ ৩৬ ॥

পাছে মুনিগণের আশ্রমের কোন প্রকার উপদ্রব হয় এই ভয়ে অতি অল্প-সংখ্যক অনুযাত্রিক সঙ্গে লইলেন; কিন্তু তাঁহাদের চরিত্রের

moved on with a deep but pleasing rattle—looking like the divine elephant *Airavata* and the bright lightening riding together on a dark cloud.

37. Fearing lest there should be any disturbance of the

* প্রাবৃষেণ্যং—প্রাবৃট্ বর্ষাকালঃ প্রাবৃষি ভবং প্রাবৃষেণ্যং, প্রাবৃষ এণ্যঃ ৪।৩। ১৭।—*Panini.*

† অনুভাববিশেষাৎ—অনুভাবয়তি জ্ঞাপয়তি অনেন ইতি অনুভাবঃ

सेव्यमानौ सुखस्पर्शैः शालनिर्य्यासगन्धिभिः ।
पुष्परेणूत्किरैर्वातैराधूतवनराजिभिः ॥ ३८ ॥
मनोऽभिरामाः शृण्वन्तौ रथनेमिस्वनोन्मुखैः ।

सेव्यमानाविति। पुनः कथम्भूतौ? सुखः शीतलत्वात् प्रियः स्पर्शः येषां तैः, शालनिर्य्यासगन्धिभिः सर्जतरुनिस्यन्दनगन्धवद्भिः, उत्किरन्ति विक्षिपन्ति इति उत्किराः पुष्परेणूनाम् उत्किराः तैः, आधूताः मान्द्यात् ईषत् कम्पिताः वनराजयः यैः तैः, वातैः सेव्यमानौ ॥ ३८ ॥

मन इति। रथनेमिस्वनोन्मुखैः मेघध्वनिशङ्कया उन्नमितमुखैः

প্রভাবগুণে এইরূপ বোধ হইতে লাগিল যেন সৈন্যসামন্তে বেষ্টিত হইয়া চলিয়াছেন ॥ ৩৭ ॥

তাঁহারা যত অগ্রসর হইতে লাগিলেন ততই শালতরুর নির্য্যাস-গন্ধে আমোদিত, পুষ্পসকলের পরাগবাহী সমীরণ, বনরাজিকে বিকম্পিত করিয়া প্রবাহিত হইয়া তাঁহাদের শরীরকে শীতল করিতে লাগিল ॥ ৩৮ ॥

তাঁহাদের রথচক্রের ধ্বনি শ্রবণ করিয়া ময়ূরগণ উন্মুখ হইয়া দুই

---

peace of the hermitage, they took only a limited number of attendants with them; but on account of the dignity and majesty of their personal presence, it seemed as if they had an army about them.

38. The cool air, fragrant with the odorous milk of *Sal* trees and surcharged with the pollen-grains of a thousand flowers, fanned them, as they passed through rows of trees, gently shaken by the breeze.

39. How they listened to the music of flights of wild

कोषदण्डादिजाता राज्ञां प्रभुशक्तिः—the mysterious power and prestige of a prince, born of a vigorous and prosperous rule.

षड्जसंवादिनीः केका*द्विधाभिन्नाः शिखण्डिभिः॥३९॥
परस्पराक्षिसादृश्यम् अदूरोज्झितवर्त्मसु ।
मृगद्वन्द्वेषु पश्यन्तौ स्यन्दनाबद्धदृष्टिषु ॥ ४० ॥

इत्यर्थः, शिखण्डिभिः मयूरैः, द्विधाभिन्नाः शुद्धविकृतभेदेन आविष्कृताऽवस्थायां च्युताच्युतभेदेन वा षड्जः द्विविधः, तदनुसारादस्यात् केका अपि द्विधा भिन्ना इत्युच्यते, अतएवाह षड्जसंवादिनीरिति, षड्भ्यः स्थानेभ्यः जातः षड्जः (तदुक्तम्, "नासां कण्ठमुरस्तालुजिह्वादन्तांश्च संस्पृशन् । षड्भ्यः सञ्जायते यस्मात् तस्मात् षड्ज इति स्मृतः ॥ स च तन्त्रीकण्ठजन्मा स्वरविशेषः ("निषादर्षभगान्धारषड्जमध्यमधैवताः । पञ्चमश्चेत्यमी सप्त तन्त्रीकण्ठोत्थिताः स्वराः" इत्यमरः ।) षड्जेन संवादिनीः सदृशीः मनोऽभिरामाः मनसः प्रियाः इति केकाः मयूरवाचः ताः केकाः शृण्वन्तौ इति श्लोकार्थः ॥ ३९ ॥

परस्परेति । विश्वम्भात् अदूरं समीपं यथा भवति तथा उज्झितं वर्त्म यैः तेषु, स्यन्दनाबद्धदृष्टिषु स्यन्दने रथे आबद्धा आसञ्जिता दृष्टिः

দলে কেকা ধ্বনি করিতে লাগিল, তাহারা সেই ষড়জস্বরের অনুকারী মোহন ধ্বনি শ্রবণ করিতে লাগিলেন ॥ ৩৯ ॥

হরিণগণ রথের পথ পরিত্যাগ পূর্ব্বক অদূরে দাঁড়াইয়া অনিমেষ-

peacocks ! who, roused by the rattling noise of the chariot, uttered their shrill cries with extended necks,—one party responding to the notes of another,—as if in imitation of the notes of the *sharjaraga*.

40. How they were delighted to look at the large eyes of the deer, charming like their own, as the animals left the

* द्विधाभिन्नाः—Mallinath explains it by describing the shrill cries of the peacocks, as divided into two parts, शुद्ध and विकृत, literally "pure" and "impure" but there is

श्रेणीबन्धाद्वितन्वद्भिरस्तम्भां * तोरणस्रजम् ।
सारसैः कलनिर्ह्रादैः क्वचिदुन्नमिताननौ ॥ ४१ ॥

नेत्रं येः तेषु (कौतुकवशादूर्ध्वासक्तदृष्टिषु इत्यर्थः) मृगेषु मृगाश्च तेषां द्वन्द्वेषु मिथुनेषु परस्पराक्ष्णां स्वाक्ष्णां सादृश्यं पश्यन्तौ। इदमत्ररहस्या-मर्थात् मृगीषु सुदक्षिणाक्षिसादृश्यं दिलीपाक्षिसादृश्यं मृगेषु इत्येवं विवेक्तव्यम् ॥ ४० ॥

श्रेणीति। श्रेणीबन्धात् पङ्क्तिबन्धनात् हेतोः, अस्तम्भाम् आधार-स्तम्भरहितां, तोरणं बहिर्द्वारम् तत्र या स्रक् विरच्यते तां तोरणस्रज,

নেত্রে রথের প্রতি চাহিয়া রহিল ; তাঁহারা সেই কালে মৃগমিথুনের নয়নে আপনাদের সুবিশাল নয়নের সাদৃশ্য দর্শন করিতে লাগিলেন ॥৪০॥

কোন স্থানে বা সারসকুল শ্রেণীবদ্ধ হইয়া স্তম্ভবিহীন পুষ্পমালার

public road and retreated on both sides, from the chariot's path, watching the car with steadfast gaze.

41. How they looked, with up-turned eyes, at the flights

another explanation which would add greater beauty to the passage—It is this, it is the custom of these birds to respond to the cries of each other ; in accordance with that custom the peacocks raised their shrill cries, one party responding to another, as the chariot-wheels rattled on past by them.

* **तोरणस्रजं—तोरण** is a gate or triumphal arch erected for welcoming a prince ; hence the sense of the passage is the flights of *sarush* cranes flying in the air, resembled garlands of flowers hung up on triumphal arches, as if a welcome was thereby accorded to the great king.

पवनस्यानुकूलत्वात्*प्रार्थनासिद्धिशंसिनः ।
रजोभिस्तुरगोत्कीर्णैः † अस्पृष्टालकवेष्टनौ ॥४२॥

वितन्वद्भिः इव दृश्यैः, कलनिनादैः अव्यक्तमधुरध्वनिभिः, सारसैः पक्षिविशेषैः ऊर्द्धैः क्वचित् उन्नमिताननौ ॥ ४१ ॥

पवनस्येति । प्रार्थनासिद्धिशंसिनः अनुकूलत्वात् एव मनोरथसिद्धि-सूचकस्य, पवनस्य अनुकूलत्वात् गन्तव्यदिगभिमुखत्वात् तुरगोत्कीर्णैः रजोभिः अस्पृष्टाः अलकाः देव्याः, वेष्टनम् उष्णीषम् राज्ञः, ययोः तौ तथोक्तौ ॥ ४२ ॥

শোভা বিস্তার করিয়া উড়িয়া যাইতেছে, তাঁহারা উভয়ে উর্দ্ধমুখ হইয়া দর্শন করিতে লাগিলেন ॥ ৪১ ॥

রথসংযুক্ত অশ্বগণের খুরোত্থিত ধূলিরাশি, অনুকূল পবনের দ্বারা তাড়িত হইয়া তাঁহাদের অগ্রে অগ্রেই ছুটিল ; রাজমহিষীর কুন্তলজালে কিম্বা দিলীপের উষ্ণীষে সংলগ্ন হইল না ; বায়ুর অনুকূলতা দেখিয়া তাঁহারা বুঝিলেন যে তাঁহাদের মনোরথ পূর্ণ হইবে ॥ ৪২ ॥

---

of *sarush* cranes, cackling melodiously and forming by their peculiar motion triumphal garlands, suspended in the air.

42. The breeze was favourable to them and betokened the early fulfilment of their desire ; and it was so swift that the dust raised by the hoofs of their horses did stick neither on the locks of the queen nor on the coronet of the king.

* प्रार्थनासिद्धिशंसिनः—प्रार्थनायाः पुत्रकामनायाः सिद्धिः फललाभः तां शंसति सूचयति यः स प्रार्थनासिद्धिशंसी तस्य—the favourable breeze that indicated the approaching fruition of their desire.

† अलकवेष्टनौ –The chariot was moving with so much speed that the dust raised by the hoofs of the horses could

সরসীষ্বরবিন্দানাং বীচিবিক্ষোভশীতলম্ ।
আমোদমুপজিঘ্রন্তৌ* স্বনিঃশ্বাসানুকারিণম্ ॥ ৪৩ ॥
গ্রামেষ্বাত্মবিসৃষ্টেষু যূপচিহ্নেষু যজ্বনাম্ ।
অমোঘাঃ প্রতিগৃহ্নন্তৌ অর্ঘ্যানুপদমাশিষঃ ॥ ৪৪ ॥

সরসীষ্বিতি । সরসীষু বীচিবিক্ষোভশীতলম্ ঊর্ম্মিসঙ্ঘট্টনেন শীতলং, স্বনিঃশ্বাসম্ অনুকর্ত্তুং শীলমস্যেতি স্বনিঃশ্বাসানুকারিণম্, (এতেন তয়োরুত্তমস্ত্রীপুংসজাতীয়ত্বমুক্তম্) অরবিন্দানাম্ আমোদম্ উপজিঘ্রন্তৌ ঘ্রাণেন গৃহ্নন্তৌ ॥ ৪৩ ॥

গ্রামেষ্বিতি । আত্মবিসৃষ্টেষু স্বদত্তেষু, যূপঃ নাম সংস্কৃতপশুবন্ধায় দারুবিশেষঃ যূপাঃ এব চিহ্নানি যেষাং তেষু, গ্রামেষু অমোঘাঃ সফলাঃ

সরোবরজলে পদ্ম সকল তরঙ্গের দ্বারা আন্দোলিত হইয়া চতুর্দ্দিকে অতি সুস্নিগ্ধ সুগন্ধতার বিস্তার করিতেছে, তাঁহারা স্বীয় স্বীয় সুরভি-নিঃশ্বাসের অনুরূপ সেই গন্ধ সুখে আঘ্রাণ করিতে লাগিলেন ॥ ৪৩ ॥

তাঁহারা যে সকল গ্রাম ব্রাহ্মণদিগকে দান করিয়াছিলেন, যূপ কাষ্ঠের দ্বারা চিহ্নিত সেই সকল গ্রামে যাজ্ঞিকগণ অর্ঘ্যাদি দ্বারা

---

43. When riding by the side of large lakes, they were delighted to inhale the fagrance of the lotus-flowers, resembling their own breath, and wafted by the breeze,—cooled by its contact with the ripples of the water.

44. As they approached the villages, previously presented by themselves as gifts to priests who had officianted at ceremonies, of which the *yupas* at several places were the signs, the latter came forward to welcome them with due

---

not settle down on the locks of the queen or the crown of the king.

* স্বনিঃশ্বাসানুকারিণং—The old Sanskrit writers on Love and

हैयङ्गवीनमादाय*घोषवृद्धानुपस्थितान् ।
†नामधेयानि पृच्छन्तौ वन्यानां‡मार्गशाखिनाम् ॥ ४५ ॥

यज्वनां विधिनेष्यताम् आशिषः आशीर्वादान्, अर्घ्यं पूजाविधिः तदर्थं द्रव्यम् अर्घ्यम् अर्घ्यञ्च अनुपदम् अन्वक् अर्घ्यस्वीकारानन्तरम्, शृण्वन्तः प्रतिगृह्णन्तौ स्वीकुर्वन्तौ । ४४ ॥

हैयङ्गवीनमिति । ह्यस्तन-गोदोहोद्भवं घृतं हैयङ्गवीनम्, ह्यः पूर्वेद्युर्भवम् तत् सद्योघृतम्, आदाय उपस्थितान् घोषवृद्धान् वन्यानां मार्गशाखिनां नामधेयानि पृच्छन्तौ ॥ कुलकम् ॥ ४५ ॥

তাঁহাদের অভ্যর্থনানন্তর অনেক আশীর্ব্বাদ করিতে লাগিলেন ; উভয়ে সেই সকল অব্যর্থ আশীর্ব্বাদ গ্রহণ করিতে লাগিলেন ॥ ৪৪ ॥

গোপপল্লীর বৃদ্ধগণ সদ্যোজাত ঘৃত লইয়া উপহার দিবার জন্য উপস্থিত হইল ; উভয়ে তাহাদিগকে পথপার্শ্ববর্ত্তী বনতরুগণের নাম জিজ্ঞাসা করিতে লাগিলেন ॥ ৪৫ ॥

homage and to honor them with their benediction. The royal couple reverentially accepted the welcome as well as the benediction.

45. As they passed by the villages of cow-herds, the old men of the villages approached them with newly-made *ghee*

Love-making divide all men and women into a number of classes according to their quality, the breath of the first class they describe as having a peculiar fragrance.

* घोषवृद्धान्—घोषः गोपपल्ली तत्र ये वृद्धाः गलित-वयसः—the old men amongst the inhabitants of a village of cowherds.

† नामधेयानि— नामान्येव इति नामधेयानि स्वार्थे धेयः, रूपनाम-भागेभ्योधेयः इति सूत्रेण धेयप्रत्ययः—Mallinath.

‡ मार्गशाखिनां—शाखा विद्यन्ते येषां ते शाखिनः वृक्षाः, मार्गे पथि

কাপ্যভিখ্যা তয়োরাসীদ্‌ ব্রজতোঃ শুদ্ধবেশয়োঃ।
হিমনির্ম্মুক্তয়োর্যোগে চিত্রাচন্দ্রমসোরিব ॥ ৪৬ ॥
তত্তদ্ভূমিপতিঃ*পত্ন্যৈ দর্শয়ন্‌ প্রিয়দর্শনঃ।
অপি লঙ্ঘিতমধ্বানং বুবুধে ন বুধোপমঃ ॥ ৪৭ ॥

কাপীতি। ব্রজতোঃ গচ্ছতোঃ শুদ্ধবেশয়োঃ উজ্জ্বলনেপথ্যয়োঃ তয়োঃ সুদক্ষিণাদিলীপয়োঃ হিমনির্ম্মুক্তয়োঃ চিত্রাচন্দ্রমসোঃ ইব যোগে সতি কা অপি অনির্ব্বাচ্যা অভিখ্যা শোভা আসীৎ। চিত্রা নক্ষত্রবিশেষঃ শিশিরাপগমে চৈত্র্যাং চিত্রাপূর্ণচন্দ্রমসোরিবেত্যর্থঃ ॥ ৪৬ ॥

তত্তদিতি। প্রিয়ং দর্শনং আকারক যস্য অসৌ প্রিয়দর্শনঃ যোগ্য-

শুদ্ধবেশধারী সেই রাজদম্পতী যখন একরথারূঢ় হইয়া এইরূপে গমন করিতে লাগিলেন তখন তাঁহাদের কি শোভাই হইল! হেমন্ত-ঋতুর অবসানে চন্দ্রের সহিত চিত্রা নক্ষত্রের মিলন হইলে এইরূপ শোভা হইয়া থাকে ॥ ৪৬ ॥

সেই প্রিয়দর্শন ও বুধোপম নরপতি পত্নীকে এটীওটী দেখাইতে দেখাইতে, যে কত পথ ছাড়াইয়া গেলেন তাহা জানিতে পারিলেন না ॥৪৭॥

and the king and the queen enquired of them the names of the wild trees standing on both sides of the road.

46. As they rode on together, dressed in a simple and pure style, how, beautiful they looked !—methinks it was like the union, at the approach of spring, of the moon and of the brilliant and beautiful star called *chitra*.

47. The king was so much absorbed in pointing out and

স্থিতাঃ শাখিনঃ মার্গশাখিনস্তেষাং মার্গশাখিনাং—trees growing on both sides of the road

* পত্ন্যৈ—The auothor of সিদ্ধান্তকৌমুদী quotes a বার্ত্তিকমত

स दुष्प्रापयशाः प्रापदाश्रमं श्रान्तवाहनः ।
सायं संयमिनस्तस्य महर्षेर्महिषीसखः ॥ ४८ ॥

दर्शनीयः दृश्यमानः, भूमिपतिः पत्न्यै तस्मात् अद्भुतं वस्तु दर्शयन् अतिक्रान्तम् अतिवाहितम् अपि अध्वानं न बुबुधे न ज्ञातवान्, बुधः सौम्यः उपमा उपमानं यस्य इति विग्रहः, इदं विशेषणं तत्सहृदयत्वा-त्सुपयोगितयैवास्य माहात्म्यख्यापनार्थम् ॥ ४७ ॥

स इति। दुष्प्रापयशाः दुष्प्रापम् अन्यदुर्लभं यशः यस्य सः तथोक्तः, श्रान्तवाहनः दूरोपगमनात् क्लान्ततुरगः, महिष्याः सखा महिषीसखः सहायान्तरनिरपेक्ष इति भावः, सः राजा सायं सायंकाले, संयमिनः नियमवतः, तस्य महर्षेः वशिष्ठस्य आश्रमं प्रापत् प्राप ॥ ४८ ॥

ক্রমে দিবা শেষ হইল ; রথের অশ্বগণ পথশ্রমে ক্লান্ত হইয়া পড়িল ; অবশেষে নরপতি মহিষীর সহিত, ব্রতধারী মহর্ষি বশিষ্ঠের আশ্রমে গিয়া পৌঁছিলেন ॥ ৪৮ ॥

explaining to his beloved queen, the several objectes that met his eyes, that he was not conscious of the length of the road he had passed.

48. At last towards the close of day, Dileep, of unrivalled

"दृशेश्च" which means that the अणिजन्त कर्त्ता of दृश becomes an objective case when the verb is changed into णिजन्त ; he also cites दर्शयति हरिम्भक्तान् as an example. According to this rule पत्न्यै should have been in the द्वितीया and not in चतुर्थी ; but the reader has to apply in this case another वार्त्तिकसूत्र,—"क्रियया यमभिप्रैति सोऽपि सम्प्रदानम्" which means,—he whose action is the point of aim of another's action, is also सम्प्रदान. Here the act of pointing out of the king has for its aim to induce the act of seeing of the queen, hence it is a case of सम्प्रदान, therefore it is in the चतुर्थी ।

वनान्तरादुपावृत्तैः समित्कुशफलाहरैः ।
पूर्य्यमाणमदृश्याग्निप्रत्युद्यातैस्तपस्विभिः ॥ ४९ ॥
आकीर्णमृषिपत्नीनामुटजद्वाररोधिभिः ।
अपत्यैरिव नीवारभागधेयोचितैर्मृगैः ॥ ५० ॥

वनान्तरादिति । वनान्तरात् अन्यस्मात् वनात्, उपावृत्तैः प्रत्यावृत्तैः, समिधश्च कुशाश्च फलानि च आहर्तुं शीलं येषाम् इति समित्कुशफलाहराः तैः, अदृश्यैः दर्शनायोग्यैः अग्निभिः वैतानिकैः प्रत्युद्याताः प्रत्युद्गताः तैः तपस्विभिः पूर्य्यमाणम् । "प्रोष्यागच्छतामाहिताग्नीनामग्नयः प्रत्युद्यान्तीति श्रूयते" । यथाह, "यथा पितरं प्रोषितं बालपुत्राः प्रत्याधावन्ति एवमेतमग्नयः प्रत्याधावन्ति सशकलान् दारूनिवाहरन्" इति ॥ ४९ ॥

आकीर्णमिति । नीवाराणां भागः एव भागधेयः अंशः, तस्य

তখন তপস্বিগণ, বনাভ্যন্তর হইতে সমিৎ কুশ ফল প্রভৃতি আহরণ করিয়া দলে দলে আশ্রমে প্রতিনিবৃত্ত হইতেছেন; এবং তাঁহাদের আহিত অগ্নিসকল অদৃশ্য ভাবে অগ্রসর হইয়া তাঁহাদিগকে অভ্যর্থনা করিতেছে ॥ ৪৯ ॥

ঋষিপত্নীদিগের দ্বারা পুত্রাধিক যত্নে প্রতিপালিত নীবার ধানের

fame, arrived with his queen, at the hermitage of the sage, who constantly lived under a system of spiritual discipline.

49. By that time the pious inmates of that hermitage were returning home from their rambles in the forest, in quest of sacrificial wood, fruits, and the sacred Kusa grass,—secretly welcomed by the sacred fire of each.

50. And the domesticated deer, loved as children by the wives of the *rishis* and used to handfuls of corn as their por-

सेकान्ते मुनिकन्याभिः तत्क्षणोज्झितवृक्षकम् ।
विश्वासाय विहङ्गानाम् आलवालाम्बुपायिनाम् ॥ ५१ ॥
आतपात्ययसंक्षिप्तनीवारासु निषादिभिः ।
मृगैर्वर्त्तितरोमन्थम् उटजाङ्गनभूमिषु ॥ ५२ ॥

उषितैः अतएव उटजानां पर्णशालानां, द्वारदेशभाग्भिः द्वाररोधकैः, वन्यैः ऋषिपत्नीनाम् अपत्यैः इव आकीर्णं व्याप्तम् ॥ ॥

सेकान्ते इति। सेकान्ते वृक्षमूलसेचनावसाने, भिः सेक्त्रीभिः आलवालेषु जलाधारप्रदेशेषु यत् अम्बु तत्पायिनाम् विहङ्गानां पक्षिणां, विश्वासाय विस्रम्भाय, तत्क्षणे सेकक्षणे, उज्झिताः वृक्षकाः ह्रस्ववृक्षाः, यस्मिन् तत्। ह्रस्वार्थे कप्रत्ययः ॥ ५१ ॥

आतपेति। आतपस्य अत्यये अपगमे सति, संक्षिप्ताः राशीकृताः नीवाराः तृणधान्यानि यासु तासु, उटजानां पर्णशालानाम् अङ्गन-

অংশলাভে চিরাভ্যস্ত মৃগ সকল দলে দলে পর্ণশালার দ্বার রোধ করিয়া দাঁড়াইতেছে ॥ ৫০ ॥

মুনিকন্যাগণ নবজাত তরু সকলে জলসেচন করিয়া আলবালস্থিত জল পানে প্রয়াসী পক্ষিকুলের ভয় হরণের নিমিত্ত দূরে সরিয়া দাঁড়াই-তেছেন ॥ ৫১ ॥

কোথাও বা সন্ধ্যা সমাগত দেখিয়া নীবার ধান্য সকল পর্ণশালার

---

tion in the evening, were flocking before the cottage-doors.

51. By that time the daughters of the *rishis* were leaving the sides of the young plants, after having watered them, to allow the little birds to drink from the water-beds at the foot of the shrubs, without being afraid of their presence.

52. By that time, owing to its being the close of day the corn-grains, that had been spread out in the yard to dry, were

अभ्युत्थिताग्निपिशुनैरतिथीनाश्रमोन्मुखान् *।
पुनानं †पवनोद्धूतैर्धूमैराहुतिगन्धिभिः ॥ ५३ ॥

मुनिषु यज्ञभागेषु, निषादिभिः उपविष्टैः, मृगैः वर्त्तितः निष्पादितः रोमन्थः चर्वितचर्वणं यस्मिन् आश्रमे तम् ॥ ५२ ॥

अभ्युत्थितेति। अभ्युत्थिताः प्रज्वलिताः, होमयोग्याः इत्यर्थः, तेषाम् अग्नीनां पिशुनैः सूचकैः, पवनोद्धूतैः आहुतिगन्धः येषाम् अस्तीति आहुतिगन्धिनः तैः, धूमैः आश्रमोन्मुखान् अतिथीन् पुनानं पवित्रीकुर्वाणम् ॥ ५३ ॥

অঙ্গনে স্তূপাকার করিয়া সঞ্চয় করিয়া রাখা হইয়াছে. সেই প্রাঙ্গণের এক দিকে হরিণ সকল শয়ন করিয়া রোমন্থ করিতেছে ॥ ৫২ ॥

ইতি মধ্যেই সায়ংকালীন হোমাগ্নি প্রজ্বলিত হইয়া বায়ুতাড়িত ও আহুতির গন্ধে আমোদিত ধূমরাশির দ্বারা আশ্রমাগত অতিথিদিগকে পবিত্র করিয়া দিতেছে ॥ ৫৩ ॥

---

being collected in heaps in one part of the yard ; and close by the deer lay ruminating at their ease.

53. And volumes of smoke betokening the mounting flame, and odorous with the sacrificial offerings, came wafted by the evening breeze and sanctified by its contact the royal guests, who were now entering into the holy retreat.

---

* आश्रमोन्मुखान्—आश्रमाय आश्रममागन्तुमित्यर्थः उन्मुखाः उद्यताः आश्रमोन्मुखास्तान् आश्रमोन्मुखान्—who were about to enter the hermitage.

† पवनोद्धूतैः—पवनेन वायुना उद्धूताः ऊर्द्ध्वं प्रक्षिप्तास्तैः, उद्धूता इत्यादि, मध्यपदलोपी समासः।

अथ यन्तारमादिश्य धुर्य्यान् विश्रामयेति सः ।
तामवारोहयत् पत्नीं रथादवततार च ॥ ५४ ॥
तस्मै सभ्याः सभार्य्याय गोप्त्रे * गुप्ततमेन्द्रियाः ।
अर्हणामर्हते चक्रुः मुनयो नयचक्षुषे ॥ ५५ ॥

अथेति । अथ आश्रमप्राप्त्यनन्तरं, सः राजा यन्तारं सारथिं, धुरं वहन्ति धुर्य्याः अश्वाः, धुर्य्यान् रथाश्वान्, विश्रामय विश्रान्तान् कुरु, इति आदिश्य आज्ञाप्य, तां पत्नीं रथात् अवारोहयत् अवतारितवान्, स्वयञ्च अवततार ॥ ५४ ॥

तस्मै इति । सभायां साधवः सभ्याः, गुप्ततमेन्द्रियाः अत्यन्तनियमितेन्द्रियाः, मुनयः सभार्य्याय गोप्त्रे रक्षकाय, नयः शास्त्रम् एव चक्षुः

অনন্তর অশ্বদিগকে বিশ্রাম করাও, সারথিকে এই আদেশ করিয়া রাজা রথ হইতে নামিলেন, এবং মহিষীকে নামাইলেন । ৫৪ ॥

ভদ্রোচিত ব্যবহারজ্ঞ জিতেন্দ্রিয় মুনিগণ রাজনীতিবিশারদ সস্ত্রী-

54. Then having ordered the charioteer to tend the horses, the king alighted from the chariot and also helped the queen to alight.

55. The *Rishis*, who were perfect in their manners, and pre-

---

* गुप्ततमेन्द्रियाः—गुप्ततमानि अन्तर्निगृहीतानि इन्द्रियाणि येषां ते—those who have succeeded in withdrawing their senses from their objects ; that this is the highest state of perfection for a *yogi* will be found from the following passage of the *Bhagabatgita*.

यदा संहरते चायं कूर्म्मोऽङ्गानीव सर्व्वशः ।
इन्द्रियाणीन्द्रियार्थेभ्यस्तस्य प्रज्ञा प्रतिष्ठिता ॥

Trans.—He, who can withdraw at his pleasure all his

विधेः सायन्तनस्यान्ते स ददर्श तपोनिधिम्।
अन्वासितमरुन्धत्या स्वाहयेव* हविर्भुजम् ॥ ५६॥

तस्यावेदकं प्रमाणं, यस्य तस्मै नयचक्षुषे, अतएव अर्हते प्रशस्ताय पूज्याय इत्यर्थः, तस्मै राज्ञे अर्हणां पूजां चक्रुः ॥ ५५ ॥

विधेरिति। सः राजा सायन्तनस्य सायम्भवस्य, विधेः जपहोमाद्यनुष्ठानस्य, अन्ते अवसाने, अरुन्धत्या अन्वासितं पश्चात् उपवेशनेन उपसेवितम्, तपोनिधिं वशिष्ठं, स्वाहया स्वाहादेव्या अन्वासितं हविर्भुजम् इव ददर्श ("समित्पुष्पकुशाग्न्यम्बुमृदन्नाक्षतपाणिकः। जपहोमश्च कुर्व्वाणो नाभिवाद्यो द्विजो भवेत्।") इति अनुष्ठानस्य मध्ये अभिवादननिषेधाद्विधेरन्ते ददर्शेत्युक्तम्। अन्वासनञ्चात्र पतिव्रताधर्म्मत्वेनोक्तं न तु कर्म्माङ्गत्वेन; विधेरन्त इति कर्म्मणः समाप्त्यभिधानात् ॥ ५६ ॥

নাই রাজাকে ও মহিষীকে সমুচিত অভ্যর্থনা করিলেন ॥ ৫৫ ॥

সায়ংকালীন হোমাদির পর রাজা, স্বাহাসমন্বিত অগ্নির ন্যায় দীপ্তিশালী, অরুন্ধতী-সমন্বিত মহর্ষির সহিত সাক্ষাৎ করিলেন ॥ ৫৬ ॥

---

eminent in the virtue of self-control, gave a hearty welcome to the wise king and his beloved queen.

56. After the evening devotions Dileep waited upon the holy sage, who was accompanied by his wife Arundhati, and who accordingly resembled the god Fire attended by *Swaha*, his wife.

---

senses from their objects, as does the tortoise withdraw its limbs within its shell, can be regarded as one who has attained perfect self-control.

* हविर्भुजं—हविः होमार्थं दत्तं घृतं भुङ्क्ते यः स हविर्भुक् वह्निः तम्।

तयोर्जगृहतुः पादान् राजा राज्ञी च मागधी ।
तौ गुरुर्गुरुपत्नी च प्रीत्या प्रतिननन्दतुः ॥ ५७ ॥

तमातिथ्यक्रियाशान्तरथक्षोभपरिश्रमम् ।
पप्रच्छ कुशलं राज्ये राज्याश्रममुनिं मुनिः ॥ ५८ ॥

तयोरिति । मागधी मगधराजपुत्री, राज्ञी सुदक्षिणा, राजा च तयोः अरुन्धतीवसिष्ठयोः पादान् जगृहतुः ; पादग्रहणमभिवादनम्, गुरुपत्नी गुरुश्च कर्त्तारौ सा च स च तौ सुदक्षिणादिलीपौ कर्म्मभूतौ, प्रीत्या हर्षेण प्रतिननन्दतुः आशीर्वादादिभिः सम्भावयाञ्चक्रतुः इत्यर्थः ॥ ५७ ॥

तमिति । मुनिः अतिथ्यर्थम् आतिथ्यम्, आतिथ्यस्य क्रिया तया शान्तः रथक्षोभेण यः परिश्रमः सः यस्य स तं तथोक्तं, राज्यम् एव आश्रमः, तत्र मुनिं मुनितुल्यम् इत्यर्थः, तं दिलीपं राज्ये कुशलं पप्रच्छ, (राज्यशब्दः पुरोहितादिष्वन्तर्गततत्वाद्राजकर्म्मवचनः तथाप्यत्र सप्ताङ्गवचनः, उपपन्नं ननु शिवं सप्तस्वङ्गेषु इति उत्तरविरोधात्, तथाह मनुः, "स्वाम्यमात्यपुरं राष्ट्रं कोशदण्डौ तथा सुहृत् । सप्तैतानि समस्तानि

রাজা ও মহিষী উভয়ে তাঁহাদের চরণ বন্দনা করিলেন, তাঁহারাও উভয়ে তাঁহাদিগকে প্রীতির সহিত অভ্যর্থনা করিলেন ॥ ৫৭ ॥

আতিথ্যক্রিয়া দ্বারা রথশ্রম অপনোদিত হইলে, মহর্ষি রাজ্যাশ্রমের মুনিস্বরূপ রাজাকে রাজ্যের কুশল জিজ্ঞাসা করিলেন ॥ ৫৮ ॥

---

57. Both the king and the queen prostrated themselves at the feet of the holy couple, and they too in their turn, gave a loving welcome to their royal guests.

58. After the king had rested a while and recovered from the effects of the fatigue of the previous journey, through the kind hospitality of the sage, the latter asked the pious monarch whether every thing fared well in his kingdom.

अथाथर्वनिधेस्तस्य विजितारिपुरः पुरः ।
अर्थ्यामर्थपतिर्वाचम् आददे वदतां वरः ॥ ५९ ॥
उपपन्नं ननु शिवं सप्तस्वङ्गेषु यस्य मे ।
दैवीनां मानुषीणाञ्च प्रतिहर्त्ता त्वमापदाम् ॥ ६० ॥

लोकेऽस्मिन् राज्यमुच्यते" इति)। तत्र, "ब्राह्मणं कुशलं पृच्छेत् क्षत्रबन्धुमनामयम्। वैश्यं क्षेमं समागम्य शूद्रमारोग्यमेव च ॥" इति मनुवचने सत्यपि तस्य राज्ञो महानुभावत्वात् ब्राह्मणोचितः कुशलप्रश्न एव कृत इत्यनुसन्धेयम्, अतएवोक्तं राज्याश्रममुनिमिति ॥ ५८ ॥

अथेति। अथ प्रश्नानन्तरं, विजितारिपुरः विजितशत्रुनगरः, वदतां वक्तॄणां वरः श्रेष्ठः, अर्थपतिः राजा, अथर्वणः अथर्ववेदस्य, निधेः तस्य मुनेः पुरः अग्रे अर्थ्याम् अर्थात् अनपेताम् वाचम् आददे वक्तुम् उपक्रान्तवान् इत्यर्थः। अथर्वनिधेरित्यनेन पुरोहितकर्माभिज्ञत्वात् तत्कर्म्मनिर्वाहकत्वं मुनेरस्तीति सूच्यते। यथाह कामन्दकः, "त्रय्याञ्च दण्डनीत्याञ्च कुशलः स्यात् पुरोहितः। अथर्वविहितं कुर्य्यात् नित्यं शान्तिकपौष्टिकम् ।" इति ॥ ५९ ॥

उपपन्नमिति। हे गुरो! सप्तसु अङ्गेषु स्वाम्यमात्यादिषु, शिवं

অনন্তর শত্রুকুলের উচ্ছেদকারী সেই রাজা, অথর্ব্ববেদপারদর্শী মহর্ষিকে অর্থপূর্ণ বাক্য বলিতে লাগিলেন ॥ ৫৯ ॥

আপনি যখন স্বয়ং আমার দৈবী ও মানুষী সকল প্রকার বিপদের উদ্ধারকর্ত্তা আছেন, তখন আমার রাজ্যের সপ্তাঙ্গেই কুশল, ইহাতে সন্দেহ কি ॥ ৬০ ॥

59. Then the king, who had vanquished all his enemies, thus addressed the sage, who was versed in the rules of the Athurva Veda.

60. As long as the duty of averting all my dangers, either

तव मन्त्रकृतो मन्त्रैः दूरात् संशमितारिभिः।
प्रत्यादिश्यन्त इव मे दृष्टलक्ष्यभिदः शराः ॥६१॥

कुशलमुपपन्नं तव युक्तम् एव, तत्तु अवधारये, कथम्? इत्यत्राह, यत्र मे दैवीनां देवेभ्यः आगतानां दुर्भिक्षादीनां, मानुषीणां मनुष्येभ्यः आगतानां चौरभयादीनाम्, आपदां व्यसनानां, त्वं प्रतिकर्त्ता वारयिता असि। अत्राह कामन्दकः, "हुताशनो जलं व्याधिः दुर्भिक्षं मरणं तथा। इति पञ्चविधं दैवं मानुषं व्यसनं ततः॥ आयुक्तकेभ्यश्चौरेभ्यः परेभ्यो राजवल्लभात्। पृथिवीपतिलोभाच्च नराणां पञ्चधा मतम्" ॥६०॥

तत्र मानुषापत्प्रतीकारमाह, तवेति। दूरात् परोक्षे एव संशमितारिभिः, मन्त्रान् कृतवान् मन्त्रकृत् तस्य मन्त्रकृतः मन्त्राणां स्रष्टुः प्रयोक्तुः वा, तव मन्त्रैः कर्तृभिः, दृष्टं प्रत्यक्षं यत् लक्ष्यं तन्मात्रं भिन्दन्ति इति दृष्टलक्ष्यभिदः, मे शराः प्रत्यादिश्यन्ते इव; वयमेव समर्थाः किमेभिः पिष्टपेषकैरिति निराक्रियन्ते इव इत्युत्प्रेक्षा। त्वन्मन्त्रसामर्थ्यादेव नः पौरुषं फलतीति भावः ॥ ६१ ॥

আপনি বেদমন্ত্রের রচয়িতা, আপনার মন্ত্রসকল আমার শত্রুগণকে দূর হইতেই পরাভব করে; কিন্তু আমার বাণ সকল শত্রুগণ সম্মুখে উপস্থিত না হইলে তাহাদিগকে ভেদ করিতে পারে না; সুতরাং আপনার মন্ত্র থাকিতে আমার বাণ সকলের আর প্রয়োজন নাই ॥ ৬১ ॥

human or divine, rests with you, so long prosperity is sure to reign in all the seven departments of my state.

61. You are yourself a composer of the hymns of the Vedas, and your *hymns* are efficacious enough to thwart my enemies from a distance; consequently they have made my arrows useless, which can peirce only those who come within their mark.

हविरावर्जितं होतः ! त्वया विधिवदग्निषु ।
वृष्टिर्भवति सस्यानाम् अवग्रहविशोषिणाम् ॥६२॥
पुरुषायुषजीविन्यः निरातङ्का निरीतयः ।
यन्मदीयाः प्रजास्तस्य हेतुस्त्वद्ब्रह्मवर्च्चसम्* ॥६३॥

सम्प्रति दैविकापत्प्रतीकारमाह, हविरिति। हे होतः! त्वया विधिवत् अग्निषु आवर्ज्जितं प्रक्षिप्तं हविः आज्यादिकं कर्त्तृ, अवग्रहः वर्षप्रतिबन्धः, तेन विशोषिणां शुष्यतां सस्यानां वृष्टिः भवति वृष्टिरूपेण सस्यान्युपजीवयतीति भावः। (अत्र मनुः, "अग्नौ दत्ताहुतिः सम्यक् आदित्यमुपतिष्ठते। आदित्याज्जायते वृष्टिः वृष्टेरन्नं ततः प्रजाः) इति ॥ ६२ ॥

पुरुषेति। आयुः जीवितकालः पुरुषस्य आयुः पुरुषायुषं वर्षशतम् इत्यर्थः, मदीयाः प्रजाः पुरुषायुषं जीवन्ति इति पुरुषायुषजीविन्यः, निरातङ्काः निर्भयाः निरीतयः अतिवृष्ट्यादिरहिताः इति यत् तस्य सर्वस्य त्वद्ब्रह्मवर्च्चसं तव व्रताध्ययनसम्पत्तिः एव हेतुः। "अतिवृष्टिर-

---

হে গুরো! আপনি হোতা হইয়া অগ্নিতে যথাবিধি যে ঘৃত আহুতি দেন, তাহাই অনাবৃষ্টিবিশুষ্ক শস্য সকলের প্রাণরক্ষার্থ বৃষ্টি রূপে পরিণত হয়। ৬২ ॥

আমার প্রজাকুল যে শত বৎসর নির্ভয়ে নিরাপদে বাঁচিয়া থাকে, তাহা কেবল আপনকারই তপস্যার ফল। ৬৩ ॥

---

62. The ghee-offerings that you pour on the sacrificial fire, become converted into rain, for nourishing the parched up crops.

63. That my subjects live to the full age of man, or that

---

*ब्रह्मवर्च्चसं—ब्रह्मणः वेदस्य वर्च्चः तेजः तदेव ब्रह्मवर्च्चसम् ब्रह्महस्तिभ्यां वर्च्चसः इति समासे अच्प्रत्ययः—Mallinath.

त्वयैवं चिन्त्यमानस्य गुरुणा ब्रह्मयोनिना ।
सानुबन्धाः कथं न स्युः सम्पदो मे निरापदः ॥ ६४ ॥
किन्तु वध्वां तवैतस्याम् अदृष्टसदृशप्रजम् ।
न मामवति सद्वीपा रत्नसूरपि मेदिनी ॥ ६५ ॥

नावृष्टिः मूषिकाः शलभाः शुकाः । प्रत्यासन्नाश्च राजानः षडेता ईतयः स्मृताः ॥" इति कामन्दकः ॥ ६३ ॥

त्वयेति । ब्रह्मा योनिः कारणं यस्य तेन ब्रह्मपुत्रेण गुरुणा त्वया एवम् उक्तप्रकारेण चिन्त्यमानस्य अनुध्यायमानस्य अतएव निरापदः व्यसनहीनस्य मे सम्पदः सानुबन्धाः अनुस्यूताः अविच्छिन्नाः इति यावत्, कथं न स्युः ? स्युरेव इत्यर्थः ॥ ६४ ॥

सम्प्रति आगमनप्रयोजनमाह, किन्त्विति । किन्तु तव एतस्यां वध्वां स्नुषायाम्, अदृष्टा सदृशी अनुरूपा प्रजा येन तं, मां सद्वीपा अपि

আপনার ন্যায় ব্রহ্মার পুত্র গুরু স্বয়ং যখন মঙ্গল চিন্তা করিতেছেন, তখন কেন না আমার সকল আপদ বিদূরিত হইয়া অবিচ্ছিন্ন সম্পদ হইবে ॥ ৬৪ ॥

কিন্তু আপনার এই পুত্রবধূর ক্রোড়ে নিজের অনুরূপ পুত্রের মুখ দর্শন করিতে না পাওয়াতে, নানা দ্বীপ সমন্বিত ও রত্নের খনিস্বরূপ এই পৃথিবীর সাম্রাজ্যও আমার ভাল লাগিতেছে না ॥ ৬৫ ॥

---

they are free from fear and from all agricultural losses, are all owing to the influence of your piety and learning.

64. How could the fortunes of a man be not in a state of continued prosperity, whose interests are being taken care of by a spiritual preceptor like your venerable self—one who is descended directly from *Brahma* the creator.

65. But the sovereignty of the whole earth, with all its islands, and with all its hidden treasures, does not give me any

नूनं मत्तः परं वंश्याः पिण्डविच्छेददर्शिनः ।
न प्रकामभुजः श्राद्धे स्वधासंग्रहतत्पराः ॥ ६६ ॥
मत्परं दुर्लभं मत्वा नूनमावर्जितं मया ।
पयः पूर्वैः स्वनिःश्वासैः कवोष्णमुपभुज्यते ॥ ६७ ॥

रत्नानि सूयते इति रत्नसूः अपि, मेदिनी न अवति न प्रीणाति । रत्नसूरपीत्यनेन सर्वरत्नेभ्यः पुत्ररत्नमेव श्लाघ्यमिति सूचितम् ॥ ६५ ॥

तदेव प्रतिपादयति, नूनमिति । मत्तः परं मदनन्तरम्, पिण्डविच्छेददर्शिनः पिण्डदानविच्छेदम् उत्प्रेक्षमाणाः, वंशोद्भवाः वंश्याः पितरः, स्वधा इत्यव्ययं पितृभोज्ये वर्त्तते, तस्य संग्रहे तत्पराः आसक्ताः सन्तः श्राद्धे पितृकर्म्मणि प्रकामभुजः पर्य्याप्तभोजिनः न भवन्ति नूनं सत्यम् । निर्धना स्वामदनं कियदपि संरक्षन्तीति भावः ॥ ६६ ॥

मत्परमिति । मत्परं मदनन्तरम्, दुर्लभं दुर्लभ्यं मत्वा मया आवर्ज्जितं दत्तं पयः पूर्वैः पितृभिः स्वनिःश्वासैः दुःखजैः कवोष्णम्

আমার এমন বোধ হইতেছে, পূর্ব্বপুরুষগণ আমার পর পিণ্ডলোপের আশঙ্কা করিয়া, শ্রাদ্ধ কালে প্রদত্ত পিণ্ড সকল সঞ্চয় করিয়া রাখিবার জন্যই ব্যস্ত হইতেছেন, ভাল করিয়া আহার করিতে পারিতেছেন না ॥ ৬৬ ॥

আমার পর আর কেহ জলগণ্ডূষ দিবে না; ইহা জানিয়া বুঝিবা

---

comfort, seeing that I am denied the pleasure of seeing worthy issue, form this your daughter-in-law.

66. Methinks ! my venerable ancestors, apprehending the total cessation of the *pinda* offerings after my death, are now starving themselves, in their anxiety to store up present *pindas* as a provision for the future.

67. Methinks ; those venerable ancestors of mine are drinking the libations of water offered by me, made hot by their sighs, at

সোঽহমিজ্যাবিশুদ্ধাত্মা *প্রজালোপনিমীলিতঃ।
প্রকাশশ্চাপ্রকাশশ্চ লোকালোক ইবাচলঃ ॥৬৮॥

ঈষদুষ্ণং যথা তথা উপভুজ্যতে নূনমিতি তর্কঃ। কবোষ্ণমিতি কুমন্দস্য কবাদেশঃ। ॥ ৬৭ ॥

সোঽহমিতি। ইজ্যা যাগঃ, তয়া বিশুদ্ধাত্মা বিশুদ্ধচেতনঃ, প্রজালোপেন সন্তত্যভাবেন নিমীলিতঃ সঞ্জাতনিমীলনঃ, সঃ অহম্ লোক্যতে ইতি লোকঃ ন লোক্যতে ইতি অলোকঃ লোকশ্চ অলোকশ্চ স লোকালোকঃ ইতি, লোকশ্চাসৌ অলোকশ্চেতি বা লোকালোকঃ চক্রবালঃ অচলঃ ইব, প্রকাশতে ইতি প্রকাশশ্চ দেবঋণবিমোচনাৎ, ন প্রকাশতে ইতি অপ্রকাশশ্চ পিতৃঋণাবিমোচনাৎ, লোকালোকোঽপি অন্তঃসূর্য্যসম্পর্কাৎ বহিস্তমোব্যাপ্ত্যা চ প্রকাশশ্চাপ্রকাশশ্চেতি মন্তব্যম্ ॥ ৬৮ ॥

পূর্ব্ব পুরুষগণ আমার প্রদত্ত তর্পণের বারি দীর্ঘনিঃশ্বাস দ্বারা উষ্ণ করিয়া পান করিতেছেন। ৬৭।

একদিকে যেমন যাগ যজ্ঞাদি দ্বারা আমার দেহ মনের উজ্জ্বলতা সম্পাদিত হইতেছে, অপর দিকে অনপত্যতা নিবন্ধন তাহা নিমীলিত হইয়া যাইতেছে; অতএব আমার দশা যেন লোকালোক পর্ব্বতের ন্যায়, এক দিকে উজ্জ্বল ও অপর দিকে অনুজ্জ্বল হইতেছে। ৬৮ ॥

---

the prospect of such libations ceasing altogether after my death.

68. On the one hand my soul is purified and enlightened by sacrificial ceremonies, but on the other a cloud of despair pressess upon it, on account of the failure of issue; thus I resemble the *Lokalok* mountain, one half of which is lighted and the other half dark.

---

* ইজ্যাবিশুদ্ধাত্মা—যজ+ক্যপ্—ব্রজযজোর্ভাবে ক্যপ্ ৩। ৩। ৯৮

Panini.

लोकान्तरसुखं पुण्यं तपोदानसमुद्भवम् ।
सन्ततिः शुद्धवंश्या हि परत्रेह च शर्मणे ॥६९॥
तया हीनं विधातर्मां कथं पश्यन्न दूयसे ? ।
सिक्तं स्वयमिव स्नेहाद्वन्ध्यमाश्रमवृक्षकम् ॥७०॥

ननु तपोदानादिसम्पन्नस्य किमपत्यैरित्याह, लोकान्तरेति । समुद्भवति अस्मादिति समुद्भवः कारणं, तपोदाने समुद्भवः यस्य तत् तपोदानसमुद्भवं, यत् पुण्यं तत् लोकान्तरे परलोके सुखं सुखकरं, शुद्ध-वंशे भवा शुद्धवंश्या, सन्ततिः हि परत्र परलोके इह च लोके शर्मणे सुखाय भवतीति शेषः ॥ ६९ ॥

तयेति । हे विधातः ! स्रष्टः ! तया सन्तत्या हीनम् अनपत्यम् मां स्नेहात् प्रेम्णा स्वयम् एव सिक्तं जलसेकेन वर्द्धितं वन्ध्यम् अफलम् आश्रमस्य वृक्षकं वृक्षोत्तमम् इव पश्यन् कथं न दूयसे न परितप्यसे । विधातरित्यनेन समर्थोऽप्युपेक्षसे इति गम्यते ॥ ७० ॥

তপস্যা এবং দানাদি দ্বারা যে পুণ্য সঞ্চয় করা যায় তদ্দারা পারলৌকিক সুখই লাভ হইয়া থাকে; কিন্তু সদ্বংশজাত সচ্চরিত্র পুত্রের দ্বারা ইহ পরকালে সুখ হয় ॥ ৬৯ ॥

হে বিধাতঃ! আশ্রমবৃক্ষকে স্বয়ং জলসেচন দ্বারা পালন করিয়া, তাহাতে ফল না দেখিলে আপনার যেমন ক্লেশ হয়, তেমনি আমাকে সন্তানহীন দেখিয়া কেন ক্লেশ হইতেছে না ॥ ৭০ ॥

---

69. The virtue accruing from penances and fasts and alms-givings helps a man in the other world alone ; whereas a good and virtuous son is of use in this life as well as in the next.

70. How is it, O venerable father ! that you are not pained to see me devoid of that blessing—as you would surely be when you see a beloved tree of this hermitage, planted with your

असह्यपीडं भगवन्! ऋणमन्त्यमवेहि मे।
अरुन्तुदमिवालानम् अनिर्वाणस्य दन्तिनः ॥७१॥
तस्मान्मुच्ये यथा तात! संविधातुं तथार्हसि।
इक्ष्वाकूणां दुरापेऽर्थे त्वदधीना हि, सिद्धयः ॥७२॥

असह्येति। हे भगवन्! मे मम अन्त्यम् पैतृकम् ऋणम्, अनिर्वाणस्य मज्जनरहितस्य, दन्तिनः गजस्य, अरुः मर्म्म तुदतीति अरुन्तुदं मर्म्मस्पृक्, आलानं बन्धनस्तम्भम् इव असह्या सोढुम् अशक्या पीड़ा दुःखं यस्मिन् तत्, अवेहि दुःसहदुःखजनकम्, इत्यर्थः। निर्वाणोत्थानशयनानि त्रीणि गजकर्म्माणि इति माघकाव्ये। ("ऋणं देवस्य यागेन ऋषीणां दानकर्म्मणा। सन्तत्या पितृलोकानां शोधयित्वा परिव्रजेत्") ॥ ७१ ॥

तस्मादिति। हे तात! तस्मात् पैतृकात् ऋणात् यथा मुच्ये मुक्तो भवामि, तथा संविधातुं कर्त्तुम् अर्हसि, हि यस्मात् कारणात् इक्ष्वा-

হে ভগবন্! স্নানার্থ উৎসুক হস্তীর পক্ষে বন্ধন-স্তম্ভ যেমন ক্লেশ-কর হয়, সেইরূপ পিতৃ-পুরুষের ঋণভার আমার পক্ষে যন্ত্রণা-দায়ক হইতেছে, জানিবেন ॥ ৭১ ॥

হে পিতঃ! সেই ঋণদায় হইতে যাহাতে মুক্ত হইতে পারি, কৃপা

own hands, failing to produce any fruits, in the natural season ?

71. Be it known to you, venerable sage, that these last of my debts (viz debts to my ancestors) have become galling to my spirit ; as the state of bondage, at the tying pole, is deeply irksome to the heat-stricken elephant, panting for its daily bath.

72. Order it so then, O Father, that I may be discharged form these debts ; in every thing difficult of achievement, by

इति विज्ञापितो राज्ञा ध्यानस्तिमितलोचनः ।
क्षणमात्रमृषिस्तस्थौ सुप्तमीन इव ह्रदः ॥ ७३ ॥
सोऽपश्यत् प्रणिधानेन सन्ततेः स्तम्भकारणम् ।
भावितात्मा भुवो भर्त्तुरथैनं प्रत्यबोधयत् ॥ ७४ ॥

नृपाणाम् इक्ष्वाकुवंश्यानाम्, दुरापे दुष्प्रापे अर्थे सिद्धयः त्वदधीनाः त्वदायत्ताः । ॥ ७२ ॥

इतीति । इति राज्ञा विज्ञापितः ऋषिः ध्यानेन स्तिमिते लोचने यस्य स ध्यानस्तिमितलोचनः निश्चलाक्षः, सन् क्षणमात्रं सुप्तमीनः ह्रदः इव तस्थौ ॥ ७३ ॥

सोऽपश्यदिति । सः मुनिः प्रणिधानेन चित्तैकाग्र्येण, भावितात्मा शुद्धान्तःकरणः, भुवो भर्त्तुः नृपस्य सन्ततेः स्तम्भकारणं सन्तानप्रतिबन्धकारणम् अपश्यत्, अथ अनन्तरम् एनं नृपं प्रत्यबोधयत् स्वदृष्टं ज्ञापितवान् इत्यर्थः ॥ ७४ ॥

পূর্ব্বক এইরূপ বিধান করুন ; দুষ্প্রাপ্য সকল বিষয়ে আপনিই ইক্ষাকু-বংশীয়দিগের সিদ্ধিদাতা । ৭২ ।

রাজা এই প্রকার নিবেদন করিলে, ঋষি ক্ষণকাল মীনসঞ্চার-রহিত সরোবরের ন্যায় মুদিতনেত্রে ধ্যান-পরায়ণ হইয়া রহিলেন । ৭৩ ।

বিশুদ্ধান্তঃকরণ সেই ঋষি ধ্যানযোগে দিলীপের অপত্যোৎপত্তির বিঘ্নীভূত কারণ দর্শন করিলেন, অনন্তর তাঁহাকে বুঝাইয়া বলিলেন ।৭৪।

---

the princes of the royal line of Ikshaku, success is entirely at your disposal.

73. Thus addressed by the king, the *rishi* remained for some time in a state of trance, calm and motionless like the waters of a lake, in which the fish are asleep.

74. By second sight he discovered the cause of the obs-

पुरा शक्रमुपस्थाय तवोर्वीं प्रति यास्यतः ।
आसीत् कल्पतरुच्छायामाश्रिता सुरभिः पथि॥७५

धर्मलोपभयाद्राज्ञीम् ऋतुस्नातामिमां स्मरन् ।
*प्रदक्षिणक्रियार्हायां तस्यां त्वं साधु नाचरः॥७६

पुरेति । पुरा पूर्वं शक्रम् इन्द्रम् उपस्थाय सेवित्वा उर्वीं प्रति भुवम् उद्दिश्य यास्यतः गमिष्यतः तव पथि कल्पतरुच्छायाम् आश्रिता सुरभिः कामधेनुः आसीत् तत्र स्थिता इत्यर्थः ॥ ७५

ततः किमित्याह, धर्म्मलोपेति । ऋतुः पुष्पं रजः इति यावत्, ऋतुना निमित्तेन स्नाताम् इमां राज्ञीं सुदक्षिणां धर्म्मस्य ऋत्वभिगमनलक्षणस्य लोपात् भ्रंशात् यः भयः तस्मात् स्मरन् ध्यायन्, प्रदक्षिणक्रियार्हायां प्रदक्षिणकरणयोग्यायां तस्यां धेन्वां त्वं साधु प्रद-

---

পূর্ব্বে একসময়ে ইন্দ্রের উপাসনা করিয়া আপনি যখন পৃথিবীতে প্রতিনিবৃত্ত হইতে ছিলেন, তখন আপনার পথে সুরভিনাম্নী সুরধেনু কল্পবৃক্ষের ছায়াতে শয়ন করিয়াছিলেন ॥ ৭৫ ॥

এই মহিষী তখন ঋতুস্নাতা ছিলেন, ধর্ম্মলোপভয়ে সেই দিকেই

---

tacles lying in the way of his having progeny, and then, in an inspired mood, thus divulged the secret to the king.

75. On one occasion, when you were returning to the earth after waiting upon Indra, there was a *kalpa* tree on your way, at whose shade lay at her ease the divine cow *Surabhi*.

76. At that time, in your anxiety not to be guilty of violating a sacred obligation to this queen, who was waiting for you

---

*प्रदक्षिणक्रियार्हायां—प्रदक्षिणं मङ्गल्यमावर्त्तस्य पार्श्वतो गमनं, तदेव क्रिया प्रदक्षिणक्रिया, तस्या अर्हा योग्या तस्यां—One fit for

अवजानासि मां यस्मात् अतस्ते न भविष्यति ।
मत्प्रसूतिमनाराध्य प्रजेति त्वां शशाप सा ॥७७॥

क्रियादिसत्कारं न आचरः न आचरितवान् असि । ऋतुस्नानाभिगमने मनुः "ऋतुकालाभिगामी स्यात् स्वदारनिरतः सदा।" इति । अकरणे दोषमाह पराशरः,—"ऋतुस्नातान्तु यो भार्य्यां स्वस्थः सन्नोपगच्छति । बालगोघ्नापराधेन लिप्यते नात्र संशयः । इति ॥ ७६ ॥

अवजानासीति । यस्मात् कारणात् माम् अवजानासि तिरस्करोषि अतः कारणात् मत्प्रसूतिं मम सन्ततिम् अनाराध्य असेवयित्वा ते तव प्रजा न भविष्यतीति सा सुरभिः त्वां शशाप ॥ ७७ ॥

মন থাকাতে আপনি সেই প্রদক্ষিণক্রিয়াযোগ্যা সুরভির প্রতি সমুচিত সম্মান প্রদর্শন করেন নাই ॥ ৭৬ ॥

তুই যখন আমাকে অবজ্ঞা করিলি, তখন আমার সন্তানের সেবা না করিলে তোর সন্তান জন্মিবে না, এই বলিয়া সেই সুরভি সেই সময়ে আপনাকে শাপ দিয়াছিলেন ॥ ৭৭ ॥

after her customary monthly ablution, you did not behave respectfully towards that holy cow, who was worthy of the honor of being gone round.

77. And she cursed you by saying—"As thou hast treated me with disrespect, so thou shalt never have any issue without first propitiating my offspring."

being gone round. Our old law-books enjoin the duty of going round the following objects as a mark of respect ;

मृद्गां दैवतं विप्रं घृतं मधु चतुष्पथम् ।
प्रदक्षिणानि कुर्वीत विज्ञातांश्च वनस्पतीन् ॥ *Mallinath.*

स शापो न त्वया राजन्! न च सारथिना श्रुतः।
नदत्याकाशगङ्गायाः स्रोतस्युद्दामदिग्गजे ॥ ৭৮॥
ईप्सितं तदवज्ञानात् विद्धि सार्गलमात्मनः।
*प्रतिबध्नाति हि श्रेयः पूज्यपूजाव्यतिक्रमः ॥ ৭৯॥

कथं तदस्माभिर्न श्रुतमित्याह, स शाप इति। हे राजन्! सः शापः त्वया न श्रुतः, सारथिना च न श्रुतः। अश्रवणे हेतुमाह, क्रीडार्थम् आगताः, उद्दामानः दाम्नः उद्गताः, दिग्गजाः यस्मिन् तथोक्ते आकाशगङ्गायाः मन्दाकिन्याः स्रोतसि प्रवाहे नदति सति ॥৭৮॥

अस्तु प्रस्तुते किमायातमित्यत्राह, ईप्सितमिति। तदवज्ञानात् तस्याः धेनोः अवज्ञानात अपमानात्, आत्मनः स्वस्य आप्तुम् इष्टम्

হে রাজন্! উন্মত্ত দিগ্গজগণ কর্ত্তৃক তাড়িত মন্দাকিনীর জল-স্রোতের শব্দ হওয়াতে, আপনি অথবা সারথি কেহই সেই শাপ-বাক্য শুনিতে পান নাই ॥ ৭৮।

সেই সুরভির প্রতি অবজ্ঞা প্রদর্শনের নিমিত্তই আপনার মনোরথ পূর্ণ হইবার পথে বিঘ্ন ঘটিয়াছে জানিবেন। পূজনীয় জনের প্রতি পূজার

78. At the time, an elephant, one of the keepers of the differed corners of the heavens, was diverting itself by playing with the waters of the heavenly river ; consequently there being a great noise, niether you nor your charioteer could hear that curse, pronounced by Surabhi.

79. Know then! O Prince, that the attainment of your desire is being postponed by that insult you offered to the divine cow ; it is but meet that the non-payment of homage

* प्रतिबध्नाति हि श्रेयः—श्रेयः मङ्गलं प्रतिबध्नाति प्रतिबन्धकं करोति,—comes in the way of one's we fare.

हविषे दीर्घसत्रस्य सा चेदानीं * प्रचेतसः ।
†भुजङ्गपिहितद्वारं ‡पातालमधितिष्ठति ॥ ८० ॥

ईप्सितं मनोरथम्, तद्गतं सप्रतिबन्धं विद्धि जानीहि । तथाहि, पूज्यपूजायाः व्यतिक्रमः अतिक्रमणं श्रेयः प्रतिबध्नाति ॥ ७९ ॥

हविष इति । सा च सुरभिः इदानीं दीर्घं सत्रं चिरकालसाध्यो यागविशेषः यस्य, तस्य प्रचेतसः हविषे दध्याज्यादिहविरर्थं, भुजङ्ग-पिहितद्वारं भुजङ्गावरुद्धद्वारं ततः दुष्प्रवेशं पातालम् अधितिष्ठति पाताले तिष्ठति इत्यर्थः ॥ ८० ॥

ব্যতিক্রম হইলে কল্যাণের পথে বিঘ্ন ঘটিয়াই থাকে ॥ ৭৯ ॥

এক্ষণে সেই সুরভি বরুণকর্ত্তৃক অনুষ্ঠিত বহুকালব্যাপী যজ্ঞের ঘৃত যোগাইবার মানসে পাতালে বাস করিতেছেন ; সেই পাতালের দ্বার সর্পের দ্বারা রক্ষিত সুতরাং প্রবেশ দুর্ঘট ॥ ৮০ ॥

to those who are worthy of it should thus stand in the way of our welfare.

80. Surabhi is at present staying in the nether regions,—the gates of which are guarded by serpents,—with a view to supplying *ghee* for a sacrificial ceremony of Baruna, that would last for a long time.

---

* प्रचेतसः वरुणस्य—"प्रचेता वरुणः पाशी" इत्यमरः ।

† भुजङ्गपिहितद्वारं—भुजः कुटिलीभवन् सन् गच्छति इति भुजङ्गः सर्पः, भुजङ्गेन पिहितं आच्छादितं द्वारं यस्य तत् । पिहितं—अपि+धा+क्तः ।

‡ पातालं—अधिशीङ्स्थासां कर्म्म १।४।४६ । इति सूत्रेण आधारस्य कर्म्मत्वं—*Mallinath.*

सुतां तदीयां सुरभेः कृत्वा प्रतिनिधिं शुचिः ।
आराधय सपत्नीकः प्रीता कामदुघा हि सा ॥८१॥
इति वादिन एवास्य होतुराहुतिसाधनम् ।
अनिन्द्या नन्दिनी नाम धेनुराववृते वनात् ॥ ८२॥

तर्हि का गतिरित्यत आह, सुतामिति। तस्याः : इयं तदीया, तां सुतां सुरभेः प्रतिनिधिं कृत्वा, शुचिः शुद्धः, सह पत्न्या वर्त्तते इति सपत्नीकः सन् आराधय, हि यस्मात् कारणात्, सा प्रीता तुष्टा सती, कामान् दोग्धीति कामदुघा भवति ॥ ८१ ॥

इतीति। इति वादिनः वदतः एव, होतुः हवनशीलस्य, अस्य मुनेः आहुतीनां साधनं कारणं नन्दयतीति व्युत्पत्त्या नन्दिनी नाम, अनिन्द्या अगर्ह्या प्रशस्ता, धेनुः वनात् आववृते प्रत्यागता ॥ ८२ ॥

অতএব সেই সুরভির কন্যাকে প্রতিনিধি স্বরূপ করিয়া বিশুদ্ধ অন্তরে ভার্য্যার সহিত আরাধনা করুন, তিনি প্রীত হইলে সকল কামনার ফল বিধান করেন ॥ ৮১ ॥

এই কথা বলিতে বলিতেই তাঁহার আহুতির প্রধান সহায় নন্দিনী নাম্নী ধেনু বন হইতে ফিরিয়া আসিল ॥ ৮২ ॥

81. Make then the daughter of Surabhi her mothers' representative, and worship her accompanied by the queen. She too if pleased, can fulfil all your desires.

82. Scarcely had the *rishi* finished his speech, when the blessed Nandini, the daughter of Surabhi, and the great supplier of *ghee* for all the ceremonies of her master, returned home from her grazing rambles in the forest.

ललाटोदयमाभुग्नं पल्लवस्निग्धपाटला ।
बिभ्रती श्वेतरोमाङ्कं सन्ध्येव शशिनं नवम् ॥ ८३ ॥
भुवं कोष्णेन कुण्डोघ्नी मेध्येनावभृथादपि * ।
प्रस्रवेनाभिवर्षन्ती वत्सालोकप्रवर्त्तिना ॥ ८४ ॥

सम्प्रति धेनुं विशिनष्टि, ललाट इति । पल्लवस्निग्धा चासौ पाटला च (सन्ध्यायामप्येतद्विशेषणं योज्यम्) ललाटे उदयः यस्य सः ललाटोदयः तम्, आभुग्नम् ईषद्वक्रम् श्वेतरोमाणि एव अङ्कः तं बिभ्रती, नवं शशिनं बिभ्रती सन्ध्या इव स्थिता ॥ ८३ ॥

भुवमिति । कोष्णेन किञ्चित् उष्णेन, अवभृथात् अपि अवभृथस्नानात् अपि मेध्येन पवित्रेण, वत्सस्य आलोकेन प्रदर्शनेन प्रवर्त्तिना प्रवर्त्तता, प्रस्रवेन क्षीराभिस्यन्दनेन, भुवम् अभिवर्षन्ती सिञ्चन्ती, कुण्डम्

নন্দিনীর বর্ণ নবপল্লবের ন্যায় পাটল ; ললাটের উপরে একখণ্ড শ্বেত রোমাবলী আছে ; সন্ধ্যাকালে নূতন চন্দ্রের উদয় হইলে যেরূপ শোভা হয়, তদ্দ্বারা সেইরূপ শোভা হইতেছে ॥ ৮৩ ॥

নন্দিনীর পালানটী একটী হোমাগ্নিস্থাপনের পাত্রের ন্যায় (অর্থাৎ গামলার ন্যায়) এবং বৎসকে দেখিবামাত্র তাহা হইতে ঈষদুষ্ণ দুগ্ধ-

83. Her colour was reddish yellow, like that of a new leaf, and she bore a circle of white hair on her forhead, which gave her the apperance of the twilight hour, adorned with the newly rising moon.

84 At the sight of her young the warm milk from her teats flowed out in streams, soaking the earth, and having

* अवभृथादपि—अवभृथः मुख्ययज्ञसमाप्तौ क्रियमाणं स्नानादि कर्म्म, ablution and other minor ceremonies performed at the conclusion of the main ceromony.

रजःकणैः खुरोद्धूतैः स्पृशद्भिर्गात्रमन्तिकात्।
तीर्थाभिषेकजां शुद्धिम् आदधाना महीक्षितः॥८५॥
तां पुण्यदर्शनां दृष्ट्वा *निमित्तज्ञस्तपोनिधिः।
याज्यमाशंसितावन्ध्यप्रार्थनं पुनरब्रवीत्॥ ८६ ॥

ऊधः आपीनं यस्याः सा कुण्डोध्नी। ऊधसोऽनङिति ङीबादेशः ॥८४॥

रज इति। खुरोद्धूतैः अन्तिकात् समीपे गात्रं स्पृशद्भिः रजसां कणैः महीं क्षियते ईष्टे इति महीक्षित् तस्य, तीर्थाभिषेकेण जातां तीर्थाभिषेकजां शुद्धिम् आदधाना कुर्वाणा। (एतेन गोरजस्य स्नानत्वमुक्तम्) उक्तञ्च मनुना, "आग्नेयं भस्मना स्नानम् अवगाह्यन्तु वारुणम्। आपोहिष्ठेति च ब्राह्मं वायव्यं गोरजःकृतम् इति ॥ ८५ ॥

तामिति। निमित्तज्ञः शकुनज्ञः तपोनिधिः वशिष्ठः पुण्यं दर्शनं

ধারা বিনির্গত হইয়া পৃথিবীকে সিক্ত করিতেছে, সেই দুগ্ধধারা যজ্ঞশেষের স্নান বারি অপেক্ষা পবিত্র ॥ ৮৪ ॥

তাহার খুরোদ্গত ধূলিকণা-সকল রাজার দেহে পড়িয়া তীর্থ স্থানে স্নান দ্বারা যে পবিত্রতা লাভ করা যায়, তাহা বিধান করিল ॥ ৮৫ ॥

সেই মহর্ষি লক্ষণাদি দ্বারা ভবিষ্য ফল গণনা করিতে পারিতেন,

---

greate sanctifying effects than the ablutions during a sacrificial ceremony.

85. The dust raised by her feet settled down upon the person of the monarch and gave all the purification that he could otherwise obtain by bathing in sacred places of pilgrimage.

86. The holy sage, who was skilled in reading the mean-

* निमित्तज्ञः—निमित्तानि भाविशुभाशुभसूचकानि चिह्नानि जानाति यः सः निमित्तज्ञः—One who is skilled in interpreting

अदूरवर्त्तिनीं सिद्धिं राजन्! विगणयात्मनः।
उपस्थितेयं कल्याणी नाम्नि कीर्त्तित एव यत्॥८७॥

यस्याः तां, धेनुं दृष्ट्वा कार्यविदां मनोरथः, तस्य अवन्ध्यं सफलं प्रार्थनं यस्य तम् अवन्ध्यमनोरथम् इत्यर्थः, याजयितुं योग्यं याज्यं पार्थिवं पुनः अब्रवीत्॥ ८६॥

अदूरेति। हे राजन्! आत्मनः कार्यस्य सिद्धिम् अदूरवर्त्तिनीं विगणय विद्धि, यत् यस्मात् कारणात् कल्याणी मङ्गलमूर्त्तिः, धेनुः नाम्नि कीर्त्तिते कथिते सति एव उपस्थिता॥ ८७॥

তিনি সেই পুণ্যদর্শনা ধেনুকে সমাগত দেখিয়া বুঝিতে পারিলেন যে তাঁহার যজমানের মনোরথ পূর্ণ হইবে, সুতরাং তাঁহাকে বলিলেন। ৮৬।

হে রাজন্! নাম না করিতে করিতে এই কল্যাণী যখন উপস্থিত হইলেন, তখন আপনার অভীষ্টসিদ্ধি অদূর-বর্ত্তী বলিয়া স্থির করুন॥৮৭॥

---

ings of signs and omens, could at once see that her opportune arrival boded the speedy fulfilment of the desire of his disciple, and thus addressed the latter.

87. Depend upon it, O King, the fruition of your desires is close at hand; for at the very mention of her name as it were, this blessed cow has thus made her apperance.

supernatural signs and omens. Compare with a passage in the *Bhagavatgita*, where अर्ज्जुन, addressing कृष्ण, remarks :—

न च शक्नोम्यवस्थातुं भ्रमतीव च मे मनः।
निमित्तानि च पश्यामि विपरीतानि केशव॥

Trans—I can no longer stand; my mind reels as it were and I see, O Keshava, ominous signs on all sides.

वन्यवृत्तिरिमां शश्वदात्मानुगमनेन गाम् ।
विद्यामभ्यसनेनेव प्रसादयितुमर्हसि ॥ ८८ ॥
प्रस्थितायां प्रतिष्ठेथाः स्थितायां स्थितिमाचरेः ।
निषण्णायां निषीदास्यां पीताम्भसि पिबेरपः ॥ ८९ ॥

वन्येति । वने भवं वन्यं कन्दमूलादिकं वृत्तिः आहारः यस्य तथाभूतः सन्, इमां गां शश्वत् सदा आप्रसादात् अविच्छेदेन इत्यर्थः, आत्मनः तव कर्तुः अनुगमनेन अनुसरणेन, अभ्यसनेन अभ्यासेन विद्याम् इव, प्रसादयितुं प्रसन्नां कर्तुम् अर्हसि ॥ ८८ ॥

गवानुसरणप्रकारमाह, प्रस्थितेति । अस्यां नन्दिन्यां प्रस्थितायां प्रतिष्ठेथाः प्रयाहि, स्थितायां निवृत्तगतिकायां स्थितिम् आचरेः स्थितिं कुरु तिष्ठ इत्यर्थः, निषण्णायाम् उपविष्टायां निषीद उपविश, पीतम् अम्भः यया तस्यां पीताम्भसि सत्याम् अपः पिबेः पिब ॥ ८९ ॥

অতএব বিদ্যাকে যেমন অভ্যাসের দ্বারা অধিকার করিতে হয়, সেইরূপ বনজাত ফল মূলাদি দ্বারা উদর পূরণ পূর্ব্বক নিরন্তর অনুগমন দ্বারা ইহাকে প্রসন্ন করুন ॥ ৮৮ ॥

ইনি চলিলে আপনি চলিবেন, ইনি দাঁড়াইলে আপনি দাঁড়াইবেন, ইনি শয়ন করিলে আপনি শয়ন করিবেন, এবং জল পান করিলে পরে জল পান করিবেন ॥ ৮৯ ॥

---

88. As one has to acquire learning by constant application and self-denial, so you should try to propitiate this divine cow, by constaintly waiting upon her, and by following her,—living all the time upon the vegetable products of the forest.

89. You are to move when she moves, to stand when she stands, to sit down when she does the same, and to drink water, only after she has assuaged her thirst.

বধূর্ভক্তিমতী চৈনামর্চিতামাতপোবনাৎ।
প্রযতা প্রাতরন্বেতু সায়ং প্রত্যুদ্ব্রজেদপি ॥ ৯০ ॥
ইত্যাপ্রসাদাদস্যাস্ত্বং পরিচর্য্যাপরো ভব।
অবিঘ্নমস্তু তে স্থেয়াঃ পিতেব ধুরি পুত্রিণাম্ ॥ ৯১ ॥

বধূরিতি। বধূঃ জায়া চ ভক্তিমতী প্রযতা সতী গন্ধাদিভিঃ অর্চিতাম্ এনাং গাং প্রাতঃ আ তপোবনাৎ অন্বেতু অনুগচ্ছতু সায়ম্ অপি প্রত্যুদ্ব্রজেৎ প্রত্যুদ্গচ্ছেৎ ॥ ৯০ ॥

ইতীতি। ইত্যনেন প্রকারেণ ত্বম্ আপ্রসাদাৎ প্রসাদপর্য্যন্তম্ অস্যাঃ ধেনোঃ পরিচর্য্যাপরঃ শুশ্রূষাপরঃ ভব, তে তব অবিঘ্নং বিঘ্নস্য অভাবঃ অস্তু পিতেব পুত্রিণাং সৎপুত্রবতাম্ ধুরি অগ্রে স্থেয়াঃ তিষ্ঠেঃ। তৎ সদৃশো ভবৎপুত্রোঽস্ত্বিতি ভাবঃ ॥ ৯১ ॥

বধূমাতাও ভক্তিমতী এবং সংযতচিত্তা হইয়া প্রাতে ইঁহাকে বিধিমতে অর্চনা পূর্ব্বক তপোবনের সীমা পর্য্যন্ত সঙ্গে সঙ্গে যাইবেন, এবং সায়ংকালে অগ্রসর হইয়া অভ্যর্থনা করিয়া লইবেন ॥ ৯০ ।

এইরূপ যতদিনে ইনি প্রসন্ন না হন, ততদিন আপনাকে ইঁহার পরিচর্য্যা করিতে হইবে। আপনার সকল বিঘ্ন কাটিয়া যাইবে; এবং আপনি পুত্রবান্ দিগের অগ্রগণ্য হইবেন ॥ ৯১ ।

90. And this our daughter-in-law, should also follow her in the morning, with every mark of respect, up to the border of the grounds of this hermitage, and should also go up to that point to receive her upon her return in the evening.

91. Go on attending upon her in this wise, till she is propitiated. May your desires be crowned with success, and may you stand at the head of happy mortals, favoured with worthy children.

तथेति प्रतिजग्राह प्रीतिमान् सपरिग्रहः ।
आदेशं देशकालज्ञः शिष्यः शासितुरानतः ॥ ९२ ॥
अथ प्रदोषे दोषज्ञः संवेशाय विशाम्पतिम् ।
सूनुः सूनृतवाक् स्रष्टुः विससर्जोर्दितश्रियम् ॥ ९३ ॥

तथेति। देशकालज्ञः देशः अग्निसन्निधिः, कालः अग्निहोत्रावसानसमयः, विशिष्टदेशकालोत्पन्नमार्गं ज्ञानमव्याहतम् इति जानन्, अत एव प्रीतिमान्, शिष्यः अन्तेवासी, राजा, सपरिग्रहः सपत्नीकः, आनतः विनयनम्रः सन्, शासितुः गुरोः, आदेशम् आज्ञां, तथेति प्रतिजग्राह स्वीचकार ॥ ९२ ॥

अथेति। अथ प्रदोषे रात्रौ दोषज्ञः विद्वान् सूनृतवाक् सत्यप्रियवाक् स्रष्टुः सूनुः ब्रह्मपुत्रः मुनिः, अनेन प्रकृतकार्य्यनिर्वाहकत्वं सूचयति, उदितश्रियं विशाम्पतिं मनुजेश्वरम् संवेशाय निद्रायै विससर्ज आज्ञापयामास ॥ ९३ ॥

দেশকালজ্ঞ সেই রাজা সস্ত্রীক বিনীত ভাবে "যে আজ্ঞা" বলিয়া গুরুর আদেশ প্রীতির সহিত গ্রহণ করিলেন। ৯২ ॥

তদনন্তর ব্রহ্মপুত্র মুনিবর সৌভাগ্যশালী রাজাকে সে রাত্রের মত শয়নের নিমিত্ত বিদায় দিলেন ॥ ৯৩ ॥

92. The king and the queen, who knew the time and the place, received, in a spirit of love and humility, the instructions of their holy preceptor.

93. After this the learned *rishi* bade the mighty king to retire for the night.

सत्यामपि तपःसिद्धौ * नियमापेक्षया मुनिः।
कल्पवित् कल्पयामास वन्यामेवास्य संविधाम्॥९४॥
निर्दिष्टां कुलपतिना स पर्णशालाम्
अध्यास्य प्रयतपरिग्रहद्वितीयः।

सत्यामपीति। कल्पवित् व्रतप्रयोगाभिज्ञः, मुनिः तपःसिद्धौ सत्याम् अपि, तपसा एव राजयोग्याहारसम्पादनसामर्थ्ये सत्यपि इत्यर्थः, नियमापेक्षया तदाप्रभृति एव व्रतचर्य्यापेक्षया, अस्य राज्ञः वन्याम् एव संविधीयते अनयेति संविधां कुशादिशयनसामग्रीम्, कल्पयामास सम्पादयामास ॥ ९४ ॥

निर्दिष्टामिति। सः राजा कुलपतिना मुनिकुलेश्वरेण, वशिष्ठेन

যজ্ঞক্রিয়ার উপদেষ্টা সেই ঋষি যদিও তপোবনে রাজভোগ্য সমুদায় সুখ দিতে পারিতেন, তথাপি রাজার পক্ষে ব্রত-নিয়মে থাকা উচিত জানিয়া বনবাসীর উপযুক্ত অন্ন পান শয়নাদি বিধান করিলেন ॥ ৯৪ ॥

রাজা মুনিকুলতিলকের প্রদর্শিত পর্ণশালাতে সংযতেন্দ্রিয়া মহিষীর

---

94. Though the sage, by reason of his great proficiency in holy penances, had the power to provide comforts worthy of his royal guests, yet looking to the necessity of their exercising abstinence, as prepatory to the life they were about to lead, ordered for them only such food and such bedding as suited a forest life.

95. The king and the queen slept together on a rude carpet, made of the Kusa grass, in a cottage alloted to them by

---

* नियमापेक्षया—नियमः गोपालनरूपव्रत-धारणं तस्य अपेक्षा तद्-दृष्टिरित्यर्थः तया—having regard to the fact that henceforth they should practise asceticism.

तच्छिष्याध्ययननिवेदितावसानां
संविष्टः कुशशयने निशां निनाय ॥ ९५ ॥

इति श्रीरघुवंशे महाकाव्ये कालिदासकृतौ
वसिष्ठाश्रमगमनो नाम प्रथमः सर्गः ।

निर्दिष्टां पर्णशालाम् अध्यास्य अधिष्ठानं कृत्वा इत्यर्थः, प्रयतः नियतः परिग्रहः पत्नी द्वितीयः यस्येति सः तथोक्तः, कुशानां शयने संविष्टः सुप्तः सन् तस्य वसिष्ठस्य शिष्याणाम् अध्ययनेन अपररात्रे वेदपाठेन निवेदितम् अवसानं यस्याः तां निशां निनाय गमयामास । (अपररात्रे अध्ययने मनुः, "निशान्ते न परिश्रान्तः ब्रह्माधीत्य पुनः स्वपेत्" ।) प्रहर्षिण्युक्तमेतत् तदुक्तम्, "म्नौ ज्रौ गस्त्रिदशयतिः प्रहर्षणीयम्" ॥ ९५ ॥

इति श्रीमहामहोपाध्यायकोलाचलमल्लिनाथसूरिविरचितायां
रघुवंशटीकायां सञ्जीवनीसमाख्यायां
प्रथमः सर्गः ।

সহিত কুশশয্যাতে সুখে শয়ন করিয়া রাত্রিযাপন পূর্ব্বক প্রত্যূষে মুনি-শিষ্যগণের বেদাধ্যয়নের দ্বারা নিশার অবসান হইয়াছে জানিতে পারি-লেন ॥ ৯৫ ॥

the sage, and their slumber was so sound that they were not roused from it until the disciples of the sage had begun to read aloud their lessons in the morning.

প্রথম সর্গ সমাপ্ত ।

द्वितीयः सर्गः ।

अथ प्रजानामधिपः प्रभाते
जायाप्रतिग्राहितगन्धमाल्याम् ।
*वनाय पीतप्रतिबद्धवत्सां
†यशोधनो धेनुमृषेर्मुमोच ॥ १ ॥

অথেতি। অথ নিশানযনানন্তরং যশোধনঃ প্রজানাম্ অধিপঃ প্রজেশ্বরঃ, প্রভাতে প্রাতঃকালে, জায়য়া সুদক্ষিণয়া প্রতিগ্রাহিতে স্বীকারিতে গন্ধমাল্যে যয়া সা জায়াপ্রতিগ্রাহিতগন্ধমাল্যা তথোক্তা, পীতং পানম্ অস্যাস্তীতি পীতঃ পীতবান্ ইত্যর্থঃ পীতঃ প্রতিবদ্ধঃ বৎসঃ যস্যাঃ তাম্, ঋষেঃ ধেনুং, বনায় বনং গন্তুম্, মুমোচ মুক্তবান্ ॥ ১ ॥

অনন্তর মহাযশা নরপতি প্রভাতে উঠিয়া সুদক্ষিণার দ্বারা নন্দিনীকে গন্ধমাল্যাদি অর্পণ করিলেন এবং বৎসকে দুগ্ধ পান করাইয়া বাঁধিয়া রাখিয়া, বন গমনের নিমিত্ত তাঁহাকে ছাড়িয়া দিলেন। ১।

1. In the morning the queen worshipped Nandini with *chandana* and flowers, and her young calf was allowed its last suck, previous to her departure for the forest; after which Dileep led her out for her journey.

* বনায়—For explanation of the চতুর্থী refer to ক্রিয়ার্থোপপদস্য কর্ম্মণি স্থানিনঃ। ২।৩।১৪ —*Panini.*

† যশোধনঃ, যশ এব ধনং যস্য সঃ—One who values his honor as a treasure.

तस्याः खुरन्यासपवित्रपांसुम्
अपांसुलानां धुरि कीर्त्तनीया ।
मार्गं मनुष्येश्वरधर्म्मपत्नी
*श्रुतेरिवार्थं स्मृतिरन्वगच्छत् ॥ २ ॥

तस्या इति । पांसवः दोषाः आसां सन्तीति पांसुलाः स्वैरिण्यः, अपांसुलानां पतिव्रतानां धुरि अग्रे कीर्त्तनीया परिगणनीया, मनुष्येश्वरधर्म्मपत्नी, खुरन्यासैः पवित्राः पांसवः यस्य तम्, तस्याः धेनोः मार्गं, स्मृतिः मन्वादि वाक्यं, श्रुतेः वेदवाक्यस्य अर्थम् अभिधेयम् इव अन्वगच्छत् अनुसृतवती । यथा स्मृतिः श्रुतिमनुसृत्यैवार्थमनुसरति तथा सापि गोखुरमनुसृत्यैव मार्गमनुससार इत्यर्थः । पांसुपदसत्त्वादपांसुलानामिति विरोधालङ्कारो ध्वन्यते ॥ २ ॥

স্মৃতি যেমন শ্রুতির অনুগামিনী সেইরূপ সতী কুলের অগ্রগণ্যা দিলীপপত্নী নন্দিনীর খুরবিন্যাসের দ্বারা পবিত্রীকৃত পথের অনুসরণ করিতে লাগিলেন ॥ ২ ॥

2. The queen, who was the fairest and purest of her sex, followed the steps of Nandini, like Smriti following the steps of Sruti, as the cow moved along, sanctifying the whole path with the print of her feet.

* श्रुतेरिवार्थं स्मृतिरन्वगच्छत्—The literal meaning of the word Smriti is memory, *i. e.* something remembered ; thus the Smritis are regarded to be the echoes of the Srutis or Vedas.

निवर्त्त्य राजा*दयितां दयालुः
तां†सौरभेयीं सुरभिर्यशोभिः।
पयोधरीभूतचतुःसमुद्रां
जुगोप गोरूपधरामिवोर्वीम्॥ २॥

निवर्त्त्येति। दयालुः कारुणिकः, यशोभिः सुरभिः मनोज्ञः, राजा तां दयितां निवर्त्त्य, सौरभेयीं कामधेनुसुतां नन्दिनीं, धरन्तीति धरा, पयसां धराः पयोधराः स्तनाः, अपयोधराः पयोधराः सम्पाद्यमानाः पयोधरीभूताः, पयोधरीभूताः चत्वारः समुद्राः यस्याः ताम्, गोरूपधराम् उर्वीम् इव जुगोप ररक्ष, भूरक्षणप्रयत्नेनैव ररक्ष इति भावः। धेनुपक्षे पयसा दुग्धेन धरीभूताः चत्वारः समुद्राः यस्याः सा तथोक्ता, दुग्धतिरस्कृतसागराम् इत्यर्थः॥ २॥

মহাযশা দিলীপ প্রণয়িনীর প্রতি স্নেহবশতঃ তাঁহাকে ফিরাইয়া দিয়া পয়োধররূপী চতুঃসাগরশালিনী গোরূপধারিণী পৃথিবীর ন্যায় সুরভি-নন্দিনীকে একাকী রক্ষা করিতে লাগিলেন॥ ৩॥

3. The king having persuaded his beloved spouse to return, took the sole charge of protecting the daughter of Surabhi, who was looking, as if she was the earth incarnate, with her udder and four teats representing the four oceans.

* दयितां—दय् अनुकम्पायां भ्वा, आत्मनेपदी,—क्त,+आप् दयितां प्रणयिनीं पत्नीं।

† सौरभेयीं—सुरभेः तन्नाम्न्याः कामधेनोरपत्यं स्त्री सौरभेयी ताम् सौरभेयीं—स्त्रीभ्यो ढक्।४।१।१२०—*Panini*.

व्रताय तेनानुचरेण धेनोः
न्यषेधि शेषोऽप्यनुयायिवर्गः ।
न चान्यतस्तस्य शरीररक्षा
स्ववीर्य्यगुप्ता हि मनोः प्रसूतिः ॥ ४ ॥

आस्वादवद्भिः कवलैस्तृणानां
कण्डूयनैर्दंशनिवारणैश्च ।

व्रतायेति । व्रताय धेनोः अनुचरेण गवां जीवनार्थमिति भावः, तेन दिलीपेन शेषः सर्वावशिष्टोऽपि अनुयायिवर्गः अनुचरवर्गो न्यषेधि निवर्त्तितः, कथं तर्हि आत्मरक्षणम् ? अत आह, न चेति; तस्य दिलीपस्य शरीररक्षा च अन्यतः पुरुषान्तरात् न । कुतः ? हि यस्मात् कारणात्, मनोः प्रसूयते इति प्रसूतिः सन्ततिः, स्ववीर्य्यगुप्ता स्ववीर्य्येणैव रक्षिता, न हि स्वपरनिर्वाहकस्य परापेक्षा इति भावः ॥ ४ ॥

आस्वादवद्भिरिति । सम्राट् मण्डलेश्वरः, सः राजा आस्वादवद्भिः

ধেনুর অনুচর হইয়া তিনি ব্রতপালনের উদ্দেশে অবশিষ্ট অনুযাত্রিকদিগকেও সঙ্গে যাইতে নিষেধ করিলেন, মনুবংশীয় রাজগণ স্বীয় বলের দ্বারাই সুরক্ষিত, সুতরাং শরীর রক্ষার্থ তাঁহাদের অন্য অনুচরের প্রয়োজন নাই । ৪ ॥

কখনও বা সুস্বাদু তৃণকবল সকল আহরণ করিয়া, কখনও গাত্র

---

4. He had now entered upon a new life of spiritual discipline, accordingly he dismissed the small residue of attendents (who naturally wished to accompany him as his body-guards). He needed no guards; for the princes of the line of Manu, were guarded by their own powers.

5. The king tried to propitiate her, now by bringing her palatable morsels of grass, now by gently rubbing her sides,

अव्याहतैः स्वैरगतैः स तस्याः
*सम्राट् समाराधनतत्परोऽभूत् ॥ ५ ॥
स्थितः स्थितामुच्चलितः प्रयातां
निषेदुषीमासनबन्धधीरः ।
जलाभिलाषी जलमाददानां
छायेव तां भूपतिरन्वगच्छत् ॥ ६ ॥

रसवद्भिः स्वादुभिः इत्यर्थः, तृणानां कवलैः ग्रासैः, कण्डूयनैः खर्जनैः, दंशानां वनमक्षिकाणां निवारणैः, अव्याहतैः अप्रतिहतैः, स्वैरगतैः स्वच्छन्दगमनैश्च, तस्याः धेन्वाः, समाराधनतत्परः शुश्रूषासक्तः, अभूत्। तदेव परं प्रधानं यस्य इति तत्परः ॥ ५ ॥

स्थित इति। भूपतिः तां गां स्थितां स्थितः सन्, प्रयातां प्रस्थिताम्

কণ্ডুয়ন করিয়া দিয়া, কখন বা দংশ মশকাদি নিবারণ করিয়া, কখন বা তাঁহার স্বচ্ছন্দ গমনের ব্যাঘাত না করিয়া, এই রূপে দিলীপ নানা উপায়ে নন্দিনীর পরিচর্য্যাতে ব্রত হইলেন ॥ ৫ ॥

নন্দিনী দাঁড়াইলে তিনি দাঁড়ান, চলিলে চলেন, শয়ন করিলে

now by keeping the gnats at a distance from her body, and now by allowing her unrestrained liberty to graze as she pleased.

6. He stopped only when she stopped, moved only when

---

* सम्राट्—येनेष्टं राजसूयेन, मण्डलस्येश्वरश्च यः।
शास्ति यश्चाज्ञया राज्ञः सम्राट् इत्यमरः—*Mallinath.*

Trans—He who has held the Rajsuya ceremony, who is lord over a body of rulers, who governs other princes by his commands is an emperor.

স ন্যস্তচিহ্নামপি রাজলক্ষ্মীং
তেজোবিশেষানুমিতাং দধানঃ।
আসীদনাবিষ্কৃতদানরাজিঃ *
অন্তর্মদাবস্থ ইব দ্বিপেন্দ্রঃ॥ ৭॥

উত্থিতঃ প্রস্থিতঃ, নিষেদুষীং নিষণ্ণাম্ উপবিষ্টাম্ ইত্যর্থঃ, আসনবন্ধে উপবেশনে ধীরঃ স্থিতঃ উপবিষ্টঃ সন্ ইত্যর্থঃ, জলম্ আদদানাং পিবন্তীং জলাভিলাষী পিবন্ ইত্যর্থঃ, ইত্থং ছায়া ইব অন্বগচ্ছৎ অনুসৃতবান্॥৬॥

স ইতি। ন্যস্তানি পরিহৃতানি চিহ্নানি ছত্রচামরাদীনি যস্যাঃ তাং তথাভূতাম্ অপি, তেজোবিশেষেণ প্রভাবাতিশয়েন অনুমিতাং সর্বথা রাজা এবায়ং ভবেৎ ইতি ঊহিতাং রাজলক্ষ্মীং দধানঃ সঃ রাজা অনা-

---

তিনি উপবেশন করেন, এবং জল পান করিলে স্বয়ং জল পান করেন, এইরূপে তিনি ছায়ার ন্যায় নন্দিনীর অনুগমন করিতে লাগিলেন॥ ৬॥

যদিও তাঁহার দেহে রাজসম্পদের অনুরূপ কোন চিহ্নই ছিল না, তথাপি একপ্রকার প্রভাব বিশেষের গুণে তাঁহার রাজলক্ষ্মী অনুভূত হইতেছিল; মদজল ক্ষরণ হইবার পূর্ব্বে অন্তর্ভূত মদাবস্থাতে মত্তহস্তীর

she was in motion, and lay down only when she was lying at her ease,—thus the king followed the sacred cow, as the shadow of a man follows his body.

7. Though he had laid aside all the *insignia* of his royal office, yet a circle of ineffable glory always surrounded him, and gave him an appearance suited to that office; consequently, in this matter he resembled a proud elephant in whom the conditions of madness were all ready within, but whose tem-

---

* অনাবিষ্কৃতদানরাজিঃ—অনাবিষ্কৃতাঃ অপ্রকটিতাঃ, ন প্রত্যক্ষং দৃশ্যমানা ইত্যর্থঃ, দানস্য মদজলস্য রাজিঃ ধারা যস্য।

लतामतानोद्ग्रथितैः स * केशैः
अधिज्यधन्वा विचचार † दावम्।

विमुक्तदानराजिः बहिरप्रकटितमदरेखः, अन्तर्गता मदावस्था यस्य सः अन्तर्मदावस्थः, तथाभूतः द्विपेन्द्रः इव आसीत् ॥ ७ ॥

लतेति। लतानां, वल्लीनां प्रतानैः कुटिलतन्तुभिः, उद्ग्रथिताः उन्नमय्य ग्रथिताः ये केशाः तैः उपलक्षितः, सः राजा अधिज्यम् आरोपितमौर्वीकं धनुः यस्य सः अधिज्यधन्वा सन्, मुनिहोमधेनोः

যেরূপ ভাব হয়, তাঁহারও ভাব সেই প্রকার লক্ষিত হইতেছিল ॥ ৭ ॥

দিলীপ লতিকা সকলের শাখারজ্জু দ্বারা কেশগুচ্ছ একত্র করিয়া বাঁধিয়াছেন, এবং ধনুতে জ্যা আরোপ করিয়া বনে বেড়াইতেছেন,

ples had not yet commenced to stream out the maddening sweat

8 His hairs were tied together with strings made of temdrils of wild creepers, and he always carried his bow ready for use. It

---

* केशैः—For the तृतीया refer to इत्थम्भूतलक्षणे। २।३।२१।—

Panini.

According to this rule anything that indicates the altered condition of another, generally, has the तृतीया। Example given by भट्टोजिदीक्षितः;—जटाभिस्तापसः—जटाज्ञाप्यतापसत्वविशिष्ट इत्यर्थः—In the case of Dileep also the student may interpret the तृतीया by saying लतावद्धकेशज्ञाप्यगोरक्षणव्रतधारीत्यर्थः।

† दावं—वनं "वने च वनवह्नौ च दवो दाव इहेष्यते" इति यादवः.

Mallinath.

According to the ordinary rules of Sanskrit grammar here

रक्षापदेशान्मुनिहोमधेनोः
वन्यान् विनेष्यन्निव दुष्टसत्त्वान् ॥ ८ ॥
विसृष्टपार्श्वानुचरस्य तस्य
पार्श्वद्रुमाः पाशभृता समस्य ।

रक्षापदेशात् रक्षणव्याजात्, वन्यान् वने भवान्, दुष्टसत्त्वान् दुष्टजन्तून्, विनेष्यन् शिक्षयिष्यन् इव, दावं वनम् विचचार वने चचार इत्यर्थः ॥ ८ ॥
विसृष्टेत्यादिभिः षड्भिः श्लोकैस्तस्य महामहिमतया द्रुमादयोऽपि

দেখিলে বোধ হয় মুনির গাভীকে রক্ষা করা ছল মাত্র, বনচারী দুষ্ট জন্তুদিগকে দমন করাই তাঁহার প্রকৃত উদ্দেশ্য ॥ ৮ ॥

কুবেরোপম দিলীপ সমুদায় অনুযাত্রিককে পশ্চাতে ফেলিয়া আসিয়া-

seemed as if the protection of the *rishi's* cow was a mere pretext, his real motive being the disciplining of the inhabitants of the forest.

9. As he walked alone and unattended, strong and muscu-

is a plain case of आधारे सप्तमी ; but here the word दावं gets an objective sense by reason of its indicating a place and also of its being at the same time allied to an intransitive verb—Refer to वार्त्तिकम्—अकर्मक-धातुभिर्योगे देशः कालो भावो, गन्तव्योऽध्वा च कर्मसंज्ञक इति वाच्यम् ; as quoted by भट्टोजीदीक्षित in सिद्धान्तकौमुदी Part I. Page 255, Taranath Tarkavachaspati's edition of 1863. In connection with this also try to get by heart the following couplet by हरि.

कालभावाध्वदेशानामन्तर्भूतक्रियान्तरैः ।
सर्वैरकर्मकैर्योगे कर्मत्वमुपजायते ॥

উদীরয়ামাসুরিবোন্মদানাম্
আলোকশব্দং বয়সাং বিরাবৈঃ ॥ ৯ ॥
মরুৎপ্রযুক্তাশ্চ মরুৎসখাভং
তমর্চ্চ্যমারাদভিবর্ত্তমানম্।
অবাকিরন্ বাললতাঃ প্রসূনৈঃ
আচারলাজৈরিব পৌরকন্যাঃ ॥ ১০ ॥

রাজোপচারং চকুরিত্যাহ, বিশ্রুটেতি। বিশ্রুটাঃ পার্শ্বানুচরাঃ পার্শ্ববর্ত্তিনো জনাঃ যেন তস্য, পাশভৃতা বরুণেন সমস্য তুল্যস্য তস্য রাজ্ঞঃ পার্শ্বয়োঃ দ্রুমাঃ, উন্মদানাম্ উৎকটমদানাং, বয়সাং খগানাম্, বিরাবৈঃ শব্দৈঃ, আলোকস্য শব্দ, বাচকম আলোকয় ইতি শব্দং জয়শব্দম্ ইত্যর্থঃ, উদীরয়ামাসুরিব, ইত্যুৎপ্রেক্ষা ॥ ৯ ॥

মরুদিতি। মরুৎপ্রযুক্তাঃ বায়ুনা প্রেরিতাঃ বাললতাঃ, আরাৎ সমীপে অভিবর্ত্তমানম্, মরুতঃ বায়োঃ সখা মরুৎসখঃ অগ্নিঃ, সঃ ইব আভাতীতি মরুৎসখাভম্, অর্চ্চ্যং পূজ্যং তং দিলীপং, প্রসূনৈঃ পুষ্পৈঃ, পৌরকন্যাঃ পৌরাশ্চ তাঃ কন্যাঃ, আচারার্থৈঃ লাজৈঃ আচারলাজৈঃ ইব অবাকিরন্

ছিলেন; কিন্তু তথাপি পার্শ্বস্থিত বৃক্ষগণ আনন্দোন্মত্ত পক্ষিকুলের শব্দের দ্বারা যেন তাঁহার জয়ধ্বনি করিতে লাগিল ॥ ৯ ॥

পুরস্ত্রীগণ যেরূপ মঙ্গলসূচক লাজাঞ্জলি বর্ষণ করে, সেইরূপ অগ্নিসম তেজস্বী দিলীপ, যখন নবজাত লতিকা সকলের সম্মুখে দাঁড়াইতে

lar like king Baruna, the trees on both sides of the road acted the part of criers, with the chorus of thousands of their feathery visitors.

10. And the tender creepers of the forest, moved gently by the breeze, honored him, as he stood before them, with showers of their flowers;—thus acting the part of young girls of

धनुर्भृतोऽप्यस्य दयार्द्रभावम्
आख्यातमन्तःकरणैर्विशङ्कैः ।
विलोकयन्त्यो वपुरापुरक्ष्णां
प्रकामविस्तारफलं हरिण्यः ॥ ११ ॥

तस्योपरि विक्षिप्तवत्यः इत्यर्थः । सखा हि सखायमागतमुपचरति इति भावः ॥ १० ॥

धनुर्भृत इति । धनुर्भृतोऽपि अस्य राज्ञः, एतेन भयसम्भावना दर्शिता, तथापि विशङ्कैः निर्भीकैः, अन्तःकरणैः वृत्तिभिः, दयया करुणारसेन आर्द्रः भावः अभिप्रायः यस्य तत् दयार्द्रभावं, तत् आख्यातं दयार्द्रभावमेतदित्याख्यातम् इत्यर्थः, तथाविधं वपुः विलोकयन्त्यः हरिण्यः, अक्ष्णां प्रकामविस्तारस्य अत्यन्तविशालतायाः फलम् आपुः । "विमदं कलुषीभवच्च चेतः कथयत्येव हितैषिणं रिपुं वा" इति न्यायेन स्वान्तःकरणवृत्तिप्रामाण्यादेव विस्रब्धं ददृशुः इत्यर्थः ॥ ११ ॥

লাগিলেন, তখন তাহারা তদীয় মস্তকে পুষ্পবৃষ্টি করিতে লাগিল ॥ ১০ ॥

তাঁহার হস্তে যদিও ধনু ছিল, তথাপি হরিণীগণের মনে ভয় হইল না, তদ্দারাই তাঁহার দয়ার্দ্রভাব প্রকাশ পাইল; হরিণীগণ তাঁহার প্রতি অসংকোচে দৃষ্টিপাত করিয়া আপনাদের নেত্রযুগলের বিশালতার উপযুক্ত ফল লাভ করিল ॥ ১১ ॥

his capital, who always welcomed him back with showers of *khoi* (fried paddy) in all his public entries into the city.

11. Though he always carried a bow about him, yet his manners inspired such a confidence in the minds of the deer, that they quietly viewed him as he passed—thus obtaining a sufficient reward for having got those beautiful large eyes of theirs.

स कीचकैर्मारुतपूर्णरन्ध्रैः
कूजद्भिरापादितवंशकृत्यम्।
शुश्राव कुञ्जेषु यशः स्वमुच्चै-
रुद्गीयमानं वनदेवताभिः॥ १२॥
पृक्तस्तुषारैर्गिरिनिर्झराणाम्,
*अनोकहाकम्पितपुष्पगन्धी।

स इति। सः दिलीपः मारुतपूर्णरन्ध्रैः अत एव कूजद्भिः स्वनद्भिः, कीचकैः वेणुविशेषैः, आपादितं सम्पादितं वंशस्य कृत्यं कार्य्यं यस्मिन् कर्मणि तत् तथा, कुञ्जेषु लतागृहेषु, वनदेवताभिः उद्गीयमानम् उच्चैः गीयमानं स्वं यशः शुश्राव श्रुतवान्॥ १२॥

पृक्त इति। गिरिषु निर्झराणां वारिप्रवाहाणाम्, तुषारैः सीकरैः,

---

কোথাও বা বংশের ছিদ্র সকলে বায়ু প্রবিষ্ট হইয়া বংশীর ধ্বনির ন্যায় ধ্বনি হইতেছে; যেন বনদেবতাগণ তরুকুঞ্জে উচ্চৈঃস্বরে বংশীর ধ্বনি সহকারে তাঁহারই যশ গান করিতেছে॥ ১২॥

আতপে রাজার শরীর ক্লান্ত হইয়াছিল, এবং তাঁহার আতপত্র

---

12. As he passed he heard the sweet musical tunes issuing from the natural bamboo-holes, filled with air, as if it were the fairies of the forest, singing in notes of excellent music, his own fair fame.

13. He had no umbrella to cover his head, but the soft cooling breeze, carrying with it the particles of water from the

* अनोकहाकम्पितपुष्पगन्धी—अनसः शकटस्य अकं गतिं हन्ति यः, शकटगतिरोधकः, वृक्ष इत्यर्थः।

तमातपक्लान्तमनातपत्रम्-
आचारपूतं पवनः सिषेवे ॥ १३ ॥
शशाम वृष्ट्यापि विना दवाग्नि-
रासीत् विशेषा फलपुष्पवृद्धिः ।

युक्तः संयुक्तः, अनोकहानां वृक्षाणाम्, आकम्पितानि ईषत्कम्पितानि पुष्पाणि तेषां यः गन्धः सः अस्यास्तीति आकम्पितपुष्पगन्धी ईषत्-कम्पितपुष्पगन्धवान्, एवं शीतः मन्दः, सुरभिः पवनः वायुः, अनातपत्रं व्रतार्थं परित्यक्तच्छत्रम्, अतएव आतपक्लान्तम्, आचारेण पूतं शुद्धं, तं नृपं सिषेवे। आचारपूतत्वात् स राजा जगत्पावनस्यापि सेव्य आसीत् इति भावः ॥ १२ ॥

शशामेति। गोप्तरि तस्मिन् राज्ञि, वनं गाहमाने प्रविशति सति, वृष्ट्या विना अपि दवाग्निः शशाम, फलानां पुष्पाणाञ्च वृद्धिः, विशेष्यते इति विशेषा अतिशयिता आसीत्, सत्त्वेषु जन्तुषु मध्ये, अधिकः प्रबलः

ছিল না; কিন্তু সুমন্দ বায়ু নির্ঝরিণীর তুষার কণা সকল হরণ করিয়া ও বৃক্ষগণের বিকম্পিত পুষ্পরাশির গন্ধভার বহন করিয়া তাঁহার ব্রত-পবিত্র দেহকে সেবা করিতে লাগিল ॥ ১৩ ॥

তিনি রক্ষকরূপে বনে প্রবিষ্ট হইলে বিনা বৃষ্টিতে দাবাগ্নি প্রশান্ত হইতে লাগিল; ফল পুষ্পের বিশেষ শ্রীবৃদ্ধি দৃষ্ট হইল; এবং বলশালী

---

hill-streams, and the fragrance of many flowers, mitigated considerably the effects of the heat of the sun.

14. When he entered the forest as its protector, the wild wood-landfire became extinguished, even without any shower of rain; the trees began to blossom and to bear fruits in abundance; and the stronger amongst the animals no longer tyra-

जनं न सत्त्वेष्वधिको * बबाधे
तस्मिन् वनं †गोप्तरि गाहमाने ॥ १४॥
सञ्चारपूतानि दिगन्तराणि
कृत्वा दिनान्ते निलयाय गन्तुम् ।
‡प्रचक्रमे पल्लवरागताम्रा
प्रभा पतङ्गस्य मुनेश्च धेनुः ॥ १५ ॥

व्याघ्रादिः जनं दुर्बलं हरिणादिकं न बबाधे ॥ १४ ॥

सञ्चारपूतानीति । पल्लवस्य रागः वर्णः पल्लवरागः, सः इव ताम्रा पल्लवरागताम्रा, पतङ्गस्य सूर्य्यस्य, प्रभा कान्तिः, मुनेः धेनुश्च, दिगन्तराणि दिशाम् अवकाशान्, सञ्चारेण पूतानि शुद्धानि कृत्वा, दिनान्ते

জন্তুগণ দুর্ব্বলদিগকে পীড়ন করা পরিত্যাগ করিল ॥ ১৪ ॥

দিবা অবসান হইলে, সূর্য্যের কিরণজাল যখন অস্তাচলে গমনোন্মুখ হইল, নবপল্লবের ন্যায় তাম্রবর্ণা নন্দিনীও তখন পদসঞ্চারের দ্বারা দিগ-

---

nnised over the weaker ones.

15. When the day was ended, the mild sun-beames spread their sanctifying influence over the evening skies, and began to fade away, and the rishi's cow,—she whose colour was like

---

* बबाधे—बाधृङ् भ्वादि, आत्मनेपदी ; पीड़ने ; लिट्, third person singular.

† गोप्तरि—गुपू, भ्वादि, परस्मैपदी ; रक्षणे । तृच्, गोप्ता तस्मिन्न्यां गोप्तरि ।

‡ प्रचक्रमे—गन्तुं आरब्धवतीत्यर्थः the आत्मनेपद is to be explained by reference to प्रोपाभ्यां समर्थाभ्यां ।१।३।४२—*Panini*. as quoted by the author of सिद्धान्तकौमुदी page 251—Tarkavachaspati's edition of 1863.

তাং দেবতাপিত্রতিথিক্রিয়ার্থাম্
অন্বক্ যযৌ *মধ্যমলোকপালঃ।
বভৌ চ সা তেন † সতাং মতেন
শ্রদ্ধেব সাক্ষাদ্বিধিনোপপন্না ॥ ১৬ ॥

সায়ংকালে, নিলয়ায় আশ্রমায়, ধেনুপক্ষে আলয়ায়, গন্তুং প্রচক্রমে ॥১৫॥

তামিতি। মধ্যমলোকপালঃ ভূপালঃ, দেবতাপিত্রতিথীনাং ক্রিয়াঃ যাগশ্রাদ্ধদানানি, তাঃ এব অর্থঃ প্রয়োজনং যস্যাঃ তাং ধেনুম্, অন্বক্ অনুপদং, যযৌ। সতাং মতেন সদ্ভিঃ মান্যেন, তেন রাজ্ঞা, উপপন্না যুক্তা, সা ধেনুঃ, সতাং মতেন বিধিনা অনুষ্ঠানেন, উপপন্না যুক্তা, সাক্ষাৎ প্রত্যক্ষা, শ্রদ্ধা আস্তিক্যবুদ্ধিঃ, ইব বভৌ চ ॥ ১৬ ॥

স্তরকে পবিত্র করিয়া গৃহাভিমুখে গমনের উপক্রম করিলেন ॥ ১৫ ॥

নরপতি দেবক্রিয়া, পিতৃক্রিয়া ও অতিথিবর্গের তৃপ্তিসাধনের সহায়-ভূতা সেই নন্দিনীর অনুগমন করিতে লাগিলেন; শ্রদ্ধার সহিত অনু-ষ্ঠানের মিলন হইলে যেমন শোভা হয়, রাজা অনুগামী হওয়াতে নন্দিনীরও সেই প্রকার শোভা হইল ॥ ১৬ ॥

that of newly grown leaves,—also slowly bent her course towards the hermitage.

16. The king followed the steps of the sacred animal, who was such an invaluable help towards the rishi's discharging his duties to his gods, to his ancestors and to his guests; and when

* মধ্যমলোকপালঃ—মধ্যে স্থিতঃ মধ্যমঃ, মধ্যমো লোকঃ মধ্যমলোকঃ পৃথিবী, তং পালয়তি যঃ স মধ্যমলোকপালঃ he who holds sway over the intermediate world *i. e.* the earth; the other two being স্বর্গ and পাতাল.

† সতাং মতেন—ক্তস্য চ বর্ত্তমানে (২।৩।৬৭) ইতি ষষ্ঠী।

स पल्वलोत्तीर्णवराहयूथा-
न्यावासवृक्षोन्मुखबर्हिणानि ।
ययौ *मृगाध्यासितशाद्वलानि
श्यामायमानानि वनानि पश्यन् ॥১৭॥

स इति। सः राजा, पल्वलेभ्यः अल्पजलाशयेभ्यः उत्तीर्णानि निर्गतानि वराहाणां यूथानि कुलानि येषु तानि, बर्हाणि एषां सन्तीति बर्हिणाः मयूराः, आवासवृक्षाणाम् उन्मुखाः बर्हिणाः येषु तानि, श्यामायमानानि वराहबर्हिणादिमलिनिम्ना अश्यामानि श्यामानि भवन्तीति श्यामायमानानि, मृगैः अध्यासिताः अधिष्ठिताः शाद्वलाः येषु तानि, शादाः शष्पाणि एषु देशेषु सन्तीति शाद्वलाः शष्पश्यामदेशाः, वनानि पश्यन् ययौ ॥ ১৭ ॥

সন্ধ্যাসমাগমে কোথাও বা বরাহ দল পল্বলের জল হইতে উঠিতেছে; কোথাও বা ময়ূরগণ আবাস বৃক্ষের অভিমুখে ধাবিত হইতেছে; কোথাও বা তৃণ ক্ষেত্রে হরিণকুল শয়ন করিয়া রহিয়াছে; এই সকলের দ্বারা বনরাজি শ্যামবর্ণ ধারণ করিতেছে; রাজা দেখিতে দেখিতে গমন করিতে লাগিলেন। ১৭।

---

thus following he looked like practical piety following devotion.

17. By that time the wild boars were leaving the water of the muddy ponds; the peacocks were returning to their accustomed trees for nightly shelter; and the deer were lying down in their accustomed grassy plots, and on the whole scene the sable mantle of night was gently falling; the king enjoyed the sight as he passed.

---

* मृगाध्यासितशाद्वलानि—शादः कर्द्दमे बालतृणे च, शादाः बालतृणाः सन्ति अत्र शाद्वलः बालतृणपूर्णः प्रदेशः तद्वत्तनवने शाद्वलाः।

आपीनभारोद्वहनप्रयत्नात्
गृष्टिर्गुरुत्वाद्वपुषो नरेन्द्रः ।
उभावलञ्चक्रतुरञ्चिताभ्यां
तपोवनावृत्तिपथं गताभ्याम् ॥ १८ ॥

वसिष्ठधेनोरनुयायिनं तम्
आवर्त्तमानं वनिता वनान्तात् ।
पपौ निमेषालसपक्ष्मपङ्क्तिः
उपोषिताभ्यामिव लोचनाभ्याम् ॥१९॥

आपीनेति । गृष्टिः सकृत् प्रसूता गौः, नरेन्द्रश्च उभौ यथाक्रमम् आपीनम् ऊधः, आपीनस्य भारोद्वहने प्रयत्नात् प्रयासात्, वपुषः गुरुत्वात् आधिक्याच्च, अञ्चिताभ्यां चारुभ्यां, गताभ्यां गमनाभ्यां, तपोवनात् आवृत्तेः पन्थाः तं तपोवनावृत्तिपथम्, अलञ्चक्रतुः भूषितवन्तौ ॥ १८ ॥

वसिष्ठेति । वसिष्ठधेनोः अनुयायिनम् अनुचरं, वनान्तात् आवर्त्त-मानं प्रत्यागतं, तं दिलीपं, वनिता सुदक्षिणा, निमेषेषु अलसा मन्दा

ধেনুটী পালানের ভারে অবনত হইয়া চলিয়াছেন ; রাজাও বিপুল দেহ ভার বহন করিয়া চলিয়াছেন ; এই রূপে তাঁহাদের উভয়ের সুন্দর গতির দ্বারা তপোবন পথের সেই ভাগের কি শোভাই হইল ॥ ১৮ ॥

রাজা যখন বশিষ্ঠধেনুর সহিত বনমধ্য হইতে ফিরিয়া আসিতে-

---

18. Each moved slowly, the cow with her heavy udder and the king with his muscular and manly frame ; as the one followed the other, moving carelessly on, what a beauty did it add to that part of the forest-path. !

19. As the king returned from the forest, along with the

पुरस्कृता वर्त्मनि पार्थिवेन
प्रत्युद्गता पार्थिवधर्मपत्न्या।
तदन्तरे सा विरराज धेनुः
दिनक्षपामध्यगतेव सन्ध्या ॥ २० ॥

पक्ष्मणां पङ्क्तिः यस्याः सा निर्निमेषा सती इत्यर्थः, लोचनाभ्यां करणाभ्याम् उपोषिताभ्याम् इव, उपवासः भोजननिवृत्तिः तद्युक्ताभ्याम् इव, पपौ। यथोपोषितः अतितृष्णया जलमधिकं पिपासति, तद्वदति-तृष्णया अधिकं व्यलोकयत् इत्यर्थः ॥ १९ ॥

पुरस्कृतेति। वर्त्मनि पार्थिवेन पृथिव्याः ईश्वरेण, पुरस्कृता अग्रतः कृता, धर्मस्य पत्नी धर्मार्थपत्नी इत्यर्थः, पार्थिवस्य धर्मपत्न्या प्रत्युद्गता सा धेनुः, तदन्तरे तयोः दम्पत्योः मध्ये, दिनक्षपयोः दिनरात्र्योः मध्यगता सन्ध्या इव, विरराज ॥ २० ॥

ছিলেন, তখন সুদক্ষিণা নিমেষবিহীন তৃষিত নয়নদ্বয়ের দ্বারা তাঁহাকে যেন পান করিতে লাগিলেন ॥ ১৯ ॥

সন্ধ্যা যেমন দিন ও রাত্রির মধ্যবর্ত্তিনী হইয়া শোভা পায়, তেমনি পশ্চাতে রাজা ও সম্মুখে সুদক্ষিণা এই উভয়ের মধ্যে দণ্ডায়মান হইয়া ধেনুর এক অপূর্ব্ব শ্রী হইল। ২০ ॥

---

cow of Basista, his loving and beloved queen drank him, as it were, with her wistful and long-fasting eyes.

20. From one side the queen came forward to meet the cow and from the other the king followed behind her; thus standing between them the sacred animal looked very much like the twilight coming between day and night.

प्रदक्षिणीकृत्य पयस्विनीं तां
सुदक्षिणा * साक्षतपात्रहस्ता ।
प्रणम्य चानर्च विशालमस्याः
शृङ्गान्तरं द्वारमिवार्थसिद्धेः ॥ २१ ॥
†वत्सोत्सुकापि स्तिमिता सपर्य्यां

प्रदक्षिणीकृत्येति । अक्षतानां पात्रेण सह वर्त्तते इति साक्षतपात्रौ हस्तौ यस्याः सा, सुदक्षिणा पयस्विनीं प्रशस्तक्षीरां तां धेनुं प्रदक्षिणीकृत्य प्रणम्य, च तस्याः धेन्वाः विशालं, शृङ्गान्तरं शृङ्गमध्यम्, अर्थसिद्धेः कार्य्यसिद्धेः, द्वारं प्रवेशमार्गम् इव, आनर्च अर्च्चयामास ॥२१॥

वत्सोत्सुकेति । सा धेनुः, वत्सोत्सुकापि वत्से उत्कण्ठितापि,

সুদক্ষিণা আতপতণ্ডুলাদি পূর্ণ পাত্র হস্তে লইয়া পয়স্বিনী নন্দিনীকে প্রদক্ষিণ পূর্ব্বক মনোরথ সিদ্ধির দ্বার স্বরূপ তাঁহার শৃঙ্গদ্বয়ের বিশাল মধ্যভাগকে অর্চ্চনা করিলেন ॥ ২১ ॥

নন্দিনী স্বীয় বৎসের জন্য নিতান্ত উৎসুক থাকিলেও স্থিরভাবে পূজা

---

21. Sudaskshina, carrying in her hands things suited for a ceremony of welcome, went round the cow, as a mark of respect, bowed, and worshipped the spacious portion of her head between her two horns, which was the gate, as it were, to the fulfilment of her wishes.

22. Though she was anxious to meet her young, yet with

* साक्षतपात्रहस्ता—अक्षतानि, यवानि, आर्द्रतण्डुलानि वा, अक्षतैः सह वर्त्तमानम् साक्षतं, साक्षतं पात्रं हस्ते यस्याः सा साक्षतपात्रहस्ता ; carrying a vessel-ful of soaked rice,-an offering used in a welcoming ceremony.

† वत्सोत्सुका—वत्से वत्सेन वा उत्सुका । प्रसितोत्सुकाभ्यां तृतीया च ।२।३।४४—*Panini*.

प्रत्यग्रहीत् सेति मनन्दतुस्तौ।
भक्त्योपपन्नेषु हि तद्विधानां
प्रसादचिह्नानि पुरःफलानि ॥ २२ ॥
गुरोः सदारस्य निपीड्य पादौ
समाप्य सान्ध्यञ्च विधिं दिलीपः।

क्लिमिता निश्चला सती, सपर्य्यां पूजां, प्रत्यग्रहीत्। इति हेतोः तौ दम्पती ननन्दतुः, पूज्येषु अनुरागः भक्तिः, तया उपपन्नेषु युक्तेषु, विषये तद्विधानां तस्याः धेन्वाः विधा इव विधा प्रकारः येषां तेषां महताम् इत्यर्थः, प्रसादस्य, चिह्नानि लिङ्गानि पूजास्वीकारादीनि, पुरःफलानि पुरोगमानि प्रत्यासन्नानि फलानि येषां तानि हि। अवि-लम्बितफलसूचकलिङ्गदर्शनादानन्दो युज्यते इत्यर्थः ॥ २२ ॥

गुरोरिति। भुजोच्छिन्नरिपुः दिलीपः, सदारस्य दारैः अरुन्धत्या सह वर्त्तमानस्य, गुरोः उभयोरपि इत्यर्थः पादौ निपीड्य अभिवन्द्य,

---

গ্রহণ করিলেন, ইহা দেখিয়া তাঁহারা উভয়ে আনন্দ করিতে লাগিলেন; কারণ, শরণাগত ভক্তের প্রতি তাদৃশ মহতের অনুগ্রহ চিহ্ন দেখিলে, অচির কালের মধ্যে যে মনোরথ পূর্ণ হইবে তাহা বুঝিতে পারা যায় ॥২২॥

দিলীপ বসিষ্ঠ ও অরুন্ধতীর পদদ্বয় বন্দনা করিয়া, এবং সায়ংকালীন

patience she accepted the worship offered to her; whereupon the royal couple were exceedingly glad; for such marks of favour to a devotee, shown by a cow like that, betoken the speedy fulfilment of such a one's desires.

23. After having bowed at the feet of his spiritual preceptor and his wife, and having finished his evening devotions, Dileep, who had destroyed all his enemies with his own hands,

दोहावसाने पुनरेव दोग्ध्रीं
भेजे भुजोच्छिन्नरिपुर्निषण्णाम् * ॥ २३ ॥

तामन्तिकन्यस्तबलिप्रदीपाम्
अन्वास्य गोप्ता गृहिणीसहायः ।
क्रमेण सुप्तामनु संविवेश
सुप्तोत्थितां प्रातरनूदतिष्ठत् ॥ २४ ॥

साध्यं सन्ध्यायां विहितं, विधिम् अनुष्ठानं च, समाप्य, दोहावसाने, निषण्णाम् आसीनां, दोग्ध्रीं दोहनशीलाम्, धेनुम् एव पुनः भेजे सेवितवान् ॥ २३ ॥

तामिति । गोप्ता रक्षकः, गृहिणीसहायः पत्नीद्वितीयः सन्, अन्तिके न्यस्ताः बलयः प्रदीपाश्च यस्याः तां तथोक्तां, तां निषण्णां धेनुम्,

---

সন্ধ্যাবন্দনাদি সমাপন করিয়া, দোহনাবসানে শয়নপরায়ণা নন্দিনীর সেবাতে আবার নিযুক্ত হইলেন ॥২৩॥

রাজা সস্ত্রীক নন্দিনীর নিকটে বলি প্রদীপাদি দিয়া, নিকটে উপবেশন করিয়া থাকিলেন, এবং তিনি নিদ্রিত হইলে পরে উভয়ে নিদ্রা গেলেন, প্রাতে নন্দিনী উঠিলে গাত্রোত্থান করিলেন ॥ ২৪ ॥

---

once more waited upon the cow, who had by that time been milked, and was lying at her ease.

24. The king and the queen, placed the spices and other offerings and the evening lamp close by the sacred cow and waited till she was asleep, when they retired to their beds,

* भुजोच्छिन्नरिपुः—भुजाभ्यां बाहुबलेनेत्यर्थः उच्छिन्नाः निहताः रिपवः येन स भुजोच्छिन्नरिपुः ।

इत्थं व्रतं धारयतः प्रजार्थं
समं महिष्या महनीयकीर्त्तेः ।
सप्त व्यतीयुस्त्रिगुणानि तस्य
दिनानि दीनोद्धरणोचितस्य ॥ २५ ॥
अन्येद्युरात्मानुचरस्य भावं
जिज्ञासमाना मुनिहोमधेनुः ।

अन्वास्य अनुपविश्य, क्रमेण सुप्ताम् अनु अनन्तरं, संविवेश सुष्वाप, प्रातः सुप्तोत्थिताम् अनु उदतिष्ठत् उत्थितवान् ॥ २४ ॥

इत्थमिति । इत्थम् अनेन प्रकारेण, प्रजार्थं सन्तानाय, महिष्या समम् अभिषिक्तपत्न्या सह, व्रतं धारयतः, महनीया पूज्या कीर्त्तिः यस्य तस्य, दीनानाम् उद्धरणं दैन्यविमोचनं तत्र उचितस्य परिचितस्य, तस्य नृपस्य, त्रयः गुणाः आवृत्तयः येषां तानि त्रिगुणानि त्रिरावृत्तानि, सप्त दिनानि एकविंशतिदिनानि व्यतीयुः ॥ २५ ॥

अन्येद्युरिति । अन्येद्युः अन्यस्मिन् दिने द्वाविंशे दिने, मुनिहोमधेनुः

এই রূপে সন্তান লাভার্থ মহিষীর সহিত ব্রত ধারণ করিয়া, মহাযশা দীন জনের চিরসহায় দিলীপের একবিংশতি দিবস অতীত হইল ॥২৫ ॥

একদা নন্দিনী অনুচর দিলীপের স্বগত ভাব জানিতে ইচ্ছুক হইয়া

waking up in the morning, only after she had risen from her slumber.

25. In this manner, king Dileep, of great fame, who was the protector of the poor, lived with his noble queen in a state of strict discipline for three weeks, in the hope of getting issue.

*26. On the twenty second day, desirous of knowing how the king really felt towards her, the rishi's cow entered a cave

गङ्गाप्रपातान्तविरूढशष्पं
गौरीगुरोर्गह्वरमाविवेश ॥ २६ ॥
सा दुष्प्रधर्षा मनसापि हिंस्रैः
इत्यद्रिशोभाप्रहितेक्षणेन ।
अलक्षिताभ्युत्पतनो नृपेण
प्रसह्य सिंहः किल तां चकर्ष ॥ २७ ॥

आत्मानुचरस्य भावम् अभिप्रायं [illegible], जिज्ञासमाना ज्ञातुमिच्छन्ती, प्रपतति अस्मिन् इति प्रपातः पतनप्रदेशः, गङ्गायाः प्रपातः तस्य अन्तं समीपे, विरूढानि जातानि शष्पाणि बालतृणानि यस्मिन् तत्, गौरीगुरोः पार्वतीपितुः गह्वरं गुहाम् आविवेश ॥ २६ ॥

सेति। सा धेनुः, हिंस्रैः व्याघ्रादिभिः, मनसा अपि दुष्प्रधर्षा दुर्धर्षा, इति हेतोः अद्रिशोभायां प्रहितेक्षणेन दत्तदृष्टिना, नृपेण, अलक्षितम् अभ्युत्पतनम् आभिमुख्येन उत्पतनं यस्य सः, सिंहः तां धेनुं

হিমালয়ের এক গহ্বরে প্রবেশ করিলেন ঐ গহ্বর গঙ্গার জলপ্রপাতের প্রান্তজাত তৃণের দ্বারা আচ্ছাদিত ছিল ॥২৬॥

রাজা জানিতেন হিংস্র জন্তুগণ নন্দিনীকে চিন্তাদ্বারাও আক্রমণ করিতে পারিবে না, সুতরাং তিনি একদৃষ্টে পর্ব্বতের শোভা দেখিতে ছিলেন, ইত্যবসরে তাঁহার অজ্ঞাতসারে একটি সিংহ লম্ফ দিয়া নন্দিনীকে আক্রমণ করিল ॥ ২৭ ॥

of the Himalays, covered with long grass, growing on the sides of a cataract of the Ganges.

27. The king was quite confident that the sacred cow could not be attacked, even in thought, by any beast of prey; consequently he was absorbed in the contemplation of the beauty of

तदीयमाक्रन्दितमार्त्तसाधोः
गुहानिबद्धप्रतिशब्ददीर्घम् ।
रश्मिष्विवादाय *नगेन्द्रसक्तां
निवर्त्तयामास नृपस्य दृष्टिम् ॥ २८ ॥

स पाटलायां गवि तस्थिवांसं
धनुर्धरः केशरिणं ददर्श ।

प्रसह्य हठात्, अकार्षं, किमेतदित्यलीके ॥ २७ ॥

तदीयमिति । गुहानिबद्धेन प्रतिशब्देन प्रतिध्वनिना दीर्घं, तस्याः इदं तदीयम्, आक्रन्दितम् आर्त्तघोषणम्, आर्त्तेषु आपन्नेषु साधोः हितकारिणः, नृपस्य नगेन्द्रसक्तां दृष्टिं रश्मिषु आदाय इव धृत्वा इव निवर्त्तयामास ॥ २८ ॥

स इति । धनुर्धरः सः नृपः, पाटलायां रक्तवर्णायां, गवि तस्थि-

নন্দিনীর আর্ত্তনাদ গিরিগহ্বরে নির্গমন পথ না পাইয়া, প্রতিধ্বনি যোগে এক মহাশব্দ উত্থিত করিল ; ঐ শব্দ কাতর জনের দুঃখ নিবারণ-কর্ত্তা দিলীপের পর্ব্বতাসক্ত দৃষ্টিকে যেন বল্গার দ্বারা আকৃষ্ট করিয়া হঠাৎ ফিরাইয়া আনিল ॥ ২৮ ॥

গৈরিকধাতুময়ী অধিত্যকাতে প্রস্ফুটিত পুষ্পরাশি পরিপূর্ণ লোধ্র

---

the mountain sceneries ; in the mean time a lion sprang upon her, before he could notice it.

28. The cries of the cow at once drew to her the eyes of the king which were fastened upon the mountain, as if suddenly turning them with the help of reins.

29. The king beheld the lion sitting upon the copper-colou-

---

* नगेन्द्रसक्तां—नगेन्द्रे पर्व्वते सक्तां आसक्तां, तद्रूपदर्शनासक्तामित्यर्थः ।

अधित्यकायामिव धातुमय्यां
लोध्रद्रुमं सानुमतः प्रफुल्लम् ॥ २९ ॥
ततो मृगेन्द्रस्य मृगेन्द्रगामी
वधाय वध्यस्य शरं शरण्यः ।
जाताभिषङ्गो नृपतिर्निषङ्गात्
उद्धर्तुमैच्छत् प्रसभोद्धृतारिः ॥ ३० ॥

यांसं स्थितम्, केशरिणं सिंहं, सानुमतः अद्रेः धातोः गैरिकस्य विकारः धातुमयी तस्याम् अधित्यकायाम् ऊर्द्ध्वभूमौ, प्रफुल्लः विकसितः तम् लोध्राख्यं द्रुमम् इव ददर्श ॥ २९ ॥

तत इति। ततः सिंहदर्शनानन्तरं, मृगेन्द्रगामी सिंहगामी, शरण्यं रक्षकम्, शरणे साधुः शरण्यः, प्रसभेन बलात्कारेण उद्धृताः अरयः येन सः, नृपतिः राजा, जाताभिषङ्गः जातपराभवः सन्, वध्यस्य वधार्हस्य, मृगेन्द्रस्य वधाय निषङ्गात् तूणीरात् शरम् उद्धर्तुम् ऐच्छत् ॥ ३० ॥

বৃক্ষ যেরূপ আরূঢ় থাকে, দিলীপ সেইরূপ পাটলবর্ণা ধেনুর উপরে সমাসীন সিংহকে দর্শন করিলেন ॥ ২৯ ॥

দিলীপ আশ্রিতজন-প্রতিপালক, ও স্বীয় বলে অনেক শত্রুদমন করিয়াছেন, সুতরাং এই পরাভবে আপনাকে অপমানিত জ্ঞান করিয়া সিংহের বধার্থ তূণীর হইতে শর আকর্ষণ করিতে উদ্যত হইলেন ॥ ৩০ ॥

---

red cow, looking very much like a tree of *lodhra* flower, in its blossoming season, displaying all its beauty on a patch of *gairic* table land.

30. Then the king, whose motions were as graceful as those of a lion and who was a perfect archer and who had conquered all his enemies by his might, felt humiliated by this sudden

वामेतरस्तस्य करः प्रहर्तुः
नखप्रभाभूषितकङ्कपत्रे ।
* सक्ताङ्गुलिः सायकपुङ्ख एव
† चित्रार्पितारम्भ ‡ इवावतस्थे ॥ ३१ ॥

वामेति । प्रहर्तुः तस्य, वामेतरः दक्षिणः करः नखानां प्रभाभिः भूषितानि विस्फुरितानि कङ्कस्य पक्षिविशेषस्य पत्राणि यस्य तस्मिन्, सायकस्य पुङ्खे एव कर्त्तर्याख्ये मूलप्रदेशे, सक्ताङ्गुलिः सन् चित्रार्पितारम्भः चित्रलिखितप्रहारोद्योगः इव अवतस्थे ॥ ३१ ॥

কিন্তু প্রহার করিবার জন্য যেই কঙ্কপক্ষীর পক্ষশোভিত শরমূলে হস্ত দিয়াছেন, অমনি অঙ্গুলি তাহাতে লাগিয়া গেল, এবং হস্তখানি চিত্রার্পিত হস্তের ন্যায় স্পন্দহীন হইয়া রহিল ॥ ৩১ ॥

---

attack and tried to draw an arrow from his arrow-case for killing the lion.

31. But in his attempt to kill the lion, his right hand, (owing to some mysterious cause) stuck to the feathery handle of his arrow, and could not be moved, so that it remained there, firmly fixed, his nails reflecting their light on the feathers of the shaft ; as if the whole thing was a piece of painting.

* सक्ताङ्गुलिः—सक्ता लग्ना, आबद्धा वा अङ्गुलयो यस्य स सक्ताङ्गुलिः ।

† चित्रार्पितारम्भः—चित्रे चित्रपटे अर्पितः विन्यस्तः यः आरम्भः क्रियोद्योगः स चित्रार्पितारम्भः—Readiness for action as painted on canvass

‡ अवतस्थे—The आत्मनेपद of this verb, is to be explained by समवप्रविभ्यः स्थः ।१।३। २२ *Panini* or प्रतिज्ञा-निर्णय-प्रकाशे सं प्र अव। स्थः—*Mugdhabodha.*—अपादः ।

বাহুপ্রতিষ্টম্ভবিবৃদ্ধমন্যুঃ
অভ্যর্ণমাগস্কৃতম
রাজা স্বতেজোভিরদহ্যতান্তঃ
ভোগীব মন্ত্রৌষধিরুদ্ধবীর্য্যঃ ॥ ৩২ ॥
তমার্য্যগৃহ্যং নিগৃহীতধেনুঃ
মনুষ্যবাচা মনুবংশকেতুম্ ।

বাহ্বিতি। বাহ্বোঃ প্রতিষ্টম্ভেন প্রতিবন্ধেন, বিবৃদ্ধমন্যুঃ প্রবৃদ্ধরোষঃ, রাজা মন্ত্রৌষধিভ্যাং রুদ্ধবীর্য্যঃ প্রতিবদ্ধসামর্থ্যঃ, ভোগী সর্পঃ ইব, অভ্যর্ণম্ অন্তিকম্, আগস্কৃতম্ অপরাধকারিণম্ অস্পৃশদ্ভিঃ স্বতেজোভিঃ অন্তঃ অদহ্যত ॥ ৩২ ॥

তমিতি। নিগৃহীতা পীড়িতা ধেনুঃ যেন সঃ, সিংহঃ, আর্য্যাণাং সতাং গৃহ্যং পক্ষ্যম্, মনুবংশস্য কেতুং চিহ্নং, কেতুবৎ ব্যাবর্ত্তকম্, সিংহ ইব উরুসত্ত্বঃ মহাবলঃ তম্, আত্মনঃ বৃত্তৌ বাহুস্তম্ভরূপে ব্যাপারে অভূত-

---

হঠাৎ হস্ত আবদ্ধ হওয়াতে দিলীপের ক্রোধ দ্বিগুণ বর্দ্ধিত হইয়া উঠিল, এবং তিনি সমীপস্থ শত্রুকে শাস্তি দিতে অক্ষম হইয়া মন্ত্র অথবা ঔষধের দ্বারা হৃতবল সর্পের ন্যায় ক্রোধ ভরে মনে মনে দগ্ধ হইতে লাগিলেন ॥ ৩২ ॥

সাধুজনের চিরসহায় ও সিংহ-সমান-পরাক্রমশালী মনুকুলপ্রদীপ দিলীপকে নিজ অবস্থা দর্শনে বিস্ময়ান্বিত দেখিয়া, সিংহ মনুষ্যভাষা

---

32. This sudden restraint upon his hand further irritated the king, who began to burn internally with rage, that could not touch an enemy so much with in his reach ; as swells an infuriated cobra made powerless by an incantation or a drug.

33. Then the lion, who had attacked the cow, assuming

विस्माययन् विस्मितमात्मवृत्तौ
सिंहोरुसत्त्वं निजगाद सिंहः ॥ ३३ ॥
अलं महीपाल ! तव श्रमेण
प्रयुक्तमप्यस्त्रमितो वृथा स्यात् ।
न पादपोन्मूलनशक्ति रंहः
शिलोच्चये मूर्च्छति मारुतस्य ॥ ३४ ॥

पूर्व्वत्वात् विस्मितम्, तं दिलीपं, मनुष्यवाचा करणेन, पुनः विस्माययन् विस्मयन् आश्चर्यं प्रापयन् निजगाद ॥ ३३ ॥

अलमिति । हे महीपाल ! तव श्रमेण अलं साध्याभावात् श्रमो न कर्त्तव्यः इत्यर्थः, इतः अस्मिन् मयि प्रयुक्तम् अपि अस्त्रं वृथा स्यात्, तथाहि, पादपोन्मूलने शक्तिः यस्य तत् तथोक्तं मारुतस्य रंहः वेगः, शिलोच्चये पर्व्वते न मूर्च्छति न प्रसरति ॥ ३४ ॥

অবলম্বনপূর্ব্বক তাঁহাকে আরও বিস্মিত করিয়া এই কথা বলিল ॥ ৩৩ ॥

হে রাজন্ ! বৃথা প্রয়াসে প্রয়োজন নাই ; যদি তুমি অস্ত্র প্রয়োগও কর তথাপি তাহা আমার দেহে ব্যর্থ হইবে ; কারণ পবনের যে বেগে তরু লতাই উন্মূলিত হইতে পারে, পর্ব্বতের দেহে সে বেগ খাটে না। ৩৪

---

human speech, thus addressed the wondering monarch, who himself was a lion in courage, and a friend of the good.

34. Cease mighty king ! fruitless is all thy labour. Even if discharged, thy shafts will be of no use here. That force of the wind which is sufficient only to uproot a tree, is of no effect against a mountain.

कैलासगौरं वृषमारुरुक्षोः
पादार्पणानुग्रहपूतपृष्ठम् ।
अवेहि मां किङ्करमष्टमूर्त्तेः*
कुम्भोदरं नाम निकुम्भमित्रम् ॥ ३५॥

कैलासेति। कैलासः इव गौरः शुभ्रः तम्, वृषं वृषभम् आरुरुक्षोः आरोढुम् इच्छोः, मत्पृष्ठोपरि पदं निक्षिप्य वृषमारोहति इत्यर्थः, अष्टौ मूर्त्तयो यस्य सः तस्य अष्टमूर्त्तेः शिवस्य, पादार्पणं पादनिक्षेपः तद् एव अनुग्रहः प्रसादः तेन पूतं पृष्ठं यस्य तं तथोक्तं, निकुम्भमित्रं कुम्भोदरं नाम किङ्करं माम् अवेहि विद्धि ॥ २५ ॥

শম্ভু যখন কৈলাস পর্ব্বত সম গৌরকান্তি বৃষভে আরোহণ করেন তখন আমারই পৃষ্ঠে পদস্থাপন করিয়া আরোহণ করিয়া থাকেন; আমার পৃষ্ঠদেশ তাঁহারই চরণস্পর্শের দ্বারা পবিত্রীকৃত; আমি তাঁহার কিঙ্কর, আমি নিকুম্ভের মিত্র, আমার নাম কুম্ভোদর ॥ ৩৫ ॥

35. Be it known to thee, O prince, that this back of mine is sanctified by the footsteps of the great Siva, when mounting his great bull, which is as white as the mount Kailas. My

---

* अष्टमूर्त्तेः—Siva is said to have eight forms.

In connection with this try to get the following opening verse of अभिज्ञानशकुन्तलं by the same author explained by your Sanskrit teacher :—

या सृष्टिः स्रष्टुराद्या वहति विधिहुतं या हविर्या च होत्री,
ये द्वे कालं विधत्तः श्रुतिविषयगुणा या स्थिता व्याप्य विश्वम् ।
यामाहुः सर्व्वबीजप्रकृतिरिति यया प्राणिनः प्राणवन्तः,
प्रत्यक्षाभिः प्रपन्नस्तनुभिरवतु वस्ताभिरष्टाभिरीशः ॥

अमुं पुरः पश्यसि देवदारुं
* पुत्रीकृतोऽसौ वृषभध्वजेन ।
यो † हेमकुम्भस्तननिःसृतानां
स्कन्दस्य मातुः पयसां रसज्ञः ॥ ३६ ॥

अमुमिति। पुरः अग्रतः अमुं देवदारुं पश्यसि ? असौ देवदारुः, वृषभः ध्वजः यस्य सः तेन, शिवेन पुत्रीकृतः पुत्रत्वेन स्वीकृतः, यः देवदारुः स्कन्दस्य मातुः गौर्य्याः, हेम्नः कुम्भः एव स्तनः तस्मात् निःसृतानां पयसाम् अम्बूनां रसज्ञः स्वादज्ञः स्कन्दपक्षे हेमकुम्भः इव स्तनः इति विग्रहः, पयसां क्षीराणाम्। स्कन्दसमानप्रेमास्पदम् इति भावः ॥ ३६ ॥

এই যে সমীপে দেবদারু দেখিতেছ, ইহাকে শম্ভু স্বয়ং অপত্য-নির্বিশেষে স্নেহ করিয়া থাকেন, এবং স্বয়ং পার্ব্বতী মাতার ন্যায় হেম-কুম্ভ-নিঃসৃত বারিরূপ স্তন্য দান দ্বারা ইহাকে পালন করিয়াছেন ॥৩৬॥

---

name is Kumbhodara, and am a servant of the great god, and a friend of Nikumbha.

36. Yonder Devdaru tree, that thou seest, has been adopted as a son by Siva.—It has had the good fortune of having been nursed, by Parvati, the mother of Kartika, from out of her own golden watering-pots representing her nursing breasts as it were.

* पुत्रीकृतः—अपुत्रः पुत्रः कृतः पुत्रीकृतः अभूततद्भावे च्वि।

† हेमकुम्भस्तननिःसृतानां पयसां रसज्ञः—गौर्य्या स्वर्णकुम्भजलविन्दुनेन संवर्द्धितः स्वहस्तैः:—reared by Gouri with her own hands with water poured from her golden watering pots.

कण्डूयमानेन कटं कदाचिद्
वन्यद्विपेनोन्मथिता त्वगस्य ।
अथैनमद्रेस्तनया शुशोच
सेनान्यमालीढमिवासुरास्त्रैः ॥ ३७ ॥
तदा प्रभृत्येव वनद्विपानां
त्रासार्थमस्मिन्नहमद्रिकुक्षौ ।

कण्डूयमानेनेति । कदाचित् कटं कपोलं, कण्डूयमानेन कर्षता, वन्यद्विपेन अस्य देवदारोः त्वक् उन्मथिता, अथ अद्रेः तनया गौरी, असुरास्त्रैः आलीढं क्षतं, सेनां नयतीति सेनानीः स्कन्दः तम्, इव एनं देवदारुं शुशोच ॥ ३७ ॥

तदेति । तदा तत्कालः प्रभृति आदिः यस्मिन् कर्म्मणि तत् यथा तथा तदाप्रभृति, एव वनद्विपानां त्रासार्थं भयार्थं, शूलभृता शिवेन, अहं समीपम् आगताः प्राप्ताः सत्त्वाः प्राणिनः वृत्तिः यस्मिन् तत्, सिंहत्वं

এক দিন কোন বন্য হস্তী এই দেবদারুর দেহে নিজ গণ্ডদেশ ঘর্ষণ করিয়া ইহার ত্বক তুলিয়া ফেলিয়াছিল ; কার্ত্তিকের দেহ অসুরাস্ত্রে ক্ষত বিক্ষত হইলে, পার্ব্বতীর যেরূপ দুঃখ হয়, ইহাতেও সেই প্রকার দুঃখ হইয়াছিল ॥ ৩৭ ॥

তদবধি বন্য হস্তিদিগকে তাড়াইবার নিমিত্ত শূলপাণি, আমাকে এই গিরিক্রোড়ে নিযুক্ত করিয়াছেন। আমার প্রতি আদেশ এই, যে

---

37. On one occasion, a wild elephant rubbed its temples against that tree and made a scar on its bark; whereupon the daughter of Himalaya was deeply aggrieved as if it was her own son Kartika, wounded by the weapons of the Asuras.

38. From that day I have been appointed by the trident-bearing god to keep guard over this valley, to scare away all

व्यापारितः शूलभृता विधाय
सिंहत्वमङ्कागतसत्त्ववृत्ति * ॥ ३८ ॥
तस्यालमेषा क्षुधितस्य तृप्त्यै
प्रदिष्टकाला परमेश्वरेण ।
उपस्थिता † शोणितपारणा मे
‡ सुरद्विषश्चान्द्रमसी सुधेव ॥ ३९ ॥

विधाय, अस्मिन् अद्रिकुक्षौ गुहायाम् अहं व्यापारितः नियुक्तः ॥३८॥

तस्येति । परमेश्वरेण, प्रदिष्टः निर्दिष्टः कालः भोजनवेला यस्याः सा, उपस्थिता प्राप्ता एषा गोरूपा शोणितपारणा रुधिरस्य व्रतान्त-भोजनं, सुरद्विषः राहोः, चन्द्रमसः इयं चान्द्रमसी, सुधा इव, क्षुधितस्य बुभुक्षितस्य, तस्य अङ्कागतसत्त्ववृत्तेः, मे मम सिंहस्य, तृप्त्यै अलं पर्य्याप्ता ॥ ३९ ॥

জন্তু যদৃচ্ছাক্রমে আমার সমীপে উপনীত হইবে, তদ্দ্বারাই আমি দেহ-যাত্রা নির্ব্বাহ করিব ॥ ৩৮ ॥

অতএব চন্দ্রের সুধা যেমন রাহুর মুখে স্বতঃই উপনীত হয়, সেই-রূপ আমার ক্ষুধা নিবারণের জন্যই জগদীশ্বর যথা সময়ে এই শোণিত-পারণাকে আমার মুখে উপস্থিত করিয়াছেন, ইহার শোণিত আমার অদ্যকার পক্ষে যথেষ্ট হইবে ॥ ৩৯ ॥

---

wild animals ;—living upon such animals alone as came un-sought into my clutches.

39. To day this cow's opportune arrival is quite providen-

---

* अङ्कागतसत्त्ववृत्ति—वृत्तिर्वर्त्तनं जीवनधारणोपाय इत्यर्थः ।

† शोणित-पारणा—शोणितस्य पारणा शोणितात्मकं व्रतान्तभोजनम् ।

‡ सुरद्विषः—सुरान् देवान् द्वेष्टि यः सः सुरद्विट् राहुस्तस्य सुरद्विषः ।

स त्वं निवर्त्तस्व विहाय लज्जां
गुरोर्भवान् दर्शितशिष्यभक्तिः ।
शस्त्रेण रक्ष्यं यदशक्यरक्षं
न तद्यशः शस्त्रभृतां क्षिणोति ॥४०॥
इति * प्रगल्भं पुरुषाधिराजो

स इति । सः एवम् उपायशून्यः, त्वं लज्जां विहाय निवर्त्तस्व, त्वं गुरोः दर्शिता प्रकाशिता शिष्यस्य कर्त्तव्या भक्तिः येन सः, तथोक्तः असि । ननु सुरधेनुं विनाश्य कथं तत्समीपं गच्छेयमित्यत आह शस्त्रे-णेति, यत् रक्ष्यं धनं, शस्त्रेण आयुधेन, अशक्या रक्षा यस्य तत्, अशक्यरक्षं रक्षितुमशक्यम् इत्यर्थः, तत् रक्ष्यं नष्टम् अपि शस्त्रभृतां यशः न क्षिणोति न छिनत्ति । अशक्यार्थस्याप्रतिविधानं न दोषाय इति भावः ॥ ४० ॥

इतीति । पुरुषाणाम् अधिराजः नृपः, इति प्रगल्भं, सगर्वाधि-

অতএব তুমি ইহাকে পরিত্যাগ পূর্ব্বক নিবৃত্ত হও; গুরুর প্রতি তোমার সমুচিত ভক্তি প্রদর্শন করা হইয়াছে; যে ধন শস্ত্রের দ্বারা রক্ষা করা সম্ভব নহে, তাহা রক্ষা করিতে না পারিলে শস্ত্রধারিদিগের নিন্দা নাই ॥ ৪০ ॥

নরপতি সিংহের এই সগর্ব্ব বাক্য শ্রবণ করিয়া বুঝিতে পারিলেন

---

tial and this bloody break-fast will suffice for this day, as sufficeth the nectar of the moon to give satisfaction to Rahu.

40. Return home then. It is no disgrace to thee. Thou hast shown thy dutifulness to the sage. In ability to protect some thing, which cannot be prolicted by arms, does not in the least detract from the glory of a soldier.

41. The king, when he listened to these proud words of

---

* प्रगल्भं - सगर्व्वं—proud words.

मृगाधिराजस्य वचो निशम्य ।
प्रत्याहतास्त्रो * गिरिशप्रभावात्
आत्मन्यवज्ञां शिथिलीचकार ॥ ४१ ॥
प्रत्यब्रवीच्चैनमिषुप्रयोगे
तत्पूर्वभङ्गे वितथप्रयत्नः ।

राजस्य वचः, निशम्य श्रुत्वा, गिरिशस्य ईश्वरस्य प्रभावात्, प्रत्याहतास्त्रः कुण्ठितास्त्रः, सन् आत्मनि विषये अवज्ञाम् अपमानं, शिथिलीचकार तत्याज इत्यर्थः ; अवज्ञातोऽहमिति निर्वेदं न प्राप इत्यर्थः। समानेषु हि अशिवत्वाद्यामभिमानो न सर्वेश्वरं प्रति इति भावः ॥ ४१ ॥

प्रतीति। सः एव पूर्व्वः प्रथमः भङ्गः प्रतिबन्धः यस्य तस्मिन् तत्पूर्वभङ्गे, इषुप्रयोगे, वितथप्रयत्नः निष्फलप्रयासः, अतएव, वज्रं कुण्ठितं, शस्त्रम् मोक्तुम् इच्छन्, त्र्यम्बकं लोचनम्, त्रीणि अम्बकानि यस्य सः त्र्यम्बकः हरः, तस्य वीक्षणेन, जडीकृतः निष्पन्दीकृतः, वज्रं पाणौ

যে, মহাদেবেরই প্রভাবে তাঁহার অস্ত্রপাত-শক্তি প্রতিহত হইয়াছে, সুতরাং নিজের প্রতি আর তাঁহার পূর্ব্ববৎ ধিক্কার থাকিল না ॥ ৪১ ॥

ইহার পূর্ব্বে বাণ প্রয়োগ বিষয়ে রাজার চেষ্টা কখনও বিফল হয় নাই; সুতরাং বজ্র প্রহারের উদ্যমেই মহাদেবের দৃষ্টিপাত দ্বারা সহসা।

---

the lion, knew that his hand had been suddenly restrained by the supernatural powers of Siva, and accordingly moderated his selfreproach.

42. Never before had the king's skill in the use of arms received such a sudden check ; consequently he looked worsted like Indra, when about to discharge the thunder, but suddenly

---

* गिरिशप्रभावात्—गिरौ हिमालये शेते यः गिरिशः शिवः तस्य प्रभावः, पराक्रमस्तेन।—the mysterious power of Siva.

जडीकृतस्त्र्यम्बकवीक्षणेन
वज्रं मुमुक्षन्निव वज्रपाणिः ॥ ४२ ॥
संबद्धचेष्टस्य मृगेन्द्र ! कामं
हास्यं वचस्तद् यदहं विवक्षुः ।
अन्तर्गतं * प्राणभृतां हि वेद
सर्वं भवान् भावमतोऽभिधास्ये ॥ ४३ ॥

यथा वः वज्रपाणिः इन्द्रः, वः त्र्यम्बकवीक्षितः स्तम्भः, एवं दिलीपस्तम्भनमभवदित्यर्थः ॥४२

संरुद्धेति। हे मृगेन्द्र ! संरुद्धचेष्टस्य प्रतिबद्धव्यापारस्य, मम तत् वचः वाक्यं, कामं हास्यं परिहसनीयं, यत् वचः, अहं विवक्षुः वक्तुम् इच्छुः अस्मि। हि यतः भवान् प्राणभृताम्, अन्तर्गतं हृद्गतं वागुच्चारणात् बहिरप्रकाशितम्, एव सर्वं भावं वेद वेत्ति, अतः अहम् अभिधास्ये वक्ष्यामि, वच इति प्रकृतं कर्म सम्बध्यते। अन्ये लौकिकवचनमात्रमसम्भाविनार्थमेतदित्युपहसन्ति, अतस्त्वां मौनमेव भूषणं, त्वं तु वाङ्मन-

স্তম্ভ-শক্তি হইলে ইন্দ্রের যেরূপ ভাব হয়, সেইরূপ ভাবাপন্ন হইয়া তিনি সিংহকে প্রত্যুত্তর করিলেন ॥ ৪২ ॥

হে মৃগেন্দ্র আমার কিছু করিবার যখন উপায় নাই, তখন আমি যে কথা বলিতে যাইতেছি তাহা তোমার নিকট উপহাসেরই বিষয় হইবে জানি ; কিন্তু তুমি প্রাণিগণের মনোগত অভিপ্রায় সমুদায় অবগত

---

paralyzed by the mysterious gaze of Siva. The king then thus spoke :—

43. Under my present condition of helplessness, O mighty lion, what I am about to say will be most likely regarded as

* प्राणभृतां—प्राणान् बिभ्रति धारयन्ति ये ते, प्राणभृतस्तेषाम्।

मान्यः स मे स्थावरजङ्गमानां
* सर्गस्थितिप्रत्यवहारहेतुः।
गुरोरपीदं धनमाहिताग्ने-
र्नश्यत् पुरस्तादनुपेक्षणीयम् † ॥ ४४ ॥

ययोरेकविध एवायमिति जानासि अतोऽभिधास्ये वक्तव्योऽहं विवक्षुः इत्यर्थः ॥ ४३ ॥

मान्य इति। प्रत्यवहारः प्रलयः, स्थावराणां तरुशैलादीनां जङ्गमानां मनुष्यादीनां सर्गस्थितिप्रत्यवहारेषु हेतुः, सः ईश्वरः, मे मम मान्यः पूज्यः अलङ्घ्यशासनः इत्यर्थः, शासनञ्च सिंहत्वमङ्कागतसत्त्ववृत्तीत्युक्तरूपम्। तर्हि विसृज्य गम्यतां नेत्याह, गुरोरपीति। पुरस्तात् अग्रे नश्यत् इदम् आहिताग्नेः गुरोः धनम् अपि गोरूपम्, अनु-

আছ; সুতরাং তোমার নিকট তাহা প্রকাশ করিয়া বলিব ॥ ৪৩ ॥

সমুদায় চরাচরের সৃষ্টিস্থিতিপ্রলয়কর্ত্তা সেই মহেশ্বর আমার পূজ্য (অর্থাৎ তাঁহার আদেশ আমার শিরোধার্য্য) অথচ আহিতাগ্নি গুরুর

laughable by you, but you know the inmost secrets of men's hearts, hence it is well that I should speak.

44. True, my respect is due to the great god, who is the creator, preserver, and destroyer of all things, animate and inanimate; but it is also my duty, on the other hand, not to

* सर्ग-स्थिति-प्रत्यवहारहेतुः—सर्गः (सृज्+घञ्) सृष्टिः स्थितिः; अवस्थानञ्च, प्रत्यवहारः (प्रति + अव + हृ + घञ्) प्रलयश्च ते सर्गस्थितिप्रत्यवहाराः तेषां हेतुः कारणम्।—the author of the creation, preservation, and destruction of things.

† अनुपेक्षणीयं—उपेक्षा, नश्यतु तावत् धनं रक्षणप्रयत्नेन इति औदासीन्यबुद्धिः तद्विषयं न कर्त्तव्यमित्यर्थः।

स त्वं मदीयेन शरीरवृत्तिं
देहेन निर्वर्तयितुं प्रसीद ।
दिनावसानोत्सुकबालवत्सा
विसृज्यतां धेनुरियं महर्षेः ॥ ४५ ॥
अथान्धकारं गिरिगह्वराणां

पेक्षणीयम् । आहिताग्नेरिति विशेषणेनानुपेक्षणीयत्वं हविःसाधनत्वं सूचयति ॥ ४४ ॥

स इति । सः अङ्कागतसत्त्ववृत्तिः त्वं, मदीयेन देहेन, शरीरस्य वृत्तिं जीवनं, निर्वर्तयितुं सम्पादयितुं, प्रसीद ; दिनावसाने उत्सुकः माता समागमिष्यतीत्युत्कण्ठितः बालवत्सः यस्याः सा, महर्षेः इयं धेनुः विसृज्यताम् ॥ ४५ ॥

अथेति । अथ भूतेश्वरस्य पार्श्ववर्त्ती अनुचरः सः सिंहः, गिरेः

ধনস্বরূপ এই ধেনু যে আমার সমক্ষে নষ্ট হইবে তাহাও সহিতে পারি না ॥ ৪৪ ॥

অতএব তুমি অনুগ্রহ করিয়া আমার শরীরের দ্বারা তোমার অদ্য-কার দিনযাত্রা নির্ব্বাহ কর ; এই মুনি ধেনুর নবজাত বৎস দিনাবসানে মাতৃদর্শনের নিমিত্ত উৎসুক হইয়া রহিয়াছে, অতএব ইহাকে পরিত্যাগ কর ॥ ৪৫ ॥

শিবকিঙ্কর সেই সিংহ দংষ্ট্রাকিরণ দ্বারা গিরিগহ্বরের অন্ধকার

---

allow this property of my spiritual preceptor, who has daily to kindle his sacrificial fire, to be destroyed before my eyes.

45. Do me one favour then, appease your hunger with this body of mine, and leave, the *rishi's* cow whose young calf is anxiously looking forward for her return at the close of day.

46. Then partly chasing the darkness of the mountain-cave

* दंष्ट्रामयूखैः शकलानि कुर्वन्।
भूयः स भूतेश्वरपार्श्ववर्त्ती
किञ्चिद्विहस्यार्थपतिं बभाषे ॥ ৪৬ ॥

एकातपत्रं जगतः प्रभुत्वं
नवं वयः कान्तमिदं वपुश्च।
अल्पस्य
विचारमूढः प्रतिभासि मे त्वम् ॥ ৪৭ ॥

गह्वरोत्थां गुहागताम्, अन्धकारं ध्वान्तं, दंष्ट्रामयूखैः शकलानि खण्डानि कुर्वन् निरस्यन् इत्यर्थः, किञ्चित् विहस्य, अर्थपतिं नृपं, भूयः बभाषे। हासकारणम् अल्पस्य हेतोर्बहु हातुमिच्छन्निति वक्ष्यमाणं द्रष्टव्यम्॥৪৬॥

एकेति। एकातपत्रम् एकच्छत्रं, जगतः प्रभुत्वं स्वामित्वं, नवं वयः यौवनम्, इदं कान्तं रम्यं वपुश्च, इत्येवं बहु अल्पस्य हेतोः अल्पेन कारणेन अल्पफलाय इत्यर्थः, हातुं त्यक्तुम् इच्छन् त्वं, विचारे कार्याकार्यविमर्शे मूढो मूर्खः, मे मम प्रतिभासि ॥ ৪৭ ॥

হরণ করিয়া পুনরায় রাজাকে কহিল ॥ ৪৬ ॥

জগতে তোমার একমাত্র প্রভুত্ব; যৌবনকাল এখনও অস্তমিত হয় নাই; দেহের কান্তি এমন সুন্দর; একটী সামান্য ধেনুর জন্য, এত

---

with the reflections of his white teeth, laughed the servant of Siva; and thus replied to the king—

47. Thou dost not seem to be wise in thy decision, O Prince, in thus offering to sacrifice thy soveriegnty over the

---

* दंष्ट्रामयूखैः—दश्यते आभिः (दन्श+ष्ट्रन्) इति दंष्ट्रा; दन्तमण्डलस्व-स्वाभा मयूखाः किरणानि तैः।

भूतानुकम्पा तव चेदियं गौः
एका भवेत् स्वस्तिमती त्वदन्ते ।
जीवन् पुनः शश्वदुपप्लवेभ्यः
प्रजाः प्रजानाथ ! पितेव पासि ॥४८॥

भूतेति । तव भूतेषु अनुकम्पा कृपा चेत्, कृपैव यदि चेत् इत्यर्थः, यर्हि त्वदन्ते तव नाशे सति, इयम् एका गौः, स्वस्तिमती क्षेमवती, भवेत् जीवेत् इत्यर्थः ; हे प्रजानाथ ! जीवन् पुनः पिता इव प्रजाः उपप्लवेभ्यः विघ्नेभ्यः शश्वत् सदा पासि रक्षसि । समग्रायुष्यवेनैकधेनुरक्षणादिदं जीवितेनैव सर्वप्रजारक्षणमधिकम् इत्यर्थः ॥ ४८ ॥

সুখ বিসর্জ্জন করিতে ইচ্ছুক হইয়া, আমার মতে তুমি নির্ব্বোধের কার্য্য করিতেছ ॥ ৪৭ ॥

যদি জগতের উপকার বুদ্ধির দ্বারা বিচার কর তাহা হইলেও ভাবিয়া দেখ, তুমি বিনষ্ট হইলে, এই একমাত্র ধেনু সুখী হইবে, কিন্তু তুমি বাঁচিয়া থাকিয়া পিতার ন্যায় প্রজাকুলকে নিরন্তর নানাপ্রকার উপদ্রব হইতে রক্ষা করিতেছ ও করিবে কোনটা শ্রেষ্ঠ ? ॥ ৪৮ ॥

---

whole world, thy tender youth, and thy comely person, for a trifle like this beast.

48. If the good of other creatures be thy motive, consider which is the greater good, whether by giving up thyself, to secure the happiness of this single cow, or by saving thy life, always to protect thy people, as their father, from all their troubles.

अथैकधेनोरपराधचण्डात्
* गुरोः कृशानुप्रतिमाद्बिभेषि।
शक्योऽस्य मन्युर्भवता विनेतुं
गाः कोटिशः † स्पर्शयता ‡ घटोध्नीः॥४९॥

न धर्मलोपादियं भीतिः किन्तु गुरुभयादित्यत आह, अथेति। पक्षान्तरे अथवा एका एव धेनुः यस्य तस्मात्, अतएव अपराधे धेनो-र्धेनोरपराधे सति चण्डात् अतिकोपनात्, अतएव कृशानुः प्रतिमा उपमा यस्य तस्मात् अग्निकल्पात् गुरोः बिभेषि, अस्य गुरोः मन्युः

আর যদি এরূপ হয়, যে এই ধেনু বিনষ্ট হইলে, সেই অপরাধে গুরু তোমার প্রতি কুপিত হইবেন, যদি সেই ভয় থাকে, তাহা হইলেও তুমি তাঁহাকে বিশাল আপীনবিশিষ্ট কোটি কোটি ধেনু দিয়া তাঁহার ক্রোধ শান্ত করিতে পার ॥ ৪৯ ॥

49. But if thou fearest to meet the displeasure of thy preceptor, who will be naturally offended for the loss of his cow, it is in thy power to allay his anger by presenting thousands of cows, whose udders are ample and full like jugs of water.

* गुरोः—भीत्रार्थानां भयहेतुः (१।४।२५) इत्यपादानात् पञ्चमी—
Mallinath.

† स्पर्शयता—विश्राणनं वितरणं स्पर्शनं प्रतिपादनमित्यमरः—
Mallinath.

‡ घटोध्नीः—घटाः कलसा इव ऊधांसि आपीनानि यासां ताः घटोध्नीः।
—ऊधसोऽनङ् (५।४।१३१) इति समासान्त अनङादेशः।
तदनन्तरं बहुव्रीहेरूधसो ङीष् (४।१।२५) इति सूत्रेण ङीष्।

तदक्ष * कल्याणपरम्पराणां
भोक्तारमूर्जस्वलमात्मदेहम्।
महीतलस्पर्शनमात्रभिन्नम्
ऋद्धं हि राज्यं पदमैन्द्रमाहुः॥ ५०॥

ओघः, घटाः इव ऊधांसि यासां ताः घटोध्नीः कोटिशो गाः स्पर्शवता प्रतिपादयता, भवता विनेतुम् अपनेतुं शक्यः॥ ४९॥

तदिति। तत् तस्मात् कारणात् कल्याणपरम्पराणां भोक्तारम् ऊर्जः बलम् अस्याः अस्तीति ऊर्जस्वलम्, आत्मदेहं रक्ष, ननु गामुपेक्ष्य आत्मदेहरक्षणे स्वर्गहानिः स्यात् नेत्याह, महीतलेति, ऋद्धं समृद्धं, राज्यं, महीतलस्पर्शनमात्रेण भूतलसम्बन्धमात्रेण भिन्नम्, ऐन्द्रम् इन्द्रसम्बन्धि पदं स्थानम्, आहुः स्वर्गान्न भिद्यते इत्यर्थः॥ ५०॥

অতএব নানা প্রকার সুখোপভোগের দ্বারস্বরূপ, আপনার তেজস্বী দেহকে রক্ষা করুন; (আর যদি এজন্য অধর্ম্ম হয় তাহাতেই বা ভয় কি) আপনার রাজ্য পৃথিবীতে অবস্থিত কেবল এই মাত্র প্রভেদ নতুবা সুখ সমৃদ্ধিতে ইহা সর্ব্বাংশে ইন্দ্রপদ তুল্য॥৫০॥

---

50. Preserve then thy strong and manly body, wherewith thou enjoyest so many blessings; thy kingly power too is equal to that of Indra, with the only exception that thou holdest thy sway on the earth.

---

* कल्याणपरम्पराणाम्—कल्याणानां मङ्गलानां परम्पराः अविच्छिन्ना सन्ततिस्तासां कल्याणपरम्पराणाम्।—A succession of blessings.

एतावदुक्त्वा विरते मृगेन्द्रे
प्रतिस्वनेनास्य गुहागतेन।
शिलोच्चयोऽपि क्षितिपालमुच्चैः
प्रीत्या * तमेवार्थमभाषतेव॥ ५१॥

एतावदिति। मृगेन्द्रे एतावत् उक्त्वा विरते सति गुहागतेन अस्य सिंहस्य प्रतिस्वनेन, शिलोच्चयः शैलोऽपि, प्रीत्या तम् एव अर्थं क्षितिपालम् उच्चैः अभाषत इव इत्युत्प्रेक्षा ॥ ५१॥

মৃগেন্দ্র এই কথা বলিয়া নিরস্ত হইলে, গুহামধ্যে তাহার প্রবল প্রতিধ্বনি উত্থিত হইল; বোধ হইল পর্ব্বতও যেন প্রীতির সহিত রাজাকে উচ্চৈঃস্বরে সেই কথাই বলিল ॥৫১॥

51. When the speech of the lion ceased, its echoes resounded in the mountain caves; methinks! the rocks also repeated the same loving request to the prince.

---

* तमेवार्थमभाषतेव – In this sloka, the verb अभाषत has two objectives क्षितिपालं and अर्थं. According to the rules of Sanskrit grammar ब्रु has two objectives, भाष being of the same meaning as ब्रु has also two objectives. Refer to सिद्धान्तकौमुदी page 253 Taranath Tarkavachaspati's edition of 1863, for the following list of *dhatus* having double objectives :—

दुह्याच् पच् दण्ड् रुधि प्रच्छि चि ब्रु शासु जि मथ् मुषाम्।
कर्म्मयुक् स्यादकथितं तथा स्यान्नी हृ कृष् वहाम्॥

Trans—A noun intimately connected with the objectives of दुह्, याच्, पच्, दण्ड्, रुध्, प्रच्छ्, चि, ब्रु, शास्, जि,

निशम्य देवानुचरस्य वाचं
मनुष्यदेवः पुनरप्युवाच ।
धेन्वा तदध्यासितकातराक्ष्या
निरीक्ष्यमाणः सुतरां दयालुः ॥ ५२ ॥
क्षतात् किल त्रायत इत्युदग्रः
क्षत्रस्य शब्दो भुवनेषु रूढः

निशम्येति । देवानुचरस्य ईश्वरकिङ्करस्य, सिंहस्य वाचं निशम्य, मनुष्यदेवः राजा, पुनः अपि उवाच, तेन सिंहेन यत् अध्यासितं आक्रमणम् तेन कातरे अक्षिणी यस्याः तया, किंवा रक्षतीति भीत्येव स्थितया इत्यर्थः धेन्वा निरीक्ष्यमाणः अतएव सुतरां दयालुः सन् ॥५२॥
किमुवाचेत्याह, क्षतादिति । (क्षणु हिंसायामिति धातोः सम्पदादि-

দেবানুচর সিংহের, এই বচন শ্রবণ করিয়া রাজা পুনরায় উত্তর করিলেন ;—ইত্যবসরে নন্দিনী সিংহাক্রমণে নিপীড়িত হইয়া কাতর-নেত্রে রাজার দিকে চাহিতে লাগিল, তাহা দেখিয়া রাজার মনে অতিশয় করুণার সঞ্চার হইল ॥৫২॥
ক্ষয় অর্থাৎ নাশ হইতে ত্রাণ করে, এই জন্যই ক্ষত্রিয়দিগের

52. The king thus rejoined to the words of the servant of Siva, moved mightily by the piteous and imploring looks of the animal.

53. A Kshatriya is so called all over the world, simply be-

मन्थ्, मुष्, नी, हृ, कृष् and वह्, is also considerd an in-direct objective. Also compare the different examples, given in that book.

राज्येन किं तद्विपरीतवृत्तेः
*प्राणैरुपक्रोशमलीमसैर्वा ॥ ५३ ॥
कथं नु शक्योऽनुनयो महर्षे-
र्विश्राणनाच्चान्यपयस्विनीनाम् ।

त्वात् क्विप्, गमादीनामिति वक्तव्यादनुनासिकलोपे तुगागमे च क्षदिति रूपं सिद्धम्) क्षतः नाशात् त्रायते इति क्षत्रः उदग्रः उन्नतः क्षत्रस्य क्षत्रवर्णस्य शब्दः वाचकः क्षत्रशब्द इत्यर्थः क्षतात् त्रायते इति व्युत्पत्त्या भुवनेषु रूढः किल प्रसिद्धः खलु, नाम्बकर्णादिवत् केवलरूढः किन्तु पङ्कजादिवत् योगरूढः इत्यर्थः, ततः किमित्यत आह, तस्य क्षत्रशब्दस्य, विपरीतवृत्तेः विरुद्धव्यापारस्य क्षतः त्राणम् अकुर्वतः, पुंसः राज्येन किम्? उपक्रोशमलीमसैः निन्दामलिनैः, प्राणैर्वा किं निन्दितस्य सर्वं व्यर्थम् इत्यर्थः । एतेनैकातपत्रमित्यादिना श्लोकद्वयेनोक्तं प्रत्युक्तमिति वेदितव्यम् ॥ ५२ ॥

अथैकधेनोरित्यत्रोत्तरमाह, कथमिति । अनुनयः क्रोधापनयः

“ক্ষত্র” এই মহৎ নাম জগতে প্রসিদ্ধ ; যে ব্যক্তি সেই নামের বিরুদ্ধাচারী অর্থাৎ দুর্ব্বলের রক্ষা বিষয়ে পরাঙ্মুখ তাহার রাজ্যে প্রয়োজন কি ; এবং কাপুরুষতার কলঙ্ক লইয়া মলিন জীবন ধারণেই বা ফল কি ? ৫৩।

অন্যান্য পয়স্বিনী ধেনু দান দ্বারা মহর্ষির প্রসন্নতা সম্পাদন সম্ভব

---

cause it is his glorious privilege to protect others from death. Of what good shall my sovereignty of the world be if I act in opposition to the spirit of that privilege ? or of what good shall be my useless life, with its tarnished fame ?

54. And again how is it possible to avert the wrath of the

---

* उपक्रोशमलीमसैः—उप+क्रुश्, आह्वाने, घञ् उपक्रोशः निन्दा तेन मलीमसाः मलिनाः ;—a life sullied by a disgrace.

इमामनूनां सुरभेरवेहि
रुद्रौजसा तु प्रहृतं त्वयास्याम् ॥ ५४ ॥
सेयं स्वदेहार्पणनिष्क्रयेण
न्याय्या मया मोचयितुं भवत्तः
न पारणा स्याद्विहता तवैवं
भवेदलुप्तश्च मुनेः क्रियार्थः ॥ [illegible] ॥

महर्षेः अनुभवः या अन्यासां पयस्विनीनां दोग्ध्रीणां गवां विश्राणनात् दानात् कथं नु शक्यः ? न शक्यः इत्यर्थः, अत्र हेतुमाह, इमां गां सुरभेः कामधेनोः अनूनाम् अन्यूनाम् अवेहि जानीहि । तर्हि कथमस्याः परिभवोऽभूदित्याह, रुद्रौजसेति, अस्यां गवि त्वया कर्त्रा प्रहृतं तु प्रहारस्तु रुद्रौजसा ईश्वरसामर्थ्येन न तु स्वयम् इत्यर्थः ॥ ५४ ॥

तर्हि किं चिकीर्षितमित्यत्राह, सेयमिति । सा इयं गौः मया, निष्क्रीयते प्रत्याह्रियते अनेन परस्माद्गृहीतम् इति निष्क्रयः प्रतिशीर्षकम्, स्वदेहार्पणम् एव निष्क्रयः तेन भवतः त्वत्तः मोचयितुं न्याय्या न्यायात्

নয় ; কারণ এই ধেনুকে সুরভি হইতে হীন বলিয়া মনে করিও না, তুমি মহেশ্বরের প্রভাব গুণেই ইহাকে আক্রমণ করিতে পারিয়াছ ; নতুবা পারিতে না ॥৫৪॥

অতএব আমার পক্ষে নিজ দেহ রূপ পণ দিয়া এই ধেনুর উন্মোচন করা কোন ক্রমেই অন্যায় নয় ; এরূপ করিলে তোমারও শোণিতের

sage by offering other cows? Know that this cow is in no way inferior to Surabhi, and it is only through the influence of the great god Siva that you have been able to attack her.

55. Accordingly, I am perfectly right in proposing to liberate this cow by the offer of my body as ransom ; for thus

ভবানপীদং পরবানবৈতি,
মহান্ হি যত্নস্তব দেবদারৌ।
স্থাতুং নিয়োক্তুর্ন হি শক্যমগ্রে
বিনাশ্য রক্ষ্যং স্বয়মক্ষতেন ॥ ৫৬ ॥

অনপেতা যুক্তা ইত্যর্থঃ ; এবং সতি মম পারণা ভোজনং বিহতা ন স্যাৎ, মুনেঃ ক্রিয়া হোমাদিঃ যঃ এব অর্থঃ প্রয়োজনং স চ অলুপ্তঃ ভবেৎ। স্বপ্রাণব্যয়েনাপি স্বামিগুরুধনং সংরক্ষ্যম্ ইতি ভাবঃ ॥ ৫৫ ॥

অথ ভবানেব প্রমাণমিত্যাহ, ভবানিতি। পরবান্ স্বামিপরতন্ত্রঃ, ভবান্ অপি ইদং বক্ষ্যমাণম্, অবৈতি ভবতা অনুভূয়তে এব ইত্যর্থঃ, কস্মাৎ হেতোঃ, তব দেবদারৌ বিষয়ে মহান্ যত্নঃ মহতা যত্নেন রক্ষ্যতে ইত্যর্থঃ, ইদং বক্ষ্যমাণমর্থং দর্শয়তি, স্থাতুমিতি। রক্ষ্যং বস্তু বিনাশ্য বিনাশং গময়িত্বা স্বয়ম্ অক্ষতেন অব্রণেন নিযুক্তেন ইতি শেষঃ নিয়োক্তুঃ স্বামিনঃ অগ্রে স্থাতুং শক্যং নহি ॥ ৫৬ ॥

পারণার ব্যাঘাত হইবে না, মুনির হোমাদি কার্য্যও লোপ প্রাপ্ত হইবে না ॥৫৫॥

তুমিও পরের নিদেশ-বর্ত্তী, এই দেবদারুর রক্ষার প্রতি তোমার কত যত্ন ; তুমি একথা অনায়াসে বুঝিতে পারিবে, যে, এক জনের প্রতি যে বস্তু রক্ষার ভার আছে, তাহাকে নষ্ট হইতে দিয়া নিজে অক্ষত শরীরে প্রভুর সমীপে দণ্ডায়মান হওয়া যায় না ॥৫৬॥

---

you will have the gratification of your hunger, and the sacrificial ceremonies of the sage will also be unobstructed.

56. You are also a servant, appointed to your present duty by another ; and great is the care with which you keep guard over this tree ; consequently you will be able to understand me when I say, that it is difficult for a servant to stand

কিমপ্যহিংস্যস্তব চেন্মতোঽহং
যশঃশরীরে ভব মে দয়ালুঃ ।
একান্তবিধ্বংসিষু মদ্বিধানাং
পিণ্ডেষ্বনাস্থা খলু ভৌতিকেষু ॥ ৫৭ ॥

অথবা চেদপ্রতিকার্যমিত্যাহ, কিমিতি । কিম্ অপি কিংবা অহং তব অহিংস্যঃ অবধ্যঃ মতঃ চেত্, তর্হি মে যশঃ এব শরীরং তস্মিন্, দয়ালুঃ কারুণিকঃ ভব ; ন তু অস্মিন্ পাঞ্চভৌতিকশরীরে কোঽভিনিবেশঃ ? অত আহ একান্তেতি, মদ্বিধানাং মাদৃশানাং বিবেকিনাম্, একান্তবিধ্বংসিষু অবশ্যবিনাশিষু, ভৌতিকেষু পৃথিব্যাদিভূতবিকারেষু, পিণ্ডেষু শরীরেষু, অনাস্থা খলু অনপেক্ষা এব ॥ ৫৭ ॥

আর যদি আমার ক্ষতি না করাই তোমার উদ্দেশ্য হয়, তবে আমার যশরূপ শরীরকে রক্ষা কর ; মাদৃশ ব্যক্তির পঞ্চভূতাত্মক ও ক্ষণবিধ্বংসি দেহপিণ্ডের প্রতি এত আদর কেন ? তাহা গেল বা থাকিল তাহাতে কি ? ॥৫৭॥

before his master after having failed to protect his charge, himself unhurt and uninjured.

57. If it be your motive to avoid all injury to me, better avoid injury to my fame ; for no great care is due to the bodies of men like me,—bodies made of earth, and perishable like all other earthly things.

* सम्बन्धमाभाषणपूर्वमाहुः
वृत्तः स वां † सङ्गतयोर्वनान्ते।
तद्भूतनाथानुग! नार्हसि त्वं
सम्बन्धिनो मे ‡ प्रणयं विहन्तुम् ॥५८॥

सौहार्दं हृदयमनुसरणीयोऽसीत्याह, सम्बन्धमिति। सम्बन्धं सख्यम् आभाषणम् आलापः पूर्वं कारणं यस्य तम् आहुः; सः तादृक् सम्बन्धः, वनान्ते सङ्गतयोः, वां आवयोः वृत्तः जातः, तत् ततः हेतोः हे भूतनाथानुग! शिवानुचर! एतेन तस्य महत्त्वं सूचयति, अतएव सम्बन्धिनः मित्रस्य मे प्रणयं याच्ञां विहन्तुं न अर्हसि ॥ ५८ ॥

সজ্জনের বন্ধুতা আলাপ মাত্রেই হয়, এই কথা লোকে বলিয়া থাকে; এই বন-মধ্যে মিলিত হইয়া তোমার ও আমার মধ্যে সেই বন্ধুতা জন্মিয়াছে, অতএব হে শিবকিঙ্কর! আমি তোমার বন্ধু, বন্ধুর প্রার্থনা বিফল করা উচিত নয়। ৫৮।

---

58. The friendship of good people springs up at the first acquaintance, they say; accordingly we are friends now, after our meeting in this forest; do not refuse, then, O. servant of Siva, to comply with this friendly request of mine.

---

* सम्बन्धमाभाषणपूर्वमाहुः—There is a similar passage in popular Sanskrit saying—सतां हि सख्यं साप्तपदीनमुच्यते—meaning,—the friendship between good people arises after the exchange of a few words only.

† सङ्गतयोः—सम्पूर्वकात् गमेः क्तः मिलनार्थकः तयोः सङ्गतयोः—those who have come together.

‡ प्रणयं विहन्तुं,—याच्ञां विफलां कर्त्तुं—to refuse a prayer.

तथेति गामुक्तवते दिलीपः
सद्यः प्रतिष्टम्भविमुक्तबाहुः ।
स न्यस्तशस्त्रो हरये स्वदेहम्
उपानयत् पिण्डमिवामिषस्य ॥ ५९ ॥
तस्मिन् क्षणे पालयितुः प्रजानाम्
उत्पश्यतः * सिंहनिपातमुग्रम् ।

तथेति । तथा इति गाम् उक्तवते हरये दिलीपः सद्यः तत्क्षणे प्रतिष्टम्भात् प्रतिबन्धात् विमुक्तः बाहुः यस्य सः दिलीपः न्यस्तशस्त्रः त्यक्तायुधः सन् स्वदेहम् आमिषस्य मांसस्य पिण्डं कवलम् इव उपानयत् समर्पितवान् । एतेन निर्ममत्वमुक्तम् ॥ ५९ ॥

तस्मिन्निति । तस्मिन् क्षणे उग्रं सिंहनिपातम् उत्पश्यतः उत्प्रेक्षमाणस्य तर्कयतः अवाङ्मुखस्य अधोमुखस्य प्रजानां पालयितुः

সিংহ বলিল ;—আচ্ছা তবে তাহাই হউক ; অমনি দিলীপের হস্তের বন্ধন খুলিয়া গেল ; এবং তিনি অস্ত্র শস্ত্র পরিত্যাগ পূর্ব্বক সামান্য মাংস খণ্ডের ন্যায় স্বীয় দেহকে সিংহের আহারার্থ অর্পণ করিলেন । ৫৯ ।

সিংহের উল্লম্ফনের অপেক্ষা করিয়া রাজা অধোমুখ হইয়া আছেন,

---

59. Be it so, the lion replied, and instantly the king's arm was disengaged ; who laying down his arms offered his body to the lion, as if it was a piece of flesh belonging to some other being.

60. Expecting the up-springing of the lion he sat with his face looking downwards, and instantly showers of

---

* उग्रं अतिदारुणं—the fatal attack of the lion.

আবাঙ্মুখস্যোপরি পুষ্পবৃষ্টিঃ
পপাত বিদ্যাধরহস্তমুক্তা ॥ ৬০ ॥

উত্তিষ্ঠ বৎসেত্যমৃতায়মানং *
বচো নিশম্যোত্থিতমুত্থিতঃ সন্ ।
দদর্শ রাজা জননীমিব স্বাং
গামগ্রতঃ প্রস্রবিণীং ন সিংহম্ ॥ ৬১ ॥

রাজ্ঞঃ উপরি উপরিষ্টাৎ বিদ্যাধরাণাং দেবযোনিবিশেষাণাং হস্তৈঃ মুক্তা পুষ্পবৃষ্টিঃ পপাত ॥ ৬০ ॥

উত্তিষ্ঠেতি । রাজা, অমৃতমিব আচরতীতি অমৃতায়মানং, উত্থিতম্ উদগতং হে বৎস ! উত্তিষ্ঠ ইতি বচঃ, নিশম্য শ্রুত্বা, উত্থিতঃ সন্,

---

এমন সময়ে আকাশ হইতে বিদ্যাধরগণের হস্তবিসৃষ্ট পুষ্পবৃষ্টি তাঁহার উপরে পতিত হইতে লাগিল । ৬০ ।

"বাছা উঠ"—অমৃত সমান এই মধুর বচন শ্রবণ করিয়া রাজা গাত্রোত্থান করিলেন ; উঠিয়া সিংহকে দেখিতে পাইলেন না ; কেবল-

---

of flowers fell upon him from the sky, scattered by the hands of Vidyadharas,

61. "Rise up my son,"—some one sweetly exclaimed ; whereupon the king, raised his head, and looked around to see whence the voice proceeded, when lo ! there was no lion, but in its stead

* অমৃতায়মানং—অমৃতমিব আচরতি অমৃতায়তে, তস্য শানচ্
অমৃতায়মানং—অমৃতশব্দাৎ আচারার্থে ক্যঙ্। কর্ত্তুঃ ক্যঙ্ সলোপশ্চ—৩।১।১১। *Panini.*

तं विस्मितं धेनुरुवाच साधो !
मायां मयोद्भाव्य परीक्षितोऽसि ।
*ऋषिप्रभावान्मयि †नान्तकोऽपि
प्रभुः प्रहर्तुं किमुतान्यहिंस्राः ॥ ६२ ॥

अग्रतः अग्रे प्रस्रवः क्षीरस्रावः अस्ति यस्याः सा तां प्रस्रविणीं गां, स्वां जननीम् इव ददर्श, न सिंहं ददर्श ॥ ६१ ॥

तमिति । विस्मितम् आश्चर्यं गतम्, तं दिलीपं धेनुः उवाच ; किमित्यत्राह, साधो ! मया मायाम्, उद्भाव्य कल्पयित्वा, परीक्षितः असि, ऋषि-प्रभावात् मयि, अन्तकः यमः अपि, प्रहर्तुं न प्रभुः न समर्थः, अन्ये हिंस्राः श्वापदाः, किम् उत ? स्तुतु न प्रभवः ॥ ६२ ॥

মাত্র জননী সদৃশ সেই ধেনুকে সমীপে দণ্ডায়মান দেখিলেন, তাহার পালান হইতে স্নেহে দুগ্ধ ক্ষরণ হইতেছে ॥ ৬১ ॥

রাজাকে বিস্মিত দেখিয়া ধেনু কহিল, হে সাধো ! আমি মায়ার সৃষ্টি করিয়া তোমাকে পরীক্ষা করিয়াছি ; নতুবা মুনির প্রভাব গুণে অন্য হিংস্র জন্তুর কথা দূরে থাকুক যমও আমাকে পরাভব করিতে পারে না ॥ ৬২ ॥

---

there was the cow standing alone, her milk streaming out from affection, as if she was his own mother.

62. The cow thus addressed the wondering monarch :—I invented that illusion to test thy faith, my good man. be at peace, such is the influence of the sage, that even death has no control over me, far less such beasts of prey.

---

* ऋषिप्रभावात्—ऋषेः वशिष्ठस्य प्रभावः तपःस्वाध्यायसमुत्पन्नो तेजोविशेषः तस्मात् ।

† अन्तं शेषं ध्वंसं वा करोति यः अन्तकः यमः ।

भक्त्या गुरौ मय्यनुकम्पया च
प्रीतास्मि ते पुत्र! वरं वृणीष्व।
न केवलानां पयसां प्रसूतिम्
अवेहि मां कामदुघां प्रसन्नाम्॥ ६३॥

ततः समानीय स * मानितार्थी
हस्तौ स्वहस्तार्जितवीरशब्दः।

भक्त्येति। हे पुत्र! गुरौ भक्त्या, मयि अनुकम्पया च, ते तुभ्यं प्रीता अस्मि; वरं देवेभ्यो वरणीयम् अर्थम्, वृणीष्व स्वीकुरु; तथाहि, मां केवलानां पयसां, प्रसूतिं कारणं, न अवेहि न विद्धि, किन्तु प्रसन्नां मां, कामान् दोग्धीति कामदुघा ताम्, अवेहि॥ ६३॥

तत इति। ततः मानितार्थी, स्वहस्तार्जितः वीरः इति शब्दः

তোমার গুরু-ভক্তি ও আমার প্রতি দয়া দেখিয়া আমি প্রীত হইয়াছি, অতএব বৎস তুমি বর প্রার্থনা কর; জানিও, আমি যে কেবল দুগ্ধ দান করি তাহা নহে, প্রসন্ন হইলে সকল কামনা পূর্ণ করিতে পারি॥ ৬৩॥

অনন্তর রাজা যে হস্তদ্বয়ের সাহায্যে পৃথিবীতে বীর যশ উপার্জ্জন

---

63. I am pleased with thy dutifulness to thy master, and also with thy compassion for me; ask any favour of me, my son, it is not milk alone that I can give, if propitiated I can also grant the fulfilment of one's all desires.

64. Then the king folded both his hands,—those very hands

---

* मानितार्थी—मानिताः प्रार्थनापूरणेन सम्मानिताः अर्थिनो येन स मानितार्थी।

वंशस्य कर्त्तारमनन्तकीर्त्तिं
सुदक्षिणायां तनयं ययाचे ॥ ६४ ॥
सन्तानकामाय तथेति कामं
* राज्ञे प्रतिश्रुत्य पयस्विनी सा ।
दुग्ध्वा पयः पत्रपुटे मदीयं
पुत्रोपभुङ्क्ष्वेति तमादिदेश ॥ ६५ ॥

येन सः, (एतेनास्य दाक्षत्वं दैन्यराहित्यं बोध्यम्) सः राजा, हस्तौ समानीय सन्धाय, अञ्जलिं बद्ध्वा इत्यर्थः, वंशस्य कर्त्तारं प्रवर्त्तयितारम्, अतएव रघुकुलमिति प्रसिद्धः, अनन्तकीर्त्तिं स्थिरयशसं, तनयं सुदक्षिणायां ययाचे ॥ ६४ ॥

सन्तानेति । सा पयस्विनी गौः, सन्तानं कामयते इति सन्तानकामः, तस्मै राज्ञे तथेति काम्यते इति कामः वरः, तं प्रतिश्रुत्य प्रतिज्ञाय,

---

করিয়াছিলেন, সেই হস্তদ্বয় অঞ্জলি বদ্ধ করিয়া—"সুদক্ষিণার গর্ভে অনন্তকীর্ত্তিশালী বংশধর পুত্র হউক" এই বর প্রার্থনা করিলেন ॥ ৬৪ ॥

"তোমার কামনা পূর্ণ হউক" এই কথা বলিয়া, নন্দিনী সন্তানার্থী

---

with the aid of which he had acquired a world-wide fame for valour—and prayed for the birth from Sudakshina, of a son, who would be the founder of his dynasty.

65. Be it so, cried the sacred cow, of copious milk, and

---

* राज्ञे प्रतिश्रुता—Here, the चतुर्थी is to be explained by the application of प्रत्याङ्भ्यां श्रुवः पूर्वस्य कर्त्ता । १ । ४ । ४० *Panini—Vide* सिद्धान्तकौमुदी Page 279 Taranath's edition of 1863.

वत्सस्य होमार्थविधेश्च शेषम्
ऋषेरनुज्ञामधिगम्य मातः ! ।
औधस्यमिच्छामि तवोपभोक्तुं
षष्ठांशमुर्व्या इव रक्षितायाः ॥ ६६ ॥

हे पुत्र ! मदीयं पयः, पत्रपुटे पत्रनिर्मिते पात्रे, दुग्ध्वा उपभुङ्क्ष्व पिब इति, तम् आदिदेश आज्ञापितवती ॥ ६५ ॥

वत्सस्येति । हे मातः ! वत्सस्य वत्सपीतस्य, शेषं वत्सपीतावशिष्टम्, इत्यर्थः, होमः एव अर्थः, तस्य विधिः अनुष्ठानं, तस्य शेषं होमावशिष्टम् इत्यर्थः, तव ऊधसि भवम् औधस्यं क्षीरम्, रक्षितायाः उर्व्याः, षष्ठांशं षष्ठभागम् इव, ऋषेः अनुज्ञाम् अधिगम्य उपभोक्तुम् इच्छामि ॥ ६६ ॥

রাজাকে পত্রনির্ম্মিত পাত্রে নিজদুগ্ধ দোহন করিয়া পান করিতে আদেশ করিলেন ॥ ৬৫ ॥

রাজা বলিলেন—"জননি! বৎসের পানকার্য্য শেষ হইয়া, এবং হোমার্থ দোহন কার্য্য সমাধা হইয়া যে দুগ্ধ অবশিষ্ট থাকিবে, মহর্ষির অনুজ্ঞানুসারে তাহাই পান করিব; এইরূপেই আমি পৃথিবীকে রক্ষা করিয়া প্রজাকুলের আয়ের ষড়্ভাগ মাত্র গ্রহণ করি ॥ ৬৬ ॥

ordered the king to make a vessel of leaves of plants to milch her in, and to drink its contents.

66. "I shall drink your milk, O sacred mother, with the permission of the sage, and after your calf has been fed, and after the requisite quantity for sacrificial ceremony has been milched out, in pursuance of my custom to take only the 6th part of the product of the earth as my share of the revenue, but not now".

इत्थं क्षितीशेन वसिष्ठधेनुः
विज्ञापिता प्रीततरा बभूव ।
* तदन्विता हैमवताच्च कुक्षेः
प्रत्याययावाश्रममश्रमेण ॥ ६७ ॥
तस्याः प्रसन्नेन्दुमुखः प्रसादं
गुरुर्नृपाणां गुरवे निवेद्य ।

इत्थमिति । इत्थं क्षितीशेन विज्ञापिता वसिष्ठस्य धेनुः प्रीततरा, पूर्वं शुश्रूषया प्रीता, सम्प्रति एतया विज्ञापनया प्रीततरा अतिसन्तुष्टा बभूव ; तदन्विता तेन दिलीपेन अन्विता, हैमवतात् हिमवत्सम्बन्धिनः, कुक्षेः गुहायाः सकाशात्, अश्रमेण अनायासेन, आश्रमं प्रत्याययौ आगता च ॥ ६७ ॥

तस्या इति । प्रसन्नेन्दुरिव मुखं यस्य सः, नृपाणां गुरुः दिलीपः, प्रहर्षचिह्नैः मुखरागादिभिः, अनुमितम् ऊहितं, तस्याः धेनोः, प्रसादम्

রাজা এই কথা নিবেদন করিলে বশিষ্ঠধেনু সমধিক প্রীত হইলেন ; এবং রাজাকে পশ্চাতে লইয়া, সচ্ছন্দচিত্তে আশ্রমাভি-মুখে প্রতিনিবৃত্ত হইলেন ॥ ৬৭ ॥

রাজার মুখচন্দ্র আজ সুপ্রসন্ন, তিনি কুলগুরুর নিকট নন্দিনীর

---

67. Basista's cow became still more pleased with the above answer of the king, and returned without fatigue to the hermitage, from the valley of the mountain, followed by the king.

68. The king with a countenance beaming with joy, com-

---

* तदन्विता—तेन राज्ञा अन्विता, अनुगता ।

प्रहर्षचिह्नानुमितं प्रियायै
शशंस वाचा पुनरुक्तयेव ॥ ६८ ॥

स नन्दिनीस्तन्यमनिन्दितात्मा
सद्वत्सलो वत्सहुतावशेषम् ।
पपौ वसिष्ठेन कृताभ्यनुज्ञः
शुभ्रं यशो मूर्त्तमिवातितृष्णः ॥ ६९ ॥

अनुपदं, प्रहर्षचिह्नैरेव ज्ञातत्वात् पुनरुक्तया एव वाचा गुरवे निवेद्य विज्ञाप्य. पश्चात् प्रियायै शशंस। ॥६८॥

स इति। अनिन्दितात्मा अगर्हितस्वभावः, सत्सु वत्सलः प्रेमवान् सद्वत्सलः, वसिष्ठेन कृताभ्यनुज्ञः कृतानुमतिः, सः राजा, वत्सस्य हुतस्य च अवशेषं पीतहुतावशिष्टं, नन्दिन्याः, स्तन्यं क्षीरं, शुभ्रं मूर्त्तं परिच्छिन्नं यशः इव, अतितृष्णः सन् पपौ ॥ ६९ ॥

প্রসন্নতার বার্ত্তা নিবেদন করিয়া প্রিয়াকে সমুদায় কথা জ্ঞাপন করিলেন। বশিষ্ঠ এবং সুদক্ষিণা রাজার হর্ষের চিহ্ন দেখিয়া পূর্ব্বেই বুঝিতে পারিয়াছিলেন, সুতরাং রাজার বাক্যগুলি তাঁহাদের নিকট পুনরুক্তিমাত্র হইল ॥ ৬৮ ॥

সচ্চরিত্র ও সাধু বৎসল সেই রাজা গুরুর অনুজ্ঞাক্রমে স্বীয় যশের ন্যায় শুভ্রবর্ণ, বৎসের পীতাবশিষ্ট, ও হোমক্রিয়ার্থ দোহনাবশিষ্ট নন্দিনীর দুগ্ধ পান করিলেন ॥ ৬৯ ॥

---

municated to his master, the happy news of the favour shown to him by Nandini, and also related it to his queen, both of whom had nearly guessed every thing by the evident marks of gladness in his looks.

69. With the permission of Basista, the king, of unsullied famé, drank such milk of Nandini, as remained after feeding

প্রাতর্যথোক্তব্রতপারণান্তে
প্রাস্থানিকং স্বস্ত্যয়নং প্রযুজ্য।
তৌ দম্পতী স্বাং প্রতি রাজধানীং
প্রস্থাপয়ামাস বশী বশিষ্ঠঃ ৭০ ॥

প্রদক্ষিণীকৃত্য হুতং হুতাশম্
অনন্তরং ভর্তুররুন্ধতীঞ্চ।

প্রাতরিতি। বশী বশিষ্ঠঃ, প্রাতঃ যথোক্তস্য পূর্বোক্তস্য ব্রতস্য গোসেবারূপস্য, অন্তর্ভূতা বা পারণা, তস্যাঃ অন্তে প্রাস্থানিকং প্রস্থানকালে ভবং তৎকালোচিতম্ স্বস্ত্যয়নং, ঈর্যতে প্রাপ্যতে অনেনেতি অয়নং স্বস্ত্যয়ন শুভাবহম্ আশীর্বাদ, প্রযুজ্য তৌ দম্পতী স্বাং রাজধানীং পুরীং প্রতি প্রস্থাপয়ামাস ॥ ৭০ ॥

প্রদক্ষিণীকৃত্যেতি। নৃপঃ, হুতং তর্পিতম্, হুতম্ অশ্নাতীতি হুতাশঃ

পরদিন প্রাতে ব্রত পারণার অবসানে, বশী বশিষ্ঠ প্রস্থানকালোপযোগী স্বস্ত্যয়নের ব্যবস্থা করিয়া, সেই রাজদম্পতীকে স্বীয় রাজধানীর উদ্দেশে প্রেরণ করিলেন ॥ ৭০ ॥

রাজা হোমাগ্নিকে, গুরুকে, অরুন্ধতীকে ও সবৎসা নন্দিনীকে

---

the young calf and also after supplying the requisite amount for the sacrificial ceremony—the white milk looking like his own fame incarnate.

70. The next morning, after having ordered their meals, suited to the finishing ceremony of their vow, Basista duly performed the protective ceremonies on his guests and dismissed them to return to their capital.

71. The king went round the secrificial fire, his veneurable

ধেনুং সবৎসাঞ্চ নৃপঃ প্রতস্থে
* সন্মঙ্গলোদগ্রতরপ্রভাবঃ ॥ ৭১ ॥

শ্রোত্রাভিরামধ্বনিনা রথেন
স ধর্ম্মপত্নীসহিতঃ সহিষ্ণুঃ ।
যযাবনুদ্ঘাতসুখেন মার্গং
স্বেনেব পূর্ণেন মনোরথেন ॥ ৭২ ॥

অগ্নিঃ, তং ভর্ত্তুঃ মুনেঃ অনন্তরং প্রদক্ষিণানন্তরম্ ইত্যর্থঃ, অরুন্ধতীঞ্চ সবৎসাং ধেনুঞ্চ প্রদক্ষিণীকৃত্য, প্রগতো দক্ষিণং প্রদক্ষিণম্, অপ্রদক্ষিণং প্রদক্ষিণং সম্পদ্যমানং কৃত্বা প্রদক্ষিণীকৃত্য, সদ্ভিঃ মঙ্গলৈঃ প্রদক্ষিণাদিভিঃ মঙ্গলাচারৈঃ, উদগ্রতরপ্রভাবঃ নৃপঃ প্রতস্থে ॥ ৭১ ॥

শ্রোত্রেতি। ধর্ম্মপত্নীসহিতঃ সহিষ্ণুঃ ব্রতাদিদুঃখসহনশীলঃ, সঃ নৃপঃ, শ্রোত্রাভিরামধ্বনিনা কর্ণাহ্লাদকরস্বনেন, অনুদ্ঘাতঃ

প্রদক্ষিণ করিয়া প্রস্থান করিলেন, এই সকল মঙ্গলানুষ্ঠানদ্বারা তাঁহার প্রভাব যেন আরও বর্দ্ধিত হইল ॥ ৭১ ॥

সহিষ্ণুতাগুণে শ্রেষ্ঠ নরপতি ধর্ম্মপত্নীর সহিত রথারোহণ করিয়া, কর্ণের তৃপ্তিকর চক্রধ্বনি শ্রবণ করিতে করিতে গমন করিতে লাগিলেন;

---

master and his wife, and also the sacred cow with her calf, after which he started on his journey with his prowess redoubled by the protective rites.

72. Once more his chariot-wheels rattled on with their peculiar music, and the king and the queen enjoyed the jour-

* উদগ্রতরপ্রভাবঃ—উৎ ঊর্দ্ধং অগ্রং যস্য স উদগ্রঃ উন্নতিমান্ ইত্যর্থঃ, অতিশয়েন উদগ্রঃ; উদগ্রতরঃ পূর্ব্বাপেক্ষয়া বিস্তৃততরঃ প্রভাবঃ প্রতাপো যস্য সঃ—whose power has been augmented.

तमाहितौत्सुक्यमदर्शनेन
प्रजाः प्रजार्थव्रतकर्शिताङ्गम्।
नेत्रैः पपुस्तृप्तिमनाप्नुवद्भिः
नवोदयं नाथमिवौषधीनाम्॥ ७३॥

पाषाणाद्यप्रतिघातरहितः, अतएव सुखयतीति सुखः तेन, रथेन स्वेन पूर्णेन सफलेन, मनोरथेन इव, मार्गम् अध्वानं ययौ। मनोरथपक्षे अनुद्घातः प्रतिबन्धनिवृत्तिः ॥ ७२ ॥

तमिति। अदर्शनेन प्रवासनिमित्तेन, आहितौत्सुक्यं जनितदर्शनोत्कण्ठं, प्रजार्थेन सन्तानार्थेन, व्रतेन नियमेन, कर्शितं कृशीकृतम्, अङ्गं यस्य तं, नवोदयं नवाभ्युदयं, ओषधीनां नाथं सोमम् इव, प्रजाः तृप्तिम् अनाप्नुवद्भिः अतितृष्णुभिः. नेत्रैः, तं राजानं पपुः अत्यासक्त्या ददृशुः इत्यर्थः। चन्द्रपक्षे अदर्शनं कलाक्षयनिमित्तं, प्रजार्थं लोक-

আজ রথের গতি তাঁহার সফল মনোরথের ন্যায় আর আঘাত প্রাপ্ত হইতেছে না ॥ ৭২ ॥

সন্তান কামনায় ব্রতপালন করিয়া রাজার অঙ্গ কৃশভাব ধারণ করিয়াছে, এবং তিনি প্রজাদিগকে দেখিবার জন্য উৎসুক হইয়াছেন, সেই কৃশ দেহে ও উৎসুক হৃদয়ে তিনি রাজধানীর সন্নিকটে উপস্থিত হইলেন; লোকে নবোদিত চন্দ্রকে যেমন অনিমেষনয়নে দর্শন করে

ney, which was free from jirks and obstructions, as if they were being carried on the wings of their successful desire.

73. As the king approached his capital after a long absence, his body looking lean from the effects of his vow, his subjects began to drink him, as it were, with their thirsting eyes,

पुरन्दरश्रीः पुरमुत्पताकं
प्रविश्य पौरैरभिनन्द्यमानः ।
भुजे भुजङ्गेन्द्रसमानसारे
भूयः स भूमेर्धुरमाससञ्ज ॥ ७४ ॥

क्षितार्थं व्रतं देवताभ्यः कलादाननियमः, उदयः आविर्भावः, अन्यत् समानम् ॥ ७२ ॥

पुरन्दरेति । पुरः पुरीः असुराणां दारयतीति पुरन्दरः शक्रः, तस्य श्रीरिव श्रीः यस्य सः, नृपः पौरैः अभिनन्द्यमानः, उत्पताकम् उच्छ्रितध्वजम्, पुरं प्रविश्य भुजङ्गेन्द्रेण समानसारं तुल्यबले भुजे भूयः भूमेः धुरम् आससञ्ज स्थापितवान् ॥ ७४ ॥

अथेति । अथ द्यौः सुरवर्त्म, अलेः मरुद्भिः नयनयोः समुत्थम्

সেইরূপ প্রজাকুল অতৃপ্ত দৃষ্টির সহিত তাঁহাকে যেন পান করিতে লাগিল ॥ ৭৩ ॥

পুরবাসিগণের নিকট অভিনন্দন প্রাপ্ত হইয়া রাজা পতাকা-শোভিত রাজনগরে প্রবেশ করিলেন এবং পুনরায় নিজ বাহুদ্বয়ের উপরে ধরণীর ভার স্থাপন করিলেন ॥ ৭৪ ॥

gazing on him with the same delight with which men look at the rising moon.

74. Dileep, who was majestic in his appearance like Indra, was thus welcomed back into his capital by his subjects, who had decorated the city with flags; and he once more resumed hte duties of the State on his own shoulders.

अथ * नयनसमुत्थं ज्योतिरत्रेरिव द्यौः
सुरसरिदिव तेजो वह्निनिष्ठ्यूतमैशम् ।

उत्पन्नं, नयनसमुत्थम् ज्योतिः इव चन्द्रमिव इत्यर्थः, सुरसरित् गङ्गा, वह्निना निष्ठ्यूतं निक्षिप्तम् ऐशं तेजः स्कन्दम् इव इक्ष्वाकूणां सुदक्षिणा नरपतेः दिलीपस्य कुलभूत्यै सन्ततिरच्छाये गुरुभिः महद्भिः लोक-

---

अनन्तर आकाश येमन अत्रिर नयनोत्थित ज्योतिके धारण करियाछिल, गङ्गा येमन अग्नि प्रक्षिप्त ऐश तेज धारण करियाछिल.

---

75. As the skies had once concieved the moon, which sprang from the eyes of Atri, and as the Ganjes had concieved in her the divine embryo deposited by fire, so, for the good of the race of the whole line the queen concieved in time the

---

* नयनसमुत्थं ज्योतिरत्रेः—A mythological tradition ascribes the birth of the moon from a light emanating from the eyes of a Rishi called अत्रि. Anent this subject Mallinath quotes the following verses from *Harivansa*.

"नेत्राभ्यां वारि सुस्राव दशधा द्योतयद् दिशः ।
तद्गर्भविधिना हृष्टा दिशो देव्या दधुस्तदा ।
समेत्य धारयामासुर्न च ताः समशक्नुवन् ।
स ताभ्यः सहसैवाथ दिग्भ्यो गर्भः प्रभान्वितः ।
पपात भासयन् लोकान् शीतांशुः सर्वभावनः"

† तेजो वह्निनिष्ठ्यूतमैशं—In connection with this tradition Mallinatha quotes the following lines from the *Ramayan*.

ते गत्वा पर्वतं राम ! कैलासं धातुमण्डितम् ।
अग्निं नियोजयामासुः पुत्रार्थं सर्वदेवताः ।
देवकार्य्यमिदं देव ! समाधत्स्व हुताशन ।

नरपतिकुलभूत्यै गर्भमाधत्त राज्ञी
गुरुभिरभिनिविष्टं लोकपालानुभावैः॥ ७५॥

इति श्रीरघुवंशे महाकाव्ये कालिदासकृतौ
नन्दिनीवरप्रदानो नाम द्वितीयः सर्गः ।

पालानाम् अनुभावैः तेजोभिः अभिनिविष्टं गर्भम् आधत्त दधौ इत्यर्थः। अत्र मनुः, "अष्टानां लोकपालानां वपुर्धारयते नृपः" इति ।

इति श्रीमहामहोपाध्यायकोलाचलमल्लिनाथसूरिविरचितायां
रघुवंशटीकायां सञ्जीवनीसमाख्यायां द्वितीयः सर्गः ।

সেইরূপ রাজবংশের কল্যাণের নিমিত্ত মহিষী সুদক্ষিণা দিক্পালগণের তেজঃসম্ভূত গর্ভ ধারণ করিলেন ॥ ৭৫ ॥

---

coming prince, made strong by the infusion of the spirits of the lords of different quarters of the heavens.

शैलपुत्र्यां महातेजो गङ्गायां तेज उत्सृज ।
देवतानां प्रतिज्ञाय गङ्गामभ्येत्य पावकः ।
गर्भं धारय वै देवि ! देवतानामिदं प्रियम् ।
इत्येतद्वचनं श्रुत्वा दिव्यं रूपमधारयत् ।
स तस्या महिमां दृष्ट्वा समन्तादवकीर्य च ।
समन्ततस्तु तां देवीमभ्यषिञ्चत पावकः ।
सर्वस्रोतांसि पूर्णानि गङ्गाया रघुनन्दन '

तृतीयः सर्गः ।

अथेप्सितं भर्त्तुरुपस्थितोदयं*
सखीजनोद्वीक्षणकौमुदीमुखम् ।

राज्ञी गर्भमाधत्तेत्युक्तं, सम्प्रति गर्भलक्षणानि वर्णयितुं प्रस्तौति, अथेति। अथ गर्भधारणानन्तरं, सुदक्षिणा, उपस्थितोदयं प्राप्तकालं, भर्त्तुः दिलीपस्य ईप्सितं मनोरथम्, सखीजनस्य उद्वीक्षणानां दृष्टीनां कौमुदीमुखं चन्द्रिकाप्रादुर्भावम्, यद्वा, कौमुदी नाम दीपोत्सवतिथिः, तदुक्तं भविष्योत्तरे, "कौ मोदन्ते जना यस्यां तेनासौ कौमुदी मता इति। तस्या मुखं प्रारम्भम् अतएव केचित् कौमुदीमहमिति पाठं पठन्ति। इक्ष्वाकुकुलस्य सन्ततेः अविच्छेदस्य निदानं मूलकारणम्, एवंविधं दौहृदलक्षणं गर्भचिह्नं वक्ष्यमाणं दधौ। स्वहृदयेन गर्भहृदयेन च द्विहृदया गर्भिणी, यथाह वाग्भटः, "मातृजन्यस्य हृदयं मातुश्च हृदयस्य तत्। सम्बद्धं तेन गर्भिण्याः श्रेष्ठं श्रद्धाभिमाननम्॥" इति।

ক্রমে যথাকালে পতির চির আকাঙ্ক্ষিত ও ইক্ষাকুবংশের স্থিতির নিদানভূত গর্ভলক্ষণ সকল সুদক্ষিণার দেহে প্রকাশ পাইতে লাগিল;

1. In time queen Sudakshina began to show all the signs of pregnancy, a happy state for which the king had so eagerly longed, which furnished matter for exceeding delight to all her

उपस्थितोदयम्—उपस्थितः प्राप्तः आगतो वा उदयः उत्पत्ति-कालो यस्य तत्।

निदानमिक्ष्वाकुकुलस्य *सन्ततेः
सुदक्षिणा दौर्हृदलक्षणं दधौ ॥ १ ॥
†शरीरसादादसमग्रभूषणा
मुखेन सालक्ष्यत लोध्रपाण्डुना।

तत्सम्बन्धित्वाद्गर्भो दौर्हृदमित्युच्यते, सा च तद्योगात् दौर्हृदिनीति तदुक्तं संग्रहे, "द्विहृदयां नारीं दौर्हृदिनीमाचक्षते" इति ॥ १ ॥

सम्प्रति क्षामताख्यं गर्भलक्षणं वर्णयति, शरीरेति। शरीरस्य सादात् कार्श्यात्, असमग्रभूषणा परिमिताभरणा, लोध्रपुष्पेण इव पाण्डुना मुखेन उपलक्षिता सा सुदक्षिणा विचेयाः अल्पाः तारकाः यस्यां सा तथोक्ता विरलनक्षत्रा इत्यर्थः, तनुप्रकाशेन अल्पकान्तिना

সখীগণ নব চন্দ্রিকার অভ্যুদয়ের ন্যায় সেই গর্ভোদয়কে পরম আনন্দে দর্শন করিতে লাগিল ॥ ১ ॥

শরীরের অবসন্নতা বশতঃ রাজ্ঞী অলঙ্কার সকল খুলিয়া ফেলিলেন এবং তাঁহার মুখমণ্ডল লোধ্রপুষ্পের ন্যায় পাণ্ডুবর্ণ ধারণ করিল ; সুতরাং প্রভাতের প্রাক্কালে অল্পসংখ্যক তারকা-সমন্বিত ও হীনকান্তি চন্দ্র-

female attendants like the rising of the new moon and on which were also centred the hopes of the *ikshwaku* race.

2. Unable to carry on her person all her ornaments on account of extreme weakness, she put off most of them ; and her countenance became as pale as the *lodhra* flower ; consequently she

* सन्ततेः—(सम्+तन+क्तिच्) विस्तारस्य, अविच्छिन्नधारायां वा।—
the permanence or extension of a dynasty.

† शरीरसादात्—सद+घञ् सादः, अवसन्नता, शरीरस्य सादस्तस्मात्
—on account of the feebleness of her limbs.

तनुप्रकाशेन विचेयतारका
*प्रभातकल्पा शशिनेव शर्वरी ॥ २ ॥
तदाननं मृत्सुरभि क्षितीश्वरो
रहस्युपाघ्राय न तृप्तिमाययौ।
करीव सिक्तं पृषतैः पयोमुचां
†शुचिव्यपाये वनराजिपल्वलम् ॥ ३ ॥

शशिना उपलक्षिता ईषदसमाप्तप्रभाता प्रभातकल्पा प्रभातादीषदूनेत्यर्थः, शर्वरी रात्रिः इव अलक्ष्यत ॥ २ ॥

तदिति। क्षितीश्वरः रहसि मृत्सुरभि मृदा सुगन्धि तस्याः आननं तदाननं सुदक्षिणाननम्, उपाघ्राय तृप्तिं न आययौ। कः

পরিশোভিত রজনীর যেমন শোভা হয় তাঁহারও সেইরূপ শোভা হইল ॥ ২ ॥

গ্রীষ্মান্তে নবজলধরের বারিসিক্ত বনমধ্যস্থ পল্বলের গন্ধ আঘ্রাণ করিয়া করিয়া হস্তী যেমন ক্লান্ত হয় না, সেইরূপ রাজাও গোপনে

resembled the night, during the small hours of the morning, with only a few lingering stars, and with the lovely crescent of the moon grown pale upon the approach of the day.

3. The breath of her mouth, smelling earth (which she was fond of eating at this time) was so agreeable to the king

* प्रभातकल्पा—प्रायेण प्रभाता प्रभातकल्पा ईषदूनार्थे कल्पप्रत्ययः, "त्यादेश्चोने कल्पदेश्यदेशीयाः—Vide *Mugdhabodh* page 212. Girish Chandra's edition of 1882.

† शुचिव्यपाये—शुचेः ग्रीष्मस्य व्यपायः शेषः तस्मिन्।

दिवं मरुत्वानिव भोक्ष्यते भुवं
*दिगन्तविश्रान्तरथो हि तत्सुतः ।
अतोऽभिलाषे प्रथमं तथाविधे
†मनो बबन्धान्यरसान् विलङ्घ्य सा ॥४॥

कमिव ? शुचिव्यपाये ग्रीष्मावसाने पयोमुचां मेघानां पृषतैः बिन्दुभिः सिक्तम् उच्छितं वनराज्याः पल्वलम् उपाघ्राय करी गजः इव ॥ ३ ॥

दोहदलक्षणे मृद्भक्षणे हेत्वन्तरमुत्प्रेक्षते, दिवमिति । हि यस्मात् दिगन्तविश्रान्तरथः चक्रवर्त्ती तस्याः सुतः तत्सुतः मरुत्वान् इन्द्रः दिवं स्वर्गम् इव भुवं भोक्ष्यते अतः प्रथमं सा सुदक्षिणा तथाविधे भूविकारे मद्रूपे अभिलष्यते इति अभिलाषः भोग्यवस्तु तस्मिन् रसान्ते

সুদক্ষিণার মৃত্তিকা-গন্ধযুক্ত মুখমণ্ডল আঘ্রাণ করিয়া করিয়া তৃপ্তি লাভ করিতেন না, আকাঙ্ক্ষা আর মিটিত না ॥ ৩ ॥

ইন্দ্র যেরূপ স্বর্গসুখ ভোগ করেন সেইরূপ তাঁহার গর্ভজাত সন্তানও সমগ্র পৃথিবীর সুখ ভোগ করিবেন ও তাহার রথ দিগ্‌দিগন্তে ধাবিত

that he was never tired of smelling it in private, as an elephant in the wilderness is never tired of enjoying the smell of a pond of water, augmented by new showers of rain at the close of summer.

4. As Indra was the master of the whole heavens so was the

---

* दिगन्तविश्रान्तरथः—रम्यते अनेन अत्र वा रथः दिशां अन्ते विश्रान्तः स्थितः रथो दिग्विजयार्थं विनिर्गतो यानविशेषो यस्य सः—whose coquering chariot would not stop until it shall have reached the furthest ends of the earth.

† मनो बबन्ध - नितरां अभिलाषवती बभूवेत्यर्थः ।.

न मे ह्रिया शंसति किञ्चिदीप्सितं
स्पृहावती वस्तुषु केषु मागधी।
इति स्म पृच्छत्यनुवेलमादृतः
प्रियासखीरुत्तरकोशलेश्वरः ॥ ५ ॥

स्वाद्यन्ते इति रसाः भोग्यार्थाः, अन्ये च ते रसाश्च तान् विलङ्घ्य विहाय मनः बबन्ध विदधौ इत्यर्थः। दोहदहेतुकमिदं मृद्भक्षणमस्य पुत्रस्य भूभोगसूचनार्थत्वमुत्प्रेक्षते ॥ ४ ॥

नेति। मगधस्य राज्ञः अपत्यं स्त्री मागधी सुदक्षिणा, ह्रिया किञ्चित् किमपि ईप्सितम् इष्टं मे मह्यं न शंसति न आचष्टे, केषु वस्तुषु स्पृहावती इति अनुवेलम् अनुक्षणम् आदृतः आदरवान्, प्रियायाः सखीः सहचरीः उत्तरकोशलेश्वरः दिलीपः पृच्छति स्म पप्रच्छ। सखीनां विश्रम्भभूमित्वात् इति भावः ॥ ५ ॥

হইবে এই জন্যই কি সুদক্ষিণার প্রথমাবধি অন্য রস উপেক্ষা করিয়া মৃত্তিকাতে এত রুচি হইল ॥ ৪ ॥

কখন কোন পদার্থে অভিলাষ হয়, লজ্জাবশতঃ সুদক্ষিণা আমাকে সে বিষয়ে কিছু বলেন না-এই বলিয়া রাজা মহিষীর সখীদিগকে যত্ন করিয়া সর্ব্বদা জিজ্ঞাসা করিতেন ॥ ৫ ॥

prince to be born of her, destined to drive his conquering chariot to the furthest limits of the earth; was it as a sign of this destiny, that she evinced such an eagerness for eating the earth in preference to all other things of taste.

5. "Out of modesty she tells nothing about the things *she* likes." Thus did the king constantly make inquiries of her female attendants.

उपेत्य सा दोहददुःखशीलतां
यदेव वव्रे तदपश्यदाहृतम्।
न हीष्टमस्य त्रिदिवेऽपि भूपते-
रभूदनासाद्यमधिज्यधन्वनः ॥ ६ ॥

क्रमेण निस्तीर्य्य च दोहदव्यथां
*प्रचीयमानावयवा रराज सा।

उपेत्येति। दोहदं गर्भिणीमनोरथः, सा सुदक्षिणा, दोहदेन गर्भिणीमनोरथेन, दुःखशीलतां दुःखस्वभावताम्, उपेत्य प्राप्य, यत् वस्तु वव्रे आचकाङ्क्ष, तत् आहृतम् आनीतं भर्त्रा इति शेषः अपश्यत् एव अलभत इत्यर्थः। कुतः? हि यस्मात् अस्य भूपतेः त्रिदिवे अपि स्वर्गे अपि इष्टं वस्तु अनासाद्यम् अनवाप्यं न अभूत्। किं याच्ञया? नेत्याह, अधिज्यधन्वन इति। न हि वीरपत्नीनामलभ्यं नाम किञ्चिदस्ति इति भावः ॥ ६ ॥

क्रमेणेति। सा सुदक्षिणा क्रमेण दोहदव्यथाञ्च निस्तीर्य्य प्रचीय-

সুদক্ষিণা গর্ভাবস্থা-সুলভ ক্লেশ নিবারণের জন্য যাহা কিছু চাহিতেন, রাজা তৎক্ষণাৎ তাহা আনাইয়া দিতেন; তিনি ধনু ধারণ করিলে আনিতে পারেন না স্বর্গেও এমন কিছু ছিল না ॥ ৬ ॥

ক্রমে গর্ভাবস্থার প্রাক্কালসুলভ ক্লেশ সকল নিবারিত হইয়া রাজ্ঞীর

6. Whatever things she expressed a desire for, in her peculiar condition, she got without loss of time; nor was it a wonder, for there was nothing, even in heaven, which was unobtainable by Dileep, when he put the string to his bow.

7. The trying days of morning sickness were gradually

* प्रचीयमानावयवा—प्रचीयमानाः पुनरपि स्थूलतां प्राप्नुवन्तः अवयवाः करचरणादयो यस्याः सा प्रचीयमानावयवा।

पुराणपत्रापगमादनन्तरं
लतेव सन्नद्धमनोज्ञपल्लवा ॥ ७ ॥
दिनेषु गच्छत्सु नितान्तपीवरं
तदीयमानीलमुखं स्तनद्वयम् ।
तिरश्चकार भ्रमराभिलीनयोः
सुजातयोः पङ्कजकोशयोः श्रियम् ॥ ८ ॥

মানাবয়বা পুষ্যমাণাবয়বা সতী পুরাণপত্রাণাম্ অপগমাৎ নাশাৎ অনন্তরং সন্নদ্ধাঃ সঞ্জাতাঃ প্রত্যগ্রত্বাৎ মনোজ্ঞাঃ পল্লবাঃ যস্যাঃ সা লতা ইব ররাজ ॥ ৭ ॥

লক্ষণান্তরং বর্ণয়তি, দিনেষ্বিতি। দিনেষু দোহদদিবসেষু গচ্ছৎসু নিতান্তপীবরম্ অতিস্থূলম্ আ সমন্তাৎ নীলে মুখে চুচুকে যস্য তৎ তদীয়ং স্তনদ্বয়ং ভ্রমরৈঃ অভিলীনয়োঃ অভিব্যাপ্তয়োঃ সুজাতয়োঃ সুন্দরয়োঃ পঙ্কজকোশয়োঃ পদ্মমুকুলয়োঃ শ্রিয়ং তিরশ্চকার ॥ ৮ ॥

শরীর আবার পুষ্ট হইয়া অপূর্ব্ব শ্রী ধারণ করিল; পুরাতন পত্র সকল স্খলিত হইয়া নবপল্লব দেখা দিলে, লতার যেমন শোভা হয়, তাঁহারও সেই প্রকার শোভা হইল ॥ ৭ ॥

কিছু দিন গত হইলে রাজ্ঞীর স্তনদ্বয় স্থূলভাব ধারণ করিল, এবং তাহাদের চুচুক কৃষ্ণ বর্ণ হইয়া আসিল; সুন্দর দুইটী পদ্মের কোরকের

over and a singular loveliness returned to her limbs, wherewith she looked like a beautiful creeper adorned with crowns of new foliage, after the old and yellow ones had been dropped.

8. As time rolled on her breasts increased in their dimensions, and their nipples became black; thus they looked in

निधानगर्भामिव सागराम्बरां
शमीमिवाभ्यन्तरलीनपावकाम्।
नदीमिवान्तःसलिलां सरस्वतीं
नृपः ससत्त्वां महिषीममन्यत ॥ ९ ॥

प्रियानुरागस्य मनःसमुन्नतेः
भुजार्ज्जितानाञ्च दिगन्तसम्पदाम्।

निधानेति। नृपः ससत्त्वाम् आपन्नसत्त्वां गर्भिणीम् इत्यर्थः महिषीं निधानं निधिः गर्भे यस्याः तां सागराम्बरां समुद्रवसनां भूमिमिव इत्यर्थः अभ्यन्तरे लीनः पावकः यस्याः तां शमीम् इव, अन्तःसलिलाम् अन्तर्गतजलां सरस्वतीं नदीम् इव अमन्यत। एतेन गर्भस्य भाग्यवत्त्वतेजस्वित्वपावनत्वानि विवक्षितानि ॥ ९ ॥

प्रियेति। धीरः सः राजा प्रियायाम् अनुरागस्य स्नेहस्य, मनसः

উপরে দুইটী ভ্রমর বসিলে যেমন সুন্দর দেখায় সেইরূপ দেখাইতে লাগিল ॥ ৮ ॥

রাজা দেখিয়া বুঝিলেন যে পৃথিবী যেমন রত্ন সকল ধারণ করে, শমী বৃক্ষ যেমন অন্তরে অগ্নিকে ধারণ করে, সরস্বতী নদী যেমন অন্তরে জলরাশি ধারণ করে, মহিষী সেইরূপ সন্তানরত্ন ধারণ করিতেছেন ॥৯॥

পত্নীর প্রতি তাঁহার যেরূপ অনুরাগ ছিল, তাঁহার হৃদয় মন যেরূপ

---

their new beauty very much like two lovely lotus-buds surmounted by two black bees.

9. Seeing which the king at once concluded that the queen was with child, resembling in that respect the mother earth with all the valuable contents of her bowels, or the *sami* tree with the fire latent in its body, or the river Saraswati with its stream of water hidden under sand.

यथाक्रमं पुंसवनादिकाः क्रियाः
धृतेश्च धीरः सदृशीर्व्यधत्त सः ॥ १० ॥
सुरेन्द्रमात्राश्रितगर्भगौरवात्
प्रयत्नमुक्तासनया गृहागतः ।

समुन्नतेः औदार्यस्य, भुजेन भुजबलेन करेण वा अर्जितानां नतु वा पित्र्यादिना, दिगन्तेषु सम्पदां, धृतेः पुत्रो मे भविष्यतीति सन्तोषस्य च सदृशीः अनुरूपाः, पुमान् सूयते अनेनेति पुंसवनं तद् आदि यासां ताः क्रियाः यथाक्रमं क्रममनतिक्रम्य व्यधत्त कृतवान् । आदिशब्देन अनवलोभनसीमन्तोन्नयने गृह्येते । अत्र मासि द्वितीये तृतीये वा पुंसवनं यदाह । "पुंसा नक्षत्रेण चन्द्रमा युक्तः स्यात्" इति पारस्करः । "चतुर्थेऽनवलोभनम्" इति आश्वलायनः । "षष्ठेऽष्टमे वा सीमन्तः" इति याज्ञवल्क्यः ॥ १० ॥

सुरेन्द्रमात्रेति । गृहागतः नृपः, सुरेन्द्राणां लोकपालानां, मात्राभिः

উন্নত ছিল, এবং নিজভুজবলে যেরূপ সম্পদ উপার্জ্জন করিয়াছিলেন, ও তাঁহার হৃদয়ে যেরূপ আনন্দের সঞ্চার হইয়াছিল, বীরশ্রেষ্ঠ দিলীপ তদনুরূপ বাহুল্য সহকারে পুংসবনাদি সমুদায় সংস্কারের অনুষ্ঠান করিলেন ॥ ১০ ॥

রাজা গৃহে আসিলে সুদক্ষিণা দেবগণের অংশাশ্রিত গুরুতর গর্ভভারে অবনত হইয়া অতি কষ্টে গাত্রোত্থান করিতেন, এমন কি

10. The king ordered all the usual *pungsabana* and other ceremonies to be duly performed, in a manner suited to the great love he bore to the queen, to the largness of his heart, to the immense wealth acquired by his valour and also to the great joy he felt at the happy prospect of getting an issue.

11. When the king entered the queen's apartments, she

*तयोपचाराञ्जलिखिन्नहस्तया
ननन्द †पारिप्लवनेत्रया नृपः ॥ ११ ॥
कुमारभृत्याकुशलैरनुष्ठिते
भिषग्भिराप्तैरथ गर्भभर्मणि।

अर्थः, आश्रितस्य अनुप्रविष्टस्य गर्भस्य, गौरवात् प्रयत्नेन सक्तासनया आसनादुत्थितया इत्यर्थः, उपचारस्य अञ्जलौ अञ्जलिकरणे खिन्न-हस्तया पारिप्लवनेत्रया तरलाक्ष्या, तया सुदक्षिणया ननन्द। सुरेन्द्र-मात्राश्रितेत्यत्र मनुः, "अष्टाभिश्च सुरेन्द्राणां मात्राभिर्निर्मितो नृपः" इति ॥ ११ ॥

कुमारेति। अथ कुमारभृत्या बालचिकित्सा, तस्यां कुशलैः

পতির প্রতি উপচারাঞ্জলি বন্ধন করিতেও ক্লেশে তাঁহার চক্ষু দুটী ঢল ঢল করিত ; তাহা দেখিয়াই রাজা পরম প্রীতি লাভ করিতেন॥১১॥

শিশুচিকিৎসা কুশল বৈদ্যগণের দ্বারা গর্ভের পোষণোপযোগী বিধি-

would raise herself, with difficulty, from her seat, so great was the pressure of her new and divinely animated burden, and as she joined her hands as a mark of respect to her husband, they seemed to be too feeble even for that purpose ; and there was a peculiar sense of helplessness in her looks, which immensely pleased the monarch.

12. In course of time after the usual protective measures

---

* उपचाराञ्जलिखिन्नहस्तया—उपचारः सेवा पत्युरिति शेषः तदर्थः यः अञ्जलिः उपचाराञ्जलिः उपचाराञ्जलौ तद्बन्धनेनेत्यर्थः खिन्नौ क्लान्तौ हस्तौ यस्याः सा उपचाराञ्जलिखिन्नहस्ता तया।

† पारिप्लवनेत्रया—पारिप्लवे, चञ्चले, आकुले वा नेत्रे अक्षिणी यस्याः सा पारिप्लवनेत्रा तया।

पतिः प्रतीतः प्रसवोन्मुखीं प्रियां
ददर्श काले दिवमभ्रितामिव ॥ १२ ॥

ग्रहैस्ततः पञ्चभिरुच्चसंश्रयैः
असूर्य्यगैः सूचितभाग्यसम्पदम् ।
असूत पुत्रं समये शचीसमा
त्रिसाधना शक्तिरिवार्थमक्षयम् ॥ १३ ॥

কৃতিভিঃ, আপ্তৈঃ হিতৈঃ, ভিষগ্ভিঃ বৈদ্যৈঃ, গর্ভস্য ভর্মণি ভরণে অনুষ্ঠিতে কৃতে সতি, কালে দশমে মাসি, অন্যত্র যোগ্যকালে, প্রসবস্য গর্ভমোচনস্য উন্মুখীম্ আসন্নপ্রসবাম্ ইত্যর্থঃ, প্রিয়াং ভার্য্যাম্ অভ্রাণি অস্যাঃ সঞ্জাতানি অভ্রিতা তাম্, দিবম্ ইব পতিঃ ভর্ত্তা প্রতীতঃ হৃষ্টঃ সন্ দদর্শ দৃষ্টবান্ ॥ ১২ ॥

গ্রহৈরিতি। ততঃ শচ্যা ইন্দ্রাণ্যা সমা, সা সুদক্ষিণা সময়ে প্রসূতিকালে সতি, দশমে মাসি ইত্যর্থঃ, উচ্চসংশ্রয়ৈঃ উচ্চসংস্থৈঃ তুঙ্গস্থা-নগৈঃ, অসূর্য্যগৈঃ অনস্তমিতৈঃ, কৈশ্চিত্ যথাসম্ভবং পঞ্চভিঃ গ্রহৈঃ সূচিতা

সকল অনুষ্ঠিত হইলে, রাজা হৃষ্টচিত্তে আসন্নপ্রসবা প্রিয়াকে বারি-বর্ষণোন্মুখ মেঘাবৃত নভোমণ্ডলের ন্যায় দর্শন করিতে লাগিলেন ॥ ১২ ॥

অনন্তর সাধনত্রয়সম্পন্ন রাজনীতি যেমন যথাকালে অক্ষয় অভীষ্ট ফলকে প্রসব করে, সেইরূপ ইন্দ্রাণীতুল্যা সুদক্ষিণা যথাসময়ে এক

---

had been taken by competent physicians, attached to the royal household, and skilled in the treatment of women during pregnancy, the queen approached the time of her confinement ; and the king looked upon her with the same satisfaction with which men behold the sky looking heavy with clouds, about to discharge their contents in the shape of a shower of rain.

13. At last, as threefold kingly power brings on sure prosperity, so the queen brought forth a son, at whose birth five

दिशः प्रसेदुर्मरुतो ववुः सुखाः
*प्रदक्षिणार्चिर्हविरग्निराददे ।
बभूव सर्वं शुभशंसि तत्क्षणं
भवो हि लोकाभ्युदयाय तादृशाम् ॥१४॥

भाग्यसम्पदं यस्य तं पुत्रं, शक्तिः प्रभावमन्त्रोत्साहात्मकानि साधनानि उत्पादकानि यस्याः सा त्रिसाधना शक्तिः अक्षयम् अर्थम् इव असूत ॥१३॥

दिश इति । तत्क्षणं तस्मिन् क्षणे दिशः प्रसेदुः प्रसन्नाः बभूवुः, मरुतः वाताः सुखाः मनोहराः ववुः, अग्निः प्रदक्षिणार्चिः सन् हविः आददे स्वीचकार, इत्थं सर्वं शुभशंसि शुभसूचकं बभूव । तथाहि,

পুত্ররত্ন প্রসব করিলেন ; প্রসবকালে পাঁচটী অনস্তমিত গ্রহ দর্শনে বুঝিতে পারা গেল যে ঐ শিশু সৌভাগ্যবান্ হইবে ॥ ১৩ ॥

এই শিশু ভূমিষ্ঠ হইবামাত্র দিক সকল প্রসন্ন হইল ; সুখকর বায়ু বহিতে লাগিল ; অগ্নি শিখামালায় আবেষ্টন করিয়া ঘৃতাহুতি গ্রহণ করিতে লাগিল ; এইরূপে চতুর্দ্দিকে মঙ্গলসূচক চিহ্ন সকল দৃষ্ট হইতে

auspicious stars occupied the highest points in the heavens and did not set ;—thus betokening the great future that lay before the new-born babe.

14. That very moment the weather cleared off ; the breeze became soft and cool ; and the sacrificial fire leapt forward, with an encircling flame, to receive the *ghee* sacrifice ; in short, every

प्रदक्षिणार्चिः—प्रदक्षिणं अर्चिः सव्यावर्तनेनास्या हुताहुतिं प्रतिः सञ्चरन्ती शिखा, इत्यर्थः, यस्य, स प्रदक्षिणार्चिः । अग्नेः प्रज्वलिततया शिखया हुताहुतिग्रहणं शुभसूचकमिति बोद्धव्यम् ।

*अरिष्टशय्यां परितो विसारिणा
सुजन्मनस्तस्य निजेन तेजसा।
निशीथदीपाः सहसा हतत्विषः
बभूवुरालेख्यसमर्पिता इव ॥ १५ ॥

रघुप्रकाराणां भवः जन्म, लोकाभ्युदयाय भवति इति भावः, ततो देवा अपि सन्नद्धाः इत्यर्थः ॥ १४ ॥

अरिष्टेति। अरिष्टे सूतिकागृहे, शय्यां तल्पं, परितः अभितः विसारिणा, सुजन्मनः शोभनोत्पत्तेः, तस्य शिशोः, निजेन नैसर्गिकेण तेजसा, सहसा हतत्विषः क्षीणकान्तयः, निशीथदीपाः अर्धरात्रप्रदीपाः, आलेख्यसमर्पिताः चित्रार्पिता इव बभूवुः। निशीथशब्दो दीपानां प्रभाधिक्यसम्भावनार्थः ॥ १५ ॥

লাগিল; কারণ তাদৃশ মহাপুরুষের জন্ম জগতের কল্যাণেরই জন্য ॥ ১৪ ॥

সেই সুজন্মা বালকের দেহের তেজোরাশি সূতিকাশয্যার চতুর্দ্দিকে বিকীর্ণ হইয়া মধ্যরাত্রের প্রদীপ সকলকেও নিষ্প্রভ করিয়া ফেলিল; প্রদীপগুলি যেন চিত্রার্পিত প্রদীপের ন্যায় বোধ হইতে লাগিল ॥ ১৫ ॥

---

thing had an augury of good; since it is for the good of the world that these great ones are born.

15. As the new born infant lay in its bed, a halo of light emanated from its body and quite extinguished the lustre

* अरिष्टशय्यां परितः—For explanation of the द्वितीया in this passage try to have the following explained by your teacher :—

जनाय शुद्धान्तचराय शंसते
कुमारजन्मामृतसम्मिताक्षरम्* ।
अदेयमासीत् त्रयमेव भूपतेः
शशिप्रभं छत्रमुभे च चामरे ॥ १६ ॥

जनायेति । नृपतेः दिलीपस्य, अमृतसम्मिताक्षरम् अमृतसमानाक्षरम्, कुमारजन्म पुत्रोत्पत्तिं, शंसते कथयते, शुद्धान्तचराय अन्तःपुरचारिणे जनाय, त्रयम् एव अदेयम् आसीत् । किं तत् ? शशिप्रभम् उज्ज्वलं छत्रम्, उभे चामरे च । छत्रादीनां राज्ञः प्रधानाङ्गत्वात् इति भावः ॥ १६ ॥

অন্তঃপুরবাসিগণ যখন অমৃত সমান কুমারের জন্মবার্ত্তা রাজাকে শুনাইল, তখন (এতই আনন্দ হইল) যে, চন্দ্রতুল্য শোভাশালী ছত্র ও চামর দ্বয় এই তিনটী মাত্র তাঁহার অদেয় রহিল ॥ ১৬ ॥

---

of the midnight lamps, making them look like lights painted on canvass.

16. When the messengers of the ladies' apartments announced to the king the birth of his son, so great was his joy, that there were only three things that he could not give away as marks of his exceeding pleasure—his white imperial umbrella, and his two *chamars.*

उभसर्व्वतसोः कार्य्याधिगुपर्य्यादिषु त्रिषु ।
द्वितीयाम्रेडितान्तेषु ततोऽन्यत्रापि दृश्यते ॥

And अभितः परितः समया निकषा हा प्रतियोगेऽपि ।

Also refer to सिद्धान्तकौमुदी page 262, Taranath's edition of 1863

* अमृतसम्मिताक्षरं—अमृतेन, अथवा सम्मितानि तुलितानि सा-

নিবাতপদ্মস্তিমিতেন চক্ষুষা
নৃপস্য কান্তং পিবতঃ সুতাননম্।
মহোদধেঃ পূর ইবেন্দুদর্শনাৎ
গুরুঃ প্রহর্ষঃ প্রবভূব নাত্মনি ॥ ১৭ ॥

নিবাতেতি। নিবাতঃ নির্বাতপ্রদেশঃ, তত্র যৎ পদ্মং তদ্বৎ স্তিমিতেন নিষ্পন্দেন, চক্ষুষা নেত্রেণ, কান্তং সুন্দরং সুতাননং পুত্রমুখং, পিবতঃ তৃষ্ণয়া পশ্যতঃ, নৃপস্য, গুরুঃ উৎকটঃ, প্রহর্ষঃ ইন্দুদর্শনাৎ মহোদধেঃ পূরঃ জলৌঘঃ ইব, আত্মনি শরীরে ন প্রবভূব আত্মানং ন শশাক অন্তঃ ন মাতি স্ম ইতি যাবৎ। নশ্বস্যাধারে অধিকং লীয়তে ইতি ভাবঃ। যদ্বা হর্ষঃ আত্মনি স্বস্মিন্ বিষয়ে ন প্রবভূব, আত্মানং নিয়ন্তুং ন শশাক, কিন্তু বহির্নির্জগাম ইত্যর্থঃ ॥ ১৭ ॥

নরপতি বায়ুসঞ্চাররহিত পদ্মপলাশসদৃশ স্পন্দন-বিহীন নেত্রে নব-জাত শিশুর সুন্দর মুখ যখন দর্শন করিতে লাগিলেন, তখন চন্দ্রদর্শনে উচ্ছলিত জলরাশি যেমন সাগরে ধরে না তেমনি প্রবল আনন্দ তাঁহার অন্তরে ধরিল না ॥ ১৭ ॥

---

17. As the king gazed on the lovely little face, with eyes, motionless like lotus-leaves in a breezeless tank, his great joy overflew all its bounds, as overflows the sea at the sight of the moon.

শানি বা অবধি যস্য তৎ অন্ততঃ সম্মিতাম্বরং সুধাস্তৈক-সমং আহ্লাদপরনির্বর্ণঃ।

स जातकर्मण्यखिले तपस्विना
तपोवनादेत्य पुरोधसा कृते ।
दिलीपसूनुर्मणिराकरोद्भवः
प्रयुक्तसंस्कार इवाधिकं बभौ ॥ १८ ॥
सुखश्रवा मङ्गलतूर्य्यनिस्वनाः
प्रमोदनृत्यैः सह वारयोषिताम् ।

स इति। सः दिलीपसूनुः, तपस्विना पुरोधसा पुरोहितेन, वशिष्ठेन, तपस्वित्वात् तदनुष्ठितं कर्म्म सवीर्य्यं स्यात् इति भावः, तपोवनात् एत्य आगत्य, अखिले समग्रे जातकर्म्मणि जातस्य कर्त्तव्यसंस्कारविशेषे, कृते सति, प्रयुक्तः संस्कारः शाणोल्लेखनादिः यस्य सः तथोक्तः, आकरोद्भवः खनिप्रभवः मणिः इव, अधिकं बभौ, वशिष्ठमन्त्रप्रभावात् तेजिष्ठोऽभूत् इत्यर्थः। अत्र मनुः, "प्राङ्नाभिवर्द्धनात् पुंसो जातकर्म्म विधीयते" इति ॥ १८ ॥

सुखश्रवा इति। सुखः सुखकरः श्रवः श्रवणं येषां ते सुखश्रवाः

রাজপুরোহিত তপোবন হইতে আসিয়া জাতকর্ম্মসংক্রান্ত সমুদায় অনুষ্ঠান করিয়া গেলে, দিলীপকুমার আকরোদ্ভূত ও পরিমার্জ্জিত মণির ন্যায় শোভা পাইতে লাগিলেন ॥ ১৮ ॥

কেবল যে দিলীপেরই গৃহে নানাপ্রকার মঙ্গলসূচক বাদ্যযন্ত্রের

---

18. After all the post-birth ceremonies had been performed by the holy sage Basista, who came from the hermitage for that purpose, the infant prince assumed a new glory like unto a piece of precious metal dug out of the caves of the earth, after it had undergone the process of refining.

19. Not only in the palace of the king there was sweet

न केवलं सद्मनि मागधीपतेः
पथि व्यजृम्भन्त दिवौकसामपि ॥१९॥
न संयतस्तस्य बभूव
विसर्ज्जयेद् यं सुतजन्महर्षितः
ऋणाभिधानात् स्वयमेव केवलं
तदा पितॄणां मुमुचे स बन्धनात् ॥ २० ॥

श्रुतिसुखाः इत्यर्थः, मङ्गलतूर्य्यनिस्वना मङ्गलवाद्यध्वनयः, वारयोषितां वेश्यानाम्, प्रमोदनृत्यैः हर्षनर्त्तनैः, सह मागधीपतेः दिलीपस्य, सद्मनि केवलं गृहे एव, न व्यजृम्भन्त, किन्तु द्यौः ओकः येषां ते दिवौकसः देवाः तेषां पथि आकाशेऽपि व्यजृम्भन्त। तस्य देवांशत्वात् देवोपकारित्वाच्च देवदुन्दुभयोऽपि नेदुः इति भावः ॥ १९ ॥

नेति। रक्षितुः सम्यक्पालनशीलस्य, तस्य दिलीपस्य, अतएव चौराद्यभावात् संयतः बद्धः, न बभूव न अभूत्; किं तेनात आह, विसर्जयेदिति, सुतजन्मना हर्षितः तोषितः, सन् सः यं बद्धं विसर्जयेत्

ধ্বনি ও বারাঙ্গনাদিগের নৃত্য চলিতে লাগিল, তাহা নহে, আকাশমার্গে দেবতাগণও আনন্দসূচক বাদ্যধ্বনি করিতে লাগিলেন ॥ ১৯ ॥

এমন কারাবাসী ছিল না, যাহাকে দিলীপ এই আনন্দের দিনে ছাড়িয়া দেন, তবে নিজে পিতৃঋণরূপ বন্ধন হইতে মুক্তিলাভ করিলেন এই মাত্র ॥ ২০ ॥

music attended with the dancing of public women, but also in the mansions of the gods.

20. There were no prisoners, whom the king could liberate as a mark of his joy on account of the birth of his son :

श्रुतस्य यायादयमन्तमर्भकः
तथा परेषां युधि चेति पार्थिवः ।
अवेक्ष्य धातोर्गमनार्थमर्थवित्
चकार नाम्ना रघुमात्मसम्भवम् ॥२१॥

विमोचयेत्, किन्तु सः राजा, तदा पितॄणाम् ऋणाभिधानात् बन्धनात् केवलम् एकं यथा तथा स्वयम् एव एक एव इत्यर्थः ; स्वस्यैव स्वयमेव मुक्तः इत्यर्थः। अस्मिन्नर्थे "एषवा अनृणो यः पुत्री" इतिः श्रुतिप्रमाणम्॥२०॥

श्रुतस्येति। अर्थवित् शब्दार्थज्ञः, पार्थिवः पृथिवीश्वरः, दिलीपः, अयम् अर्भकः बालकः, श्रुतस्य शास्त्रस्य, अन्तं पारं यायात्, तथा युधि, परेषां शत्रूणाम्, अन्तं पारञ्च यायात् यातुं शक्नुयात् इत्यर्थः, इति हेतोः धातोः "लघिवघिमघिगत्यर्थाः" इति लघिधातोः गमनाख्यम् अर्थम् अर्थवित्त्वात् अवेक्ष्य आलोच्य, आत्मसम्भवं पुत्रं नाम्ना रघुं चकार। लङ्घिवह्योर्नलोपश्चेत्युपसंख्यये बालमूललघ्वलमङ्गुलीनां वा लोरत्वमापद्यते इति वैकल्पिके रेफादेशे रघुरिति रूपं सिद्धम्। अत्र शङ्खः, "अशौचे तु व्यतिक्रान्ते नामकर्म विधीयते" इति ॥ २१ ॥

সেই বালক সকল শাস্ত্রের পারে এবং রণক্ষেত্রে শত্রুসৈন্যেরও পারে গমন করিবে, ইহা অনুভব করিয়া, শব্দার্থজ্ঞ রাজা গমনার্থ লঘ ধাতুকে অবলম্বন পূর্ব্বক তাঁহার নবজাত কুমারের নাম রঘু রাখিলেন ॥ ২১ ॥

---

the only act of liberation that took place was his own ;—namely, that from his debts to his forefathers.

21. Feeling that the boy was destined to go to the furthest limits of learning and also of military valour in his wars with his enemies, Dileep called him *Raghu*,—a word formed from a verb-root meaning the act of going.

पितुः प्रयत्नात् स समग्रसम्पदः
शुभैः शरीरावयवैर्दिने दिने ।
पुपोष वृद्धिं *हरिदश्वदीधितेः
अनुप्रवेशादिव बालचन्द्रमाः २२ ॥
उमावृषाङ्कौ शरजन्मना यथा
यथा जयन्तेन शचीपुरन्दरौ ।

पितुरिति । सः रघुः, समग्रसम्पदः पूर्णैश्वर्यशालिनः, पितुः दिलीपस्य, प्रयत्नात् शुभैः मनोहरैः, शरीरावयवैः हरिदश्वदीधितेः सूर्य्यरश्मेः, अनुप्रवेशात् बालचन्द्रमाः इव, दिने दिने प्रतिदिनम् वृद्धिं पुपोष । अत्र वराहसंहितावचनम्, "सलिलमये शशिनि रवेर्दीधितयो मूर्च्छितास्तमो नैशम् । क्षपयन्ति दर्पणोदरनिहिता इव मन्दिरस्यान्तः ।" इति ॥ २२ ॥

उमेति । उमावृषाङ्कौ पार्वतीवृषभध्वजौ, शरजन्मना कार्त्तिकेयेन,

सूर्य्यরশ্মির অনুপ্রবেশদ্বারা প্রতিপদের চন্দ্র যেমন দিন দিন বর্দ্ধিত হয়, সেইরূপ সমৃদ্ধিশালী পিতার যত্নে সেই শিশু সুন্দর দেহাবয়ব প্রাপ্ত হইয়া দিন দিন বাড়িতে লাগিল । ২২ ॥

হরপার্ব্বতী কার্ত্তিককে প্রাপ্ত হইয়া যেরূপ আনন্দিত হইয়াছিলেন,

---

22. As by the reflection of the sun's rays, the crescent of the moon waxes larger and larger every day, so the little boy throve in all his limbs, under the care of his royal father.

23. As Siva and Parvati were delighted to have *Kartika*,

* हरिदश्वदीधितेः—हरितः हरिद्वर्णाः अश्वा यस्य स हरिदश्वः सूर्य्यस्तस्य दीधितिः किरणं तस्य । compare with १० श्लोक ।

तथा नृपः सा च सुतेन मागधी
ननन्दतुस्तत्सदृशेन तत्समौ ॥ २३ ॥

रथाङ्गनाम्नोरिव भावबन्धनं
बभूव यत् प्रेम परस्पराश्रयम् ।
विभक्तमप्येकसुतेन तत् तयोः
परस्परस्योपरि पर्य्यचीयत ॥ २४ ॥

यथा ननन्दतुः, शचीपुरन्दरौ जयन्तेन पाकशासनिना, यथा ननन्दतुः, तथा तत्समौ ताभ्याम् उमावृषाङ्काभ्यां शचीपुरन्दराभ्यां, च समौ समानौ, सा मागधी नृपश्च, तत्सदृशेन ताभ्यां कुमार-जयन्ताभ्यां सदृशेन सुतेन ननन्दतुः ॥ २३ ॥

रथाङ्गेति। रथाङ्गनाम्नी च रथाङ्गनामा च रथाङ्गनामानौ चक्रवाकौ तयोः इव, तयोः दम्पत्योः, भावबन्धनं हृदयाकर्षकं, परस्पराश्रयम् अन्योन्यविषयं, यत् प्रेम बभूव, तत् एकेन केवलेन ताभ्याम् अन्येन वा सुतेन, विभक्तम् अपि कृतविभागम् अपि, परस्परस्योपरि पर्य्यचीयत ववृधे। अकृत्रिमत्वात् स्वयमेव उपचितम् इत्यर्थः। यदेकाधारं वस्तु,

---

কিংবা শচীপুরন্দর জয়ন্তকে লাভ করিয়া যেরূপ আপনাদিকে সুখী বোধ করিয়াছিলেন, দিলীপ ও সুদক্ষিণা রঘুকে পাইয়া সেইরূপ আনন্দ লাভ করিলেন ॥ ২৩ ॥

চক্রবাক মিথুনের ন্যায় রাজা ও রাজ্ঞীর পরস্পরের প্রতি যে গভীর

---

and as Indra and Sachi, his wife, were delighted to have Jayanta, as their son, so the king and the queen were happy to have the little prince as their heir.

24. Their love for each other, which was as cordial as that of a pair of *chakrabacks* (birds proverbial for their conjugal

উবাচ ধাত্র্যা প্রথমোদিতং বচো
যযৌ তদীয়ামবলম্ব্য চাঙ্গুলিম্ ।
অভূচ্চ নম্রঃ প্রণিপাতশিক্ষয়া
পিতুর্মুদং তেন ততান সোঽর্ভকঃ ॥ ২৫ ॥

তদাধারদ্বয়ে বিভজ্যমানং হীয়তে, অত্র তু তয়োঃ সংক্রান্তকর্ত্তৃকমেকৈক বিষয়ং প্রেম অন্যত্র দ্বিতীয়বিষয়াভাবেঽপি নাহীয়ত, প্রত্যুত উপচিতমেবাভূৎ ইতি ভাবঃ ॥ ২৪ ॥

উবাচেতি । সঃ অর্ভকঃ শিশুঃ, ধাত্র্যা উপমাত্রা, প্রথমম্ উদিতম্ উপদিষ্টং, বচঃ উবাচ, তদীয়াম্ অঙ্গুলিম্ অবলম্ব্য যযৌ চ, প্রণিপাতস্য শিক্ষয়া উপদেশেন, নম্রঃ অভূৎ চ, ইতি যৎ তেন পিতুঃ মুদং ততান ॥ ২৫ ॥

প্রেম ছিল, তাহা সেই একমাত্র পুত্রে বিভক্ত হইয়াও পরস্পরের প্রতি যেন আরও গাঢ়ভাব ধারণ করিল ॥ ২৪ ॥

ক্রমে সেই বালক পরিচারিকা কর্ত্তৃক প্রথমোচ্চারিত বাক্য সকল বলিতে আরম্ভ করিল; তাহাদিগের অঙ্গুলি ধরিয়া চলিতে আরম্ভ করিল; এবং প্রণাম কর প্রণাম কর বলিলে, মস্তক নত করিতে শিখিল; দেখিয়া রাজার কতই আনন্দ বাড়িতে লাগিল ॥ ২৫ ॥

affection) increased in its intensity, when shared by their new-born child.

25. Gradually little Raghu began to lisp out the words taught by his nurses, and to exercise his little legs in walking by holding the proffered finger of the nurse, and also gently lowered his head in obediance to the nurse's command to bow to a superior ;—all these little ways of the boy Raghu were a source of pleasure to the king.

तमङ्कमारोप्य शरीरयोगजैः
सुखैर्निषिञ्चन्तमिवामृतं त्वचि ।
*उपान्तसंमीलितलोचनो नृपः
चिरात् †सुतस्पर्शरसज्ञतां ययौ ॥२६॥
अमंस्त चानेन परार्ध्यजन्मना
स्थितेरभेत्ता स्थितिमन्तमन्वयम् ।

तमिति । शरीरयोगजैः सुखैः, त्वचि त्वगिन्द्रिये, अमृतं निषिञ्चन्तम् इव, तं सुतम् अङ्कम् आरोप्य, सुखातिशयात् उपान्तयोः प्रान्तयोः, संमीलितलोचनः सन्, नृपः चिरात् सुतस्पर्शरसज्ञतां ययौ । वंशः स्थम् ॥ १२ ॥

তাহাকে ক্রোড়ে করিয়া তাহার কোমলাঙ্গের স্পর্শজনিত সুখে নিমীলিত নেত্র হইয়া, রাজা এত দিনের পর সন্তান ক্রোড়ে করার সুখ যে কি তাহার আস্বাদন লাভ করিতে লাগিলেন ॥ ২৬ ॥

সৃষ্টিকর্ত্তা যেমন নিজের সত্ত্বগুণের অবতার স্বরূপ বিষ্ণুর দ্বারা নিজ

---

26. As the king clasped his son to his bosom, his whole frame thrilled with intense emotion and with eyes closed at their corners with extreme pleasure, he experienced the long-desired joys of caressing his own child.

27. As the creator of the world considers the preservation

---

* उपान्तसंमीलितलोचनः—उपान्ते प्रान्तभागे संमीलिते कुञ्चिते (ईषन्मिलितमितत्) लोचने नेत्रे यस्य सः ईदृशः ईषन्मीलि-तास्य इत्यर्थः ।

† सुतस्पर्शरसज्ञतां—सुतस्य पुत्रस्य स्पर्शस्य यो रसः स्वादस्तं जानाति यः स सुतस्पर्शरसज्ञस्तस्य भावः सुतस्पर्शरसज्ञता ताम् ।

*স্বমূর্ত্তিভেদেন গুণাগ্র্যবর্ত্তিনা
পতিঃ প্রজানামিব সর্গমাত্মনঃ ॥২৭॥
স বৃত্তচূলশ্চলকাকপক্ষকৈ-
রমাত্যপুত্রৈঃ সবয়োভিরন্বিতঃ

অথবা ভবৃত্তজন্মনা, অনেন রঘুণা, আত্মীয়ং বংশং, প্র[illegible] পতি ব্রহ্মা গুণাঃ সত্ত্বাদয়ঃ, তেষু অগ্র্যেণ মুখ্যেন সত্ত্বেন, বর্ত্ততে [illegible]প্রবর্ত্তত ইতি গুণাগ্র্যবর্ত্তী, তেন স্বস্য মূর্ত্তিভেদেন অবতারবিশেষেণ, বিষ্ণুনা, আত্মনঃ সর্গং সৃষ্টিম্ ইব, স্থিতিমন্তং প্রতিষ্ঠাবন্তম্ অমংস্ত মন্যতে স্ম। অত্র উপমানোপমেয়য়োরিতরেতরবিশেষণানীতরেতরত্র যোজ্যানি, তত্র রঘুপক্ষে গুণাঃ বিদ্যাবিনয়াদয় ॥ ২৭ ॥

স ইতি। 'চূড়া কার্য্যা দ্বিজাতীনাং সর্ব্বেষামেব ধর্ম্মতঃ। প্রথমেঽব্দে তৃতীয়ে বা কর্ত্তব্যা শ্রুতিচোদনাৎ ॥" ইতি মনুস্মরণাৎ তৃতীয়ে বর্ষে

সৃষ্টিকে সুরক্ষিত বলিয়া অনুভব করেন; সেইরূপ লোক স্থিতি রক্ষক দিলীপ সেই সুজন্মা পুত্রের দ্বারা আপন বংশকে সুরক্ষিত বলিয়া অনুভব করিতে লাগিলেন ॥ ২৭ ॥

ক্রমে চূড়াকর্ম্ম সমাপন হইলে, কাকপক্ষধর রঘু সমবয়স্ক অমাত্য-

---

of his creation secured by the incarnation of his own self in the shape of Vishnu, so did king Dileep feel the continuance of his line certain by reason of the birth of his son.

28. In course of time the first shaving ceremony was

---

* স্বমূর্ত্তিভেদেন গুণাগ্র্যবর্ত্তিনা—ত্রয়ো গুণাঃ সত্ত্বরজস্তমআত্মকাঃ তেষাং মধ্যে আদৌ বর্ত্ততে যঃ সত্ত্বগুণ ইত্যর্থঃ তদ্বর্ত্তী বিষ্ণুঃ স চ ব্রহ্মণ এব মূর্ত্তিভেদঃ অবতারবিশেষঃ। ত্রিধা বিভক্তস্য

लिपेर्यथावद्ग्रहणेन वाङ्मयं
नदीमुखेनेव समुद्रमाविशत् ॥ २८ ॥
अथोपनीतं विधिवद्विपश्चितः
विनिन्युरेनं गुरवो गुरुप्रियम्।

वृत्तचूलः निष्पन्नचूडाकर्मा सन्, "प्राप्ते तु पञ्चमे वर्षे विद्यारम्भञ्च कारयेत्" इति वचनात् पञ्चमे वर्षे समानकालजातैः पञ्चवर्षवयस्कैः सवयोभिः स्निग्धैः अमात्यपुत्रैः अन्वितः सन्, लिपेः पञ्चाशद्वर्णात्मिकायाः मातृकायाः यथावत् ग्रहणेन सम्यक् बोधेन उपायभूतेन, वाङ्मयं शब्दजातं, नद्याः मुखं द्वारम्, तेन कश्चित् मकरादिः समुद्रम् इव, आविशत् प्रविष्टः ज्ञातवान् इत्यर्थः ॥ २८ ॥

अथेति। "गर्भाष्टमेऽब्दे कुर्वीत ब्राह्मणस्योपनायनम्। गर्भादे-

পুত্রদিগের সহিত মিলিত হইয়া নদীর দ্বারা লোকে যেমন সমুদ্রে প্রবেশ করে সেই রূপ বর্ণপরিচয়ের দ্বারা শাস্ত্র-বিদ্যাতে প্রবিষ্ট হইলেন ॥ ২৮ ॥

অনন্তর উপনয়ন কার্য্য সমধা হইলে সুপণ্ডিত অধ্যাপকগণ রাজ-

performed, and the prince of undulating locks, in company with boys of the same age, the sons of his father's courtiers, learnt his letters and entered thereby, as if through a river, into the great ocean of learing.

29. After the prince had been duly invested with the

परमेश्वरस्य ब्रह्मविष्णुमहेश्वरादयो रूपभेदा एवेति पुराण-प्रसिद्धिः—Compare with another passage of this book.

नमो विश्वसृजे पूर्वं विश्वं तदनु बिभ्रते।
अथ विश्वस्य संहर्त्रे तुभ्यं त्रेधास्थितात्मने ॥

दशमः सर्गः १६ श्लोकः।

अवन्ध्ययत्नाश्च बभूवुरत्र ते
क्रिया हि वस्तूपहिता प्रसीदति ॥२८॥
धियः समग्रैः स गुणैरुदारधीः
क्रमाच्चतस्रश्चतुरर्णवोपमाः।
ततार *विद्याः पवनातिपातिभिः
दिशो हरिद्भिर्हरितामिवेश्वरः ॥ ३० ॥

कादशे राज्ञः षष्ठपि द्वादशे विशः॥" इति मनुस्मरणात् अथ गर्भै-
कादशे वर्षे विधिवत् उपनीतं गुरुप्रियम् एनं रघुं, शिष्यहितः विद्वांसः
गुरवः विनिन्युः शिक्षितवन्तः; ते गुरवः अत्र अस्मिन् रघौ, अवन्ध्यय-
त्नाश्च बभूवुः; तथाहि क्रिया शिक्षा वस्तूनि पात्रभूते उपहिता
प्रयुक्ता प्रसीदति फलति ॥ २८ ॥

धिय इति। उदारधीः उत्कृष्टबुद्धिः, सः रघुः समग्रैः धियः
गुणैः, चतस्रः अर्णवा उपमा यासां ताः चतुरर्णवोपमाः, चतस्रः

কুমারকে যথাবিধি শিক্ষা দিতে লাগিলেন; তাঁহাদের যত্নও সকল
হইতে লাগিল; হইবেই ত, প্রকৃত পাত্রে নিযুক্ত হইলে সকল ক্রিয়াই
ফলদায়ক হয়॥ ২৯॥

সূর্য্য যেমন পবন অপেক্ষা দ্রুতগামী অশ্বের সাহায্যে দিক সকল

sacred thread, he was placed under learned teachers, who trained him carefully in their respective branches of learning. Nor were they unsuccessful in their labours :—for efforts when directed to proper objects seldom fail.

30. Aided by the extraordinary qualities of his intellect

* विद्याः—आन्वीक्षिकी, त्रयी, वार्त्ता दण्डनीतिश्चेति चतस्रः विद्याः।

ত্বচং স মেধ্যাং পরিধায় রৌরবীম্
অশিক্ষতাস্ত্রং পিতুরেব মন্ত্রবৎ।
ন কেবলং তদ্গুরুরেকপার্থিবঃ
ক্ষিতাবভূদেকধনুর্দ্ধরোঽপি সঃ ॥ ৩১ ॥

বিদ্যাঃ, হরিতাং দিশাম্, ঈশ্বরঃ সূর্য্যঃ, পবনাতিপাতিভিঃ হরিদ্ভিঃ নিজাশ্বৈঃ চতস্রঃ দিশঃ ইব, ক্রমাৎ ততার। চতুরর্ণবোপমত্বং দিশামপি দ্রষ্টব্যম্ ॥ ৩০ ॥

ত্বচমিতি। সঃ রঘুঃ, "কার্ষ্ণরৌরববাস্তানি চর্ম্মাণি ব্রহ্মচারিণঃ। বসীরন্নানুপূর্ব্ব্যেণ শাণক্ষৌমাবিকানি চ ॥" ইতি মনুস্মরণাৎ মেধ্যাং শুদ্ধাং, রৌরবীং রুরুসম্বন্ধিনীম্, ত্বচং চর্ম্ম, পরিধায় বসিত্বা, মন্ত্রবৎ সমন্ত্রকম্, অস্ত্রম্ আগ্নেয়াদিকং, পিতুঃ এব উপাধ্যায়াৎ অশিক্ষত অভ্যস্তবান্, পিতুরেবেত্যবধারণমুপপাদয়তি,

---

অতিক্রম করিয়া যান, সেইরূপ প্রতিভাশালী রঘু সর্ব্বতোমুখীন প্রতিভার গুণে চতুঃসাগর সমান বিদ্যাচতুষ্টয়ের পারদর্শী হইলেন ॥ ৩০ ॥

বিদ্যা চতুষ্টয় যথা—আন্বীক্ষিকী, ত্রয়ী, বার্ত্তা, দণ্ডনীতি।

সেই রঘু পবিত্র রুরু মৃগের চর্ম্ম পরিধান করিয়া স্বীয় পিতারই

---

he soon acquired mastery over the four reputed branches of learning, resembling four oceans ;—his progress being as rapid as the career of the sun through the skies.

31 Clad in the sacred skin of the *ruru* deer, he learnt the art of war with all its mysterious incantations from his father

---

With regard to these there is the following saying in old Sanskrit Literature :—"আন্বীক্ষিকী ত্রয়ী বার্ত্তা দণ্ডনীতিশ্চ শাশ্বতী, বিদ্যাশ্চৈতাশ্চতস্রস্তু ইতি।

মহোক্ষতাং বৎসতরঃ স্পৃশন্নিব
দ্বিপেন্দ্রভাবং কলভঃ শ্রয়ন্নিব।
রঘুঃ ক্রমাদ্যৌবনভিন্নশৈশবঃ*
পুপোষ †গাম্ভীর্য্যমনোহরং বপুঃ ॥ ৩২ ॥

নেতি। তদ্ভুবঃ একঃ অদ্বিতীয়ঃ, পার্থিবঃ কেবলং পৃথিবীশ্বরঃ এব ন অভূত্ কিন্তু ক্ষিতৌ সঃ দিলীপঃ একঃ ধনুর্ধরঃ অপি অভূত্ ॥ ৩১ ॥

মহোক্ষতামিতি। রঘুঃ ক্রমাত্ যৌবনেন ভিন্নশৈশবঃ নিরস্তশিশু-ভাবঃ সন্, মহান্ উক্ষা মহোক্ষঃ মহর্ষভঃ তস্য ভাবঃ তত্তা তাং স্পৃশন্ গচ্ছন্, বৎসতরঃ দম্যঃ ইব, দ্বিপেন্দ্রভাবং মহাগজত্বং শ্রয়ন্ ভজন্,

নিকটে মন্ত্রসমন্বিত অস্ত্রবিদ্যা শিক্ষা করিতে লাগিলেন, কারণ তাঁহার পিতা যে কেবল পৃথিবীতে অদ্বিতীয় রাজা ছিলেন তাহা নহে ধনুর্ধারী বীরদিগের মধ্যেও অদ্বিতীয় ছিলেন ॥ ৩১ ॥

গোবৎস যেমন কালে বৃষভতা প্রাপ্ত হয়, করিশাবক যেমন যৌবনাগমে গজ-রাজের আকার ধারণ করিতে থাকে, সেইরূপ

himself; for his royal sire was not only the first king in the whole world, but was also the best soldier.

32 As the young calf grows in time into the big bull, and the infant elephant becomes a majestic beast, so Raghu after the days of childhood stepped into the happy period of youth,

* যৌবনভিন্নশৈশবঃ—যৌবনেন তারুণ্যোদয়েন ভিন্নঃ পরিবর্ত্তিতঃ শৈশবো বাল্যদশা যস্য সঃ।

† গাম্ভীর্য্যমনোহরং—গাম্ভীর্য্যেণ বাল্যভাবাপগমাত্ ধীরতাগুণেন ভাবগাম্ভীর্য্যেণ মনোহরং, সুন্দরম্।

अथास्य गोदानविधेरनन्तरं
विवाहदीक्षां निरवर्त्तयद्गुरुः ।
नरेन्द्रकन्यास्तमवाप्य सत्पतिं
तमोनुदं दक्षसुता इवाबभुः ॥ ३३ ॥

कलभः करिपोतः इव, गाम्भीर्य्येण अचापलेन, मनोहरं वपुः पुपोष ॥ ३२ ॥

अथेति । गावः लोमानि केशाः दीयन्ते खण्ड्यन्ते अस्मिन् इति व्युत्पत्त्या गोदानं नाम ब्राह्मणादीनां षोड़शादिषु वर्षेषु कर्त्तव्यं केशान्ताख्यं कर्म्मोच्यते । तदुक्तं मनुना, "केशान्तः षोड़शे वर्षे ब्राह्मणस्य विधीयते । राजन्यबन्धोर्द्वाविंशे वैश्यस्य द्व्यधिके ततः ॥" इति । अथ गुरुः पिता, अस्य गोदानविधेः अनन्तरं विवाहदीक्षां निरवर्त्तयत् कृतवान् इत्यर्थः ; अथ नरेन्द्रकन्याः, तं रघुं, दक्षस्य सुताः रोहिण्यादयः, तमोनुदं चन्द्रम् इव, सत्पतिम् अवाप्य आबभुः । इति ॥ ३३ ॥

শৈশবের অন্ত হইয়া যৌবনের উদয় হওয়াতে রঘুরও সেই কান্তি গম্ভীর অথচ মনোহর ভাব ধারণ করিল ॥ ৩২ ॥

অনন্তর কেশান্ত নামক ক্রিয়ানুষ্ঠানের পর রাজা রঘুর পরিণয় কার্য্য সমাপন করিলেন ; দক্ষের কন্যাগণ চন্দ্রকে পতিরূপে প্রাপ্ত হইয়া যেমন শোভা পাইয়াছিল, সেইরূপ রাজকন্যাগণ রঘুকে পতি পাইয়া শোভা পাইতে লাগিলেন ॥ ৩৩ ॥

and became invested with a new dignity of appearance.

33 Then after the ceremony of cropping the hair, Dileep got his son married. Pretty princesses joined to him by wedlook, looked as though they were the daughters of Daksha married to the moon.

युवा युगव्यायतबाहुरंसलः
कपाटवक्षाः परिणद्धकन्धरः ।
वपुःप्रकर्षादजयद्गुरुं रघुः
तथापि नीचैर्विनयाददृश्यत ॥ ३४ ॥

अथास्य यौवनावस्थोन्नततामाह, युवेति । युवा युगं नाम धुर्यस्कन्धगः तस्मिन्नुद्धृतास्तो यानाङ्गभूतो दारुविशेषः, युगवत् व्यायतौ दीर्घौ बाहू यस्य सः, अंसौ अस्य स्तः इति अंसलः बलवान् मांसलश्चेति हलिकारः कपाटवक्षाः परिणद्धकन्धरः विशालग्रीवः. रघुः वपुषः प्रकर्षात् आधिक्यात् यौवनजातात् गुरुं पितरम् अजयत्, तथापि विनयात् नम्रत्वेन, नीचैः अल्पकः अदृश्यत । अनौद्धत्यस्य विवक्षितम् ॥ ३४ ॥

যৌবনে রঘুর দেহ মাংসল, বাহুদ্বয় রথাশ্ব বন্ধনের কাষ্ঠ-দণ্ডের ন্যায় দীর্ঘ, বক্ষঃস্থল কপাটের ন্যায় বিশাল; ও গ্রীবা স্থূল হইয়া উঠিল। তিনি দেহের বিপুলতাতে পিতাকে ছাড়াইয়া উঠিলেন ; কিন্তু তথাপি স্বাভাবিক বিনয় বশতঃ তাঁহাকে ছোটই দেখাইত। ৩৪।

34 Youg, loug-armed, stout, broad-chested, and of ample shoulders, Raghu excelled even his great father in height and in strength ; though always looking rather lowly from the innate modesty of his nature.

परिणद्धकन्धरः—कं शिरः धरति धारयति वा कन्धरा ग्रीवा, परिणद्धा विशाला कन्धरा यस्य स विशालग्रीवः मांसलदेहशाली, बलशालीति भावः ।

ततः प्रजानां चिरमात्मना धृतां
नितान्तगुर्वीं लघयिष्यता धुरम्।
निसर्गसंस्कारविनीत इत्यसौ
नृपेण चक्रे युवराजशब्दभाक्॥ ३५॥
नरेन्द्रमूलायतनादनन्तरं
तदास्पदं श्रीर्युवराजसंज्ञितम्।

यथाति तस्य यौवराज्यमाह, तत इति। ततः आत्मना चिरं धृतां नितान्तगुर्वीं प्रजानां धुरं पालनप्रयासं, लघयिष्यता लघुं करिष्यता, नृपेण दिलीपेन, असौ रघुः, निसर्गेण स्वभावेन, संस्कारेण शास्त्राभ्यासजनितवासनया च विनीतः नम्रः, इति हेतोः युवराजः इति शब्दं भजतीति तथोक्तम्, चक्रे कृतः। "द्विविधो विनयः स्वाभाविकः कृत्रिमश्च" इति कौटिल्यः। तदुभयसम्पन्नत्वात् पुत्रं युवराजं चकार इत्यर्थः॥ ३५॥

नरेन्द्रेति। गुणान् विनयादीन् शौर्यादीन् च अभिलष्यतीति

অনন্তর দিলীপ, আপনা কর্ত্তৃক বহুকাল ধৃত রাজ্যভার লঘু করিবার মানসে, স্বভাবজাত, ও শিক্ষা লব্ধ বিনয়ে ভূষিত রঘুকে যুবরাজ পদে প্রতিষ্ঠিত করিলেন॥ ৩৫॥

লক্ষ্মী পুরাতন কমলের শোভা হইতে যেমন নূতন কমলে গমন করিয়া

---

35 Then the king desirous of lightening the load of his duties, relating to the State, which he had borne so long, made Rughu joint sharer of those duties, seeing that he was eminently fitted for them by reason of his education and good breeding.

36 The goddess of Dileep's kingly power, enamoured of

*अगमत्सहदंशेन युवाभिलाषिणी
नवावतारं कमलादिवोत्पलम् ॥ ३६ ॥

*

गुणाभिलाषिणी, श्रीः राजलक्ष्मीः, महात्मनः च, [illegible]ः दिलीपः, एव मूलायतनं प्रधानस्थानं, तस्मात् अपादानात्, [illegible] सन्निहितं युवराजः इति संज्ञा अस्य सञ्जाता युवराजसंज्ञित[illegible] आत्मनः पदं स्थानम् आस्पदम् आस्पदं प्रतिष्ठायामिति निपातः, [illegible] रघुः इति आस्पदं तदास्पदं, कमलात् चिरोत्पलात्, नवावतारम् [illegible]चिरोत्पलम्, उत्पलम् इव अंशेन अगमत् ॥ ३६ ॥

থাকেন, সেইরূপ গুণাভিলাষিণী রাজলক্ষ্মী আদি নিকেতন দিলীপ হইতে আংশিক-রূপে যুবরাজ রঘুতে সংক্রান্ত হইল ॥ ৩৬ ॥

---

the young prince's many virtues, as it were, partly got herself transfered to him, as Laksmi gets possession of a fresh lotus from the declining beauty of an old one.·

---

* अगमत्सहदंशेन—अंशेन अगमत् For explanation of the तृतीया in this passage, refer to वार्त्तिकसूत्र,—प्रकृत्यादिभ्य उपसंख्यानम् as quoted by the author of सिद्धान्तकौमुदी page 270 Taranath's edition, of 1863. Compare it with the examples समेनैति विषमेणैति । Or the तृतीया may also be explained by the rule,

गम्यमानापि क्रिया विभक्तौ प्रयोजिका ।

सिद्धान्तकौमुदी page 274.

As in the case of मतेन मतेन पाययति पयः—the तृतीया is to be explained by reference to an implied verb

*বিভাবসুঃ সারথিনেব বায়ুনা
†ঘনব্যপায়েন গভস্তিমানিব ।
বভূব তেনাতিতরাং সুদুঃসহঃ
কটপ্রভেদেন করীব পার্থিবঃ ॥ ৩৭ ॥

বিভাবসুরিতি । সারথিনা সহায়ভূতেন বায়ুনা বিভাবসুঃ বহ্নিঃ ইব, ঘনব্যপায়েন সারথিনা গভস্তিমান্ সূর্য্যঃ ইব, কটঃ গণ্ডঃ, তস্য প্রভেদঃ স্ফুটনং মদোদয়ঃ ইত্যর্থঃ, তেন করী ইব, পার্থিবঃ দিলীপঃ, তেন রঘুণা অতিতরাম্ অত্যন্তং, সুদুঃসহঃ সুষ্ঠু অসহ্যঃ বভূব ॥ ৩৭ ॥

বায়ু সারথি হইলে অগ্নির প্রতাপ যেমন বর্দ্ধিত হয়, মেঘ অপগত হইলে সূর্য্যের দীপ্তি যেমন প্রখর হয়, এবং গণ্ডদেশ হইতে মদ ক্ষরণ আরম্ভ হইলে গজরাজ যেরূপ দুঃসহ হয় সেইরূপ যুবরাজের সহায়তা পাইয়া দিলীপের প্রতাপ দুঃসহ হইয়া উঠিল ॥ ৩৭ ॥

37 As fire blezes up when fanned by the breeze ; as the sun becomes intolerable when clouds leave its path ; and as the elephant becomes dangerous, when its temples begin to open, so the power of king Dileep increased tenfold, when Raghu became a co-sharer of his regal duties.

> পরিচ্ছিদ্য here also, the student may explain it by reference to an implied verb বিভজ্য । রাজলক্ষ্মীঃ অংশেন অগমৎ অংশেন বিভজ্য অগমদিত্যর্থঃ ।

* বিভাবসুঃ—বিভা, দীপ্তিঃ, আভা এব বসু ধনং যস্য স বিভাবসুঃ অগ্নিঃ ।

† ঘনব্যপায়েন—ঘনানাং মেঘানাং ব্যপায়ঃ বিনাশস্তেন ।

निषुज्य तं होमतुरङ्गरक्षणे
धनुर्धरं राजसुतैरनुद्रुतम् ।
अपूर्णमेकेन शतक्रतूपमः
शतं क्रतूनामपविघ्नमाप सः ॥ ३८ ॥
ततः परं तेन मखाय यज्वना
तुरङ्गमुत्सृष्टमनर्गलं पुनः ।

नियुज्येति । शतक्रतुः इन्द्रः उपमा यस्य सः शतक्रतूपमः सः दिलीपः, राजसुतैः अनुद्रुतम् अनुगतं, धनुर्धरं तं रघुं, होमतुरङ्गरक्षणे नियुज्य, एकेन क्रतुना अपूर्णम् एकोनम्, क्रतूनाम् अश्वमेधानां, शतम् अपविघ्नं अपगतविघ्नम् यथा तथा आप ॥ ३८ ॥

तत इति । ततः परम्, एकोनशततमक्रतुसमाप्त्यनन्तरं, यज्वना विधिनेष्टवता, तेन दिलीपेन, पुनः पुनः अपि, मखाय मखं कर्तुम्, उत्सृष्टं तुरगम्, अनर्गलम् अप्रतिबन्धम्, अव्याहतस्वैरगतिम् इत्यर्थः, शतक्र

ইন্দ্রসমতেজস্বী দিলীপ ধনুর্দ্ধর রঘুকে রাজপুত্রগণ সঙ্গে দিয়া যজ্ঞীয় অশ্ব রক্ষণে নিযুক্ত করতঃ একোনশত সংখ্যক অশ্বমেধ যজ্ঞ নির্বিঘ্নে সমাপন করিলেন ॥ ৩৮ ॥

তৎপরে পুনরায় শততম যজ্ঞের জন্য অশ্ব ছাড়িয়া দিলে, স্বয়ং ইন্দ্র

38 By sending out Raghu, followed by other princes of his age, in charge of the sacrificial horse, Dileep, who resembled Indra, safely brought to completion ninety nine out of his projected hundred ceremonies of horse sacrifice.

39 On the occasion of the hundredth ceremony, Indra, by covering himself under invisibility stole away, from before the

ধনুর্ভৃতামগ্রত এব রক্ষিণাং
জহার শক্রঃ কিল গূঢ়বিগ্রহঃ* ॥৩৯॥
বিষাদলুপ্তপ্রতিপত্তি বিস্মিতং
কুমারসৈন্যং সপদি স্থিতঞ্চ তৎ ।
বশিষ্ঠধেনুশ্চ যদৃচ্ছয়াগতা
শ্রুতপ্রভাবা দদৃশেঽথ নন্দিনী ॥ ৪০ ॥

ধনুর্ভৃতাং রক্ষিণাং রক্ষকাণাম্, অগ্রতঃ এব, শক্রঃ গূঢ়বিগ্রহঃ সন্ জহার কিল ইতি ঐতিহ্যে ॥ ৩৯ ॥

বিষাদেতি। তৎ কুমারসৈন্যং যেন সপদি বিষাদঃ ইষ্টনাশজন্যঃ মনোভঙ্গঃ, তেন লুপ্তা প্রতিপত্তিঃ কর্তব্যজ্ঞানং যস্য, তৎ তথোক্তং বিস্মিতম্ অশ্বনাশস্য আকস্মিকত্বাৎ আশ্চর্যান্বিতং সৎ স্থিতং তস্থৌ। অথ শ্রুতপ্রভাবা যদৃচ্ছয়া স্বেচ্ছয়া আগতা, রঘোঃ স্বপ্রসাদজনকত্বাৎ

প্রচ্ছন্নাকার হইয়া ধনুর্ধারী রক্ষকদিগের সম্মুখ হইতেই অপ্রতিহত-গতি সেই অশ্বকে হরণ করিয়া লইয়া গেলেন। ৩৯।

কুমারের সৈন্য দল হঠাৎ বিপৎপাতে বিস্মিত ও হতবুদ্ধি হইয়া

---

eyes of the guards, the sacrificial horse, that Dileep had sent out on a journey for his last ceremony.

40 This sudden disappearance of the horse filled the minds of Raghu's army with sorrow and confusiou, but fortunalety at

---

* গূঢ়বিগ্রহঃ—গূঢ়ঃ সংবৃতঃ মায়য়া দর্শনাযোগ্যঃ কৃতঃ স্বশরীরঃ, বিগ্রহঃ দেহো যস্য সঃ গূঢ়বিগ্রহঃ। who, by his divine power, has made himself invisible.

তদঙ্গনিস্যন্দজলেন লোচনে
প্রমৃজ্য পুণ্যেন পুরস্কৃতঃ সতাম্ ।
*অতীন্দ্রিয়েষ্বপ্যুপপন্নদর্শনো
বভূব ভাবেষু দিলীপনন্দনঃ ॥ ৪১ ॥

অনুজিঘৃক্ষয়া ইতি ভাবঃ, নন্দিনী নাম বশিষ্ঠধেনুঃ দদৃশে। দৌ
বনাদৌ অবিতর্কিতাগতা ॥ ৪০ ॥

তদিতি। সতাং পুরস্কৃতঃ পূজিতঃ, দিলীপনন্দনঃ রঘুঃ, পুণ্যেন তস্যাঃ নন্দিন্যাঃ, অঙ্গং বপুঃ, তস্য নিস্যন্দঃ দ্রবঃ তস্য জলং মূত্রম্ তেন লোচনে প্রমৃজ্য শোধয়িত্বা, অতীন্দ্রিয়েষু ইন্দ্রিয়াণি অতিক্রান্তেষু, ভাবেষু অপি বস্তুষু, উপপন্নদর্শনঃ সম্পন্নসাক্ষাৎকারশক্তিঃ বভূব ॥ ৪১ ॥

রহিয়াছে, এমন সময়ে যদৃচ্ছাক্রমে বশিষ্ঠের সুবিখ্যাত ধেনু নন্দিনী দেখা দিলেন ॥ ৪০ ॥

সাধুজনের আদরণীয় রঘু সেই নন্দিনীর মূত্রবারি দ্বারা নয়নদ্বয় প্রক্ষালিত করিয়া অতীন্দ্রিয় বস্তু সকলও দর্শন করিবার শক্তি লাভ করিলেন ॥ ৪১ ॥

---

that very juncture arrived Nandini, the far-famed cow of Basista.

41 The son of Dileep,—he who was honored by the good—gave a wash to his eyes with the urine of this cow, and instantly received a second sight which enabled him to view things invinsible to mortal eyes.

* অতীন্দ্রিয়েষু—অতিক্রান্তানি ইন্দ্রিয়াণি চক্ষুরাদীনি যৈস্তে অতীন্দ্রিয়া বিষয়াস্তেষু।

स पूर्वतः पर्वतपक्षशातनं

ददर्श देवं नरदेवसम्भवः।

पुनः पुनः सूतनिषिद्धचापलं

हरन्तमश्वं रथरश्मिसंयतम्॥ ৪২ ॥

शतैस्तमक्ष्णामनिमेषवृत्तिभि-

र्हरिं विदित्वा हरिभिश्च वाजिभिः।

स इति। नरदेवसम्भवः सः रघुः, पुनः पुनः सूतेन निषिद्धचापलं निवारितचौर्यं, रथस्य रश्मिभिः प्रग्रहैः, संयतं बद्धम्, अश्वं हरन्तं पर्वतपक्षाणां शातनं छेदकं, देवम् इन्द्रं, पूर्वतः पूर्वस्यां दिशि ददर्श ॥ ৪২ ॥

शतैरिति। रघुः तम् अश्वहर्तारम्, अनिमेषवृत्तिभिः निमेष-व्यापारशून्यैः, अक्ष्णां शतैः, हरिभिः हरिद्वर्णैः, वाजिभिः अश्वैश्च,

---

অনন্তর রাজকুমার পূর্ব্বদিকে দৃষ্টিপাত করিয়া দেখিতে পাইলেন যে স্বয়ং দেবরাজ যজ্ঞীয় অশ্বকে নিজের রথরশ্মি দ্বারা সংযত করিয়া লইয়া যাইতেছেন, এবং ইন্দ্র-সারথি বার বার তাহার চপলতা নিবারণ করিতেছে ॥ ৪২ ॥

রঘু সেই অশ্ব হরণকারী দেবকে নিমেষবিহীন সহস্র লোচনের দ্বারা

---

42 And looking towards the east, the prince beheld the great god Indra stealing away his horse, whom he found fastened to the chariot of the god, and constantly lashed by the divine charioteer to overcome his shyness.

43 Raghu could at once know the god to be no other than the great Indra, by his thousand eyes, that never twinkled, and also by the green colour of his horses, and with a deep and

অবোচদেনং গগনস্পৃশা রঘুঃ
স্বরেণ ধীরেণ নিবর্ত্তয়ন্নিব ॥ ৪৩ ॥
মখাংশভাজাং প্রথমো মনীষিভি-
স্ত্বমেব দেবেন্দ্র ! সদা নিগদ্যসে ।
অজস্রদীক্ষাপ্রয়তস্য মদ্গুরোঃ
*ক্রিয়াবিঘাতায় কথং প্রবর্ত্তসে ॥ ৪৪ ॥

হরিম্ ইন্দ্রং, বিদিত্বা এনম্ ইন্দ্রং, গগনস্পৃশা ব্যোমব্যাপিনা, ধীরেণ, গভীরেণ, স্বরেণ ধ্বনিনা, এব নিবর্ত্তয়ন্ ইব অবোচৎ ॥ ৪৩ ॥

মখেতি। হে দেবেন্দ্র! মনীষিভিঃ ত্বম্ এব মখাংশভাজাং যজ্ঞভাগভুজাং, প্রথমঃ সদা নিগদ্যসে কথ্যসে, তথাপি অজস্রদীক্ষায়াং নিত্যদীক্ষায়াং,

---

ও হরিদ্বর্ণ অশ্ব সকলের দ্বারা ইন্দ্র বলিয়া জানিতে পারিয়া গগনস্পর্শী গম্ভীর ধ্বনিতে তাঁহাকে প্রতিনিবৃত্ত করিয়া বলিলেন ॥ ৪৩ ॥

হে দেবরাজ! পণ্ডিতগণ আপনাকে যজ্ঞাংশভাজন দেবগণের মধ্যে সর্ব্বপ্রধান বলিয়া বর্ণন করেন; আমার পিতা নিরন্তর যজ্ঞানুষ্ঠানে রত,

---

sonorous voice he addressed the following words to him ;—suddenly arresting his progress as it were.

44 You are reputed to be the chief, O Indra, of all those gods, who have a share in the offerings of a ceremony, how is it that you seem to be bent upon obstructing the ceremony of my father, who is constantly engaged in such pious acts.

* ক্রিয়াবিঘাতায়—ক্রিয়াং বিহন্তুমিত্যর্থঃ, তুমর্থাচ্চ ভাববচনাৎ ইতি চতুর্থী।

त्रिलोकनाथेन सदा मखद्विषः
स्त्वया नियम्या ननु दिव्यचक्षुषा ।
स चेत् स्वयं कर्म्मसु धर्म्मचारिणां
त्वमन्तरायो भवसि च्युतो विधिः ॥४५॥

भवतस्तु महद्गुणस्यैव, क्रियाविघातरूपं प्रतिविधानमिव, क्रियां विहन्तुम् इत्यर्थः, कथं प्रवर्त्तसे ॥ ४४ ॥

त्रिलोकेति । त्रयाणां लोकानां नाथः त्रिलोकनाथः तेन, त्रैलोक्यनियामकेन, दिव्यचक्षुषा अतीन्द्रियार्थदर्शिना, त्वया, मखद्विषः क्रतुविघातकाः, सदा नियम्याः ननु निग्राह्याः खलु, स त्वं धर्म्मचारिणां कर्म्मसु क्रतुषु, स्वयम् अन्तरायः विघ्नः भवसि चेत्, विधिः अनुष्ठानं, च्युतः नष्टः, लोके सत्कर्मकथैवास्तमियाद् इत्यर्थः ॥ ४५ ॥

আপনি তাঁহারই অনুষ্ঠানের বিঘ্ন উৎপাদন করিতে কেন উদ্যত হইয়াছেন ॥ ৪৪ ॥

আপনি ত্রিলোকপতি, আপনি দিব্য চক্ষে সমুদায় দেখিতেছেন, যজ্ঞের বিঘ্নকারীদিগকে দমন করাই আপনার কার্য্য, তাহা না হইয়া আপনি যদি স্বয়ং ধার্ম্মিকগণের ধর্ম্মানুষ্ঠানের বিঘ্নস্বরূপ হয়, তাহা হইলে ত আর ধর্ম্ম কর্ম্ম থাকে না ॥ ৪৫ ॥

45 You are the lord of the three worlds and you have eyes to see invisible things, and it is your duty to punish such, as obstruct these sacrifical ceremonies, but instead of that if you yourself thus choose to obstruct the ceremonies of the religious then all piety is at an end.

तदङ्गमग्र्यं मघवन् महाक्रतो-
रमुं तुरङ्गं प्रतिमोक्तुमर्हसि ।
पथः श्रुतेर्दर्शयितार ईश्वरा
*मलीमसामाददते न पद्धतिम् ॥ ४६ ॥
इति प्रगल्भं रघुणा समीरितं
वचो निशम्याधिपतिर्दिवौकसाम् ।

तदङ्गमिति । हे मघवन् ! तत् तस्मात् कारणात्, महाक्रतोः अश्वमेधस्य, अग्र्यं श्रेष्ठम्, अङ्गं साधनम्, अमुं तुरङ्गं, प्रतिमोक्तुं प्रतिदातुम्, अर्हसि । यस्माद्धि श्रुतेः पथः दर्शयितारः सन्मार्गप्रदर्शकाः, ईश्वराः, महात्मानः, मलीमसां मलिनानां, पद्धतिं मार्गं, न आददते न स्वीकुर्वते, अतस्त्वमिमं मावलम्बस्व इत्यर्थः ॥ ४६ ॥

इतीति । इति रघुणा समीरितं, प्रगल्भं वचः, निशम्य आकर्ण्य,

অতএব হে মঘবন্! যজ্ঞ কার্য্যের সর্ব্বশ্রেষ্ঠ সহায় এই অশ্বকে ছাড়িয়া দিন; আপনার ন্যায় মহাত্মাগণ শ্রুতিবিহিত মার্গের পথপ্রদর্শক, তাঁহারা পাপাচারীদিগের রীতি কখনই অবলম্বন করেন না। ॥ ৪৬ ॥

দেবকুলের অধিপতি, রঘুর এই বীরোক্তিপূর্ণ বচন শ্রবণ করিয়া

---

46 Leave then that horse, O Indra, it is the principal requisite for my father's ceremony, great ones like yourself should always show us the path of right and should on no account take to the dark ways of the sinners.

47. When the ruler of the gods heard these proud words,

* मलीमसां—मल+ईमस्+सस्—मलिनानां पापजनानामित्यर्थः ;—the ways of sinful men.

निवर्त्तयामास रथं सविस्मयः
*प्रचक्रमे च प्रतिवक्तुमुत्तरम् ॥ ४७ ॥

यदात्थ राजन्यकुमार ! तत् तथा
यशस्तु रक्ष्यं परतो यशोधनैः ।
जगत्प्रकाशं तदशेषमिज्यया
भवद्गुरुर्लङ्घयितुं ममोद्यतः ॥ ४८ ॥

दिवौकसः स्वर्गौकसः तेषाम् अधिपतिः देवेन्द्रः, रघुप्रभावात् सविस्मयः सन्, रथं निवर्त्तयामास, उत्तरं प्रतिवक्तुं प्रचक्रमे च ॥ ४७ ॥

यदिति। हे राजन्यकुमार। क्षत्रियकुमार ! यत् वाक्यम् आत्थ ब्रवीषि, तत् तथा सत्यं, किन्तु यशोधनैः यशआढ्यैः, परतः शत्रुतः,

---

বিস্ময়ান্বিত হইয়া রথ ফিরাইলেন এবং প্রত্যুত্তরে বলিতে লাগিলেন ॥ ৪৭ ॥

হে ক্ষত্রিয়কুমার ! তুমি যাহা বলিলে তাহা সত্য ; কিন্তু নিজ যশকে যাঁহারা মূল্যবান মনে করেন, তাঁহাদের পক্ষে পরহস্ত হইতে সেই যশকে

---

his wonder was great, and he turned the chariot to make the following reply.

48. Whatever thou sayest, O thou son of a Kshatriya, is true, but those, who value their good name must needs strive

प्रचक्रमे—क्रम is a परस्मैपदी धातुः, but on account of the उपसर्ग प्र it becomes आत्मनेपदी, according to rule, प्रोपाभ्यां समर्थाभ्यां (१।३।४२) *Panini* or प्रोपादारम्भे—(मं ८६४) *Mugdhabodha.*

हरिर्यथैकः पुरुषोत्तमः स्मृतः
महेश्वरस्त्र्यम्बक एव नापरः ।
तथा विदुर्मां मुनयः शतक्रतुम्
द्वितीयगामी न हि शब्द एष नः ॥४९॥

यशः रक्ष्यम्। ततः किमत आह, भवद्गुरुः त्वत्पिता, जगत्प्रकाशं लोकप्रसिद्धम्, अशेषं सर्वं, मम तत् यशः, इज्यया कार्येन, बहुविधेन तिरस्कर्त्तुम् उद्यतः उद्युक्तः ॥ ४८ ॥

किं तद् यश इत्याह, हरिरिति। यथा हरिः विष्णुः, एकः एव पुरुषोत्तमः स्मृतः, यथा च त्र्यम्बकः शिवः एव महेश्वरः स्मृतः, न अपरः, अपरः पुमान् न तथा, मां मुनयः शतक्रतुं विदुः विदन्ति, नः अस्माकं हरिहरयोर्मम च इत्यर्थः, एषः त्रितयः अपि शब्दः द्वितीयगामी न हि ॥ ४९ ॥

রক্ষা করা কর্ত্তব্য। তোমার পিতা যজ্ঞানুষ্ঠান দ্বারা আমার লোক-প্রসিদ্ধ যশকে খর্ব্ব করিবার জন্য উদ্যত হইয়াছেন ॥ ৪৮ ॥

পুরুষোত্তম বলিলে যেমন একমাত্র বিষ্ণুকেই বুঝায়, ত্র্যম্বক বলিলে যেমন একমাত্র শম্ভুকেই বুঝায়, সেইরূপ মুনিগণ একমাত্র আমাকেই শতক্রতু বলিয়া জানিতেন, এই শব্দ অদ্যাপি দ্বিতীয় ব্যক্তিতে বর্ত্তে নাই ॥ ৪৯ ॥

to protect it. Consider how thy sire is bent upon robbing me of one of my world-wide distinction. by rivalling me with his sacrificial ceremonies.

49. As by the word "*Purushottam*" none other than the great Vishnu is meant ; and as by the word "*Maheshwar*" the great Siva alone is implied, so it is my sole privilege to be

अतोऽयमश्वः कपिलानुकारिणा
पितुस्त्वदीयस्य मयापहारितः।

अत इति। यतः अहम् एव शतक्रतुः, अतः त्वदीयस्य पितुः अयं शततमः अश्वः, कपिलानुकारिणा कपिलमुनितुल्येन मया अपहारितः अपहृतः, तव अत्र अश्वे प्रयत्नेन अलं, प्रयासो माकारि, निषेधस्य

অতএব মহামুনি কপিলের অনুকরণ করিয়া আমি তোমার পিতার

styled *Satakratu* (viz he who has performed hundred ceremo-mes) the term cannot be shared by any other person.

50. Accordingly, following the example of Kapila, I have

कपिलानुकारिणा—यथा पूर्वं सगरस्य राज्ञो अश्वमेधतुरङ्गमः कपिलेन महर्षिणा हृत आसीत्, तद्वत् मयापि भवत्पितुस्तुरङ्गमो हृत इत्यर्थः। In connection with this the following story is told in the *Mahabharat* (वनपर्व) :—

इक्ष्वाकूणां कुले जातः सगरो नाम पार्थिवः।
रूपसत्त्वबलोपेतः स चापुत्रः प्रतापवान् ॥ ७ ॥
स हैहयान् समुत्साद्य तालजङ्घांश्च भारत !।
वशे च कृत्वा राजन्यान् स्वराज्यमन्वशासत ॥ ८ ॥
तस्य भार्ये त्वभवतां रूपयौवनदर्पिते।
वैदर्भी भरतश्रेष्ठ ! शैब्या च भरतर्षभ ! ॥ ९ ॥
स पुत्रकामो नृपति-स्तप्यते स्म महत्तपः।
पत्नीभ्यां सह राजेन्द्र ! कैलासं गिरिमाश्रितः ॥ १० ॥
स तप्यमानः सुमहत् तपोयोगसमन्वितः।
आससाद महात्मानं त्र्यक्षं त्रिपुरमर्द्दनम् ॥ ११ ॥ * * *
तं प्रीतिमान् हरः प्राह सभार्यं नृपसत्तमम्।
यस्मिन् वृतो मुहूर्तेऽहं त्वयेह नृपते ! वरम् ॥ १४ ॥

षष्टिः पुत्रसहस्राणि शूराः समरदर्पिताः ।
एकस्यां सम्भविष्यन्ति पत्न्यां नरवरोत्तम ! ॥ १५ ॥
ते चैव सर्वे सहिताः क्षयं यास्यन्ति पार्थिव ! ।
एको वंशधरः शूर एकस्यां सम्भविष्यति ॥ १६ ॥
एवमुक्त्वा तु तं रुद्र-स्तत्रैवान्तरधीयत ।
स चापि सगरो राजा जगाम स्वं निवेशनम् ॥ १७ ॥
पत्नीभ्यां सहितस्तात सोऽतिहृष्टमनास्तदा ।
तस्य ते मनुजश्रेष्ठ ! भार्ये कमललोचने ॥ १८ ॥
वैदर्भी चैव शैब्या च गर्भिण्यौ संबभूवतुः ।
ततः कालेन वैदर्भी गर्भालाबुं व्यजायत ॥ १९ ॥
शैब्या च सुषुवे पुत्रं कुमारं देवरूपिणम् ।
तदालाबुं समुत्स्रष्टुं मनश्चक्रे स पार्थिवः ॥ २० ॥
अथान्तरीक्षाच्छुश्राव वाचं गम्भीरनिस्वनाम् ।
राजन् ! मा साहसं कार्षीः पुत्रान् न त्यक्तुमर्हसि ॥ २१ ॥
अलाबुमध्यान्निष्कृष्य बीजं यत्नेन गोप्यताम् ।
सोपस्वेदेषु पात्रेषु घृतपूर्णेषु भागशः ॥ २२ ॥
ततः पुत्रसहस्राणि षष्टिं प्राप्स्यसि भारत ! ।
अनेन क्रमयोगेन मा ते बुद्धिरतोऽन्यथा ॥ २३ ॥ * * *
एतच्छ्रुत्वान्तरीक्षाच्च स राजा राजसत्तमः ।
यथोक्तं तच्चकाराथ श्रद्दधद्भरतर्षभ ! ॥ १ ॥
एकैकशस्ततः कृत्वा बीजं बीजं नराधिपः ।
घृतपूर्णेषु कुम्भेषु तान् भागान् निदधे ततः ॥ २ ॥
धात्रीश्चैकैकशः प्रादात् पुत्ररक्षणतत्परः ।
ततः कालेन महता समुत्तस्थुर्महाबलाः ॥ ३ ॥
षष्टिः पुत्रसहस्राणि तस्याप्रतिमतेजसः ।
रुद्रप्रसादाद्राजर्षेः समजायन्त पार्थिव ! ॥ ४ ॥ * * *
ततः काले बहुतिथे व्यतीते भरतर्षभ ! ।

अलं प्रयत्नेन तवात्र मा निधाः
पदं †पदव्यां सगरस्य सन्ततेः ॥ ५० ॥

निषेधं प्रति कारणत्वात् इतीवा । सगरस्य राज्ञः सन्ततेः सन्तानस्य पदव्यां पदं मा निधाः न निधेहि। महदास्कन्दनं विनाशमूलं भवेत् इति भावः ॥ ५० ॥

এই অশ্ব হরণ করিয়াছি। তুমি এবিষয়ে বৃথা প্রয়াস পাইও না; সগর-সন্তানদিগের পদবীতে পদার্পণ করিও না ॥ ৫০ ॥

---

stolen away thy father's horse. Desist from all further struggle. Do not tempt the fate of the sons of king Sagar.

दीक्षितः सगरो राजा हयमेधेन वीर्य्यवान् ॥ ११ ॥
तस्याऽश्वो व्यचरद्भूमिं पुत्रैः सम्परिरक्षितः ।
समुद्रं स समासाद्य निस्तोयं भीमदर्शनम् ॥ १२ ॥
रक्ष्यमाणः प्रयत्नेन तत्रैवान्तरधीयत ।
ततस्ते सागरास्तात ! हृतं मत्वा हयोत्तमम् ॥ १३ ॥
आगम्य पितुराचख्यु-रदृश्यं तुरगं हृतम् ।
तेनोक्ता दिक्षु सर्व्वासु सर्व्वे मार्गत वाजिनम् ॥ १४ ॥
ततस्ते पितुराज्ञाय दिक्षु सर्व्वासु तं हयम् ।
अमार्गन्त महाराज ! सर्व्वञ्च पृथिवीतलम् ॥ १५ ॥ * * *
एवं हि खनतां तेषां समुद्रं वरुणालयम् ।
व्यतीतः सुमहान् कालो न चाऽश्वः समदृश्यत ॥ २७ ॥
ततः पूर्व्वोत्तरे देशे समुद्रस्य महीपते ! ।
विदार्य्य पातालमथ संक्रुद्धाः सगरात्मजाः ॥ २८ ॥
अपश्यन्त हयं तत्र विचरन्तं महीतले ।
कपिलञ्च महात्मानं तेजोराशिमनुत्तमम् ।
तेजसा दीप्यमानन्तु ज्वालाभिरिव पावकम् ॥ २९ ॥

† पदव्यां सगरस्य सन्ततेः—सगरपुत्रा यथा कपिलक्रोधात् विनष्टा

ततः प्रहस्यापभयः पुरन्दरं
पुनर्बभाषे तुरगस्य रक्षिता।

तत इति। ततः तुरगस्य रक्षिता रघुः, प्रहस्य प्रहासं कृत्वा, अपभयः निर्भीकः सन्, पुनः पुरन्दरं बभाषे। किमिति? हे देवेन्द्र! यदि एषः अश्वामोचनरूपः, ते तव, सर्गः निश्चयः, तर्हि शस्त्रं गृहाण;

अनन्तर निर्भीक রঘু হাস্য করিয়া ইন্দ্রকে কহিলেন, যদি তোমার

51. The fearless prince laughed at these words and thus replied :—"If that be thy decision, then take up thy arms,

आसन् तथा मम कोपाग्नौ शलभतां मा व्रज इत्यर्थः; In connection with this the following story is told in the Ramayana of *Valmiki*. (बालकाण्डम् ४० सर्गः।)

ते तु सर्वे महात्मानो भीमवेगा महाबलाः।
ददृशुः कपिलं तत्र वासुदेवं सनातनम्॥ २५॥
हयञ्च तस्य देवस्य चरन्तमविदूरतः।
प्रहर्षमतुलं प्राप्ताः सर्वे ते रघुनन्दन!॥ २६॥
ते तं यज्ञहनं ज्ञात्वा क्रोधपर्याकुलेक्षणाः।
खनित्रलाङ्गलधरा नानावृक्षशिलाधराः॥ २७॥
अभ्यधावन्त संक्रुद्धास्तिष्ठ तिष्ठेति चाब्रुवन्।
अस्माकं त्वं हि तुरगं यज्ञियं हृतवानसि॥ २८॥
दुर्मेधस्त्वं हि संप्राप्तान् विद्धि नः सगरात्मजान्।
श्रुत्वा तद्वचनं तेषां कपिलो रघुनन्दन!॥ २९॥
रोषेण महताविष्टो हुङ्कारमकरोत् तदा।
ततस्तेनाप्रमेयेण कपिलेन महात्मना।
भस्मराशीकृताः सर्वे काकुत्स्थ! सगरात्मजाः॥ ३०॥

गृहाण शस्त्रं यदि सर्ग एष ते
न खल्वनिर्जित्य रघुं कृती भवान् ॥५१॥

स एवमुक्त्वा मघवन्तमुन्मुखः
करिष्यमाणः सशरं शरासनम् ।
अतिष्ठदालीढविशेषशोभिना
वपुःप्रकर्षेण विडम्बितेश्वरः ॥ ५२ ॥

भवान् रघुं माम् अनिर्जित्य, कृतमनेनेति कृती कृतकृत्यः, न खलु ; रघुमित्यनेनात्मनो दुर्जयत्वं सूचितम् ॥ ५१ ॥

स इति । सः रघुः उन्मुखः सन्, मघवन्तम् इन्द्रम् एवम् उक्त्वा, शरासनं चापं सशरं करिष्यमाणः आलीढेन आलीढाख्येन स्थानकभेदेन, विशेषशोभिना अतिशयशोभिना, वपुप्रकर्षेण देहौन्नत्येन, विडम्बितेश्वरः अनुकृतपिनाकी सन् अतिष्ठत् । आलीढलक्षणमाह यादवः, "स्थानानि धन्विनां पञ्च तत्र वैशाखमस्त्रियाम् । त्रिवि

এইরূপই নিশ্চয়, তবে শস্ত্র গ্রহণ কর, রঘুকে জয় না করিয়া তুমি অশ্ব হরণ করিতে পারিবে না ॥ ৫১ ॥

ঊর্দ্ধমুখে ইন্দ্রকে এই কথা বলিয়া রঘু যখন শরাসনে জ্যারোপণ করিতে প্রবৃত্ত হইলেন, তখন তাঁহার সমুন্নত দেহ আলীঢ়নামক ধনু

thou must not consider thyself a successful plunderer until thou hast conquered Raghu.

52. Thus he said and as he stood, with his face turned upwords, fitting his arrows, his bow-string to the attitude of his manly frame was the same as is called *alirah* in the science of archery, by virtue of which he resembled the great god Sivæ himself, in the act of drawing his bow-string.

रघोरवष्टम्भमयेन पत्रिणा
हृदि क्षतो गोत्रभिदप्यमर्षणः ।
नवाम्बुदानीकमुहूर्त्तलाञ्छने
धनुष्यमोघं समधत्त सायकम् ॥ ५३ ॥

तस्यान्तरौ पादौ मण्डलं नीरव्याकति। अर्थं त्वात् समपदम् आलीढन्तु ततोऽपरः। दक्षिणो वाममाकुञ्च प्रत्यालीढं विपर्ययः' इति ॥ ५२ ॥

रघोरिति। रघोः अवष्टम्भमयेन स्तम्भरूपेण, पत्रिणा बाणेन, हृदि हृदये, क्षतः विद्धः, अतएव अमर्षणः असहनः क्रुद्धः इत्यर्थः, गोत्रभित् इन्द्रः अपि, नवाम्बुदानाम्, अनीकस्य वृन्दस्य, मुहूर्त्तं क्षणमात्रं, लाञ्छने चिह्नभूते, धनुषि दिव्ये धनुषि इत्यर्थः, अमोघम् अवन्ध्यं, सायकं बाणं, समधत्त संहितवान् ॥ ५३ ॥

বিদ্ধ। প্রসিদ্ধ উপবেশনপ্রণালীবশতঃ অপূর্ব্ব শ্রী ধারণ করিল, এবং ত্রিদবস্থ শত্রুর ন্যায় দেখাইতে লাগিল ॥ ৫২ ॥

রঘুর স্তম্ভরূপী বাণের দ্বারা হৃদয়ে আহত হইয়া দেবরাজ কুপিত হইলেন, এবং নবজলধরে ক্ষণকাল প্রকাশমান ধনুতে অব্যর্থ শর আরোপ করিলেন ॥ ৫৩ ॥

53. The arrow of Raghu struck like a massive pillar on the breast of Indra, who incensed at the attack put an arrow, that was sure of its mark, on the string of his famous bow, which appears as a temporary signal on a volume of new clouds,-viz the rain-bow.

दिलीपसूनोः स वृहद्भुजान्तरं
प्रविश्य भीमासुरशोणितोचितः।
पपावनास्वादितपूर्वमाशुगः
कुतूहलेनेव मनुष्यशोणितम्॥ ५४॥
हरेः कुमारोऽपि कुमारविक्रमः
सुरद्विपास्फालनकर्कशाङ्गुलौ।

दिलीपेति। भीमानां भयङ्कराणाम्, असुराणां, शोणिते रुधिरे, उचितः परिचितः, सः इन्द्रयुक्तः, आशुगः सायकः, दिलीपसूनोः रघोः, वृहत् विशालं, भुजान्तरं वक्षः, प्रविश्य, अनास्वादितपूर्वं पूर्वम् अनास्वादितम्, मनुष्यशोणितं कुतूहलेन इव पपौ॥ ५४॥

हरेरिति। कुमारस्य स्कन्दस्य विक्रमः इव विक्रमः यस्य सः, तथोक्तः कुमारः रघुः अपि, सुरद्विपस्य ऐरावतस्य, आस्फालनेन कर्कशाः अङ्गुलयः यस्य सः, तस्मिन् शच्याः पत्रविशेषकैः अङ्किते शचीपत्रविशेषकाङ्किते, हरेः इन्द्रस्य, भुजे, स्वनामचिह्नं स्वनामाङ्कितं,

প্রচণ্ড দৈত্যগণের শোণিতপানে চিরাভ্যস্ত ইন্দ্রাস্ত্র দিলীপনন্দনের সুবিশাল বক্ষঃস্থলে প্রবিষ্ট হইয়া অনাস্বাদিতপূর্ব্ব নররুধির যেন আনন্দে পান করিতে লাগিল। ৫৪।

ইন্দ্রের যে বাহুর অঙ্গুলি সকল ঐরাবতের তাড়না দ্বারা কর্কশ এবং যে বাহু শচী কর্ত্তৃক অর্পিত পত্রাবলী দ্বারা চিহ্নিত সেই বাহুতে কার্ত্তি-

---

54. That arrow, long used in drinking the blood of great Asuras, plunged deep into the bosom of Raghu, and drank, with ardour as it were, the blood of man, which it had never tasted before.

55, The prince too, who resembled the great Kartika in valour, planted an arrow, bearing his own name, on the arm

भुजे शचीपत्रविशेषकाङ्किते
स्वनामचिह्नं निचखान सायकम् ॥५५॥
जहार चान्येन मयूरपत्रिणा
शरेण शक्रस्य महाशनिध्वजम्।
चुकोप तस्मै स भृशं सुरश्रियः
प्रसह्य केशव्यपरोपणादिव ॥५६॥

सायकं निचखान निखातवान्। निष्कण्टकराज्ये शक्राय महानभिभवः इति भावः ॥ ५५ ॥

जहारेति। अन्येन मयूरपत्रिणा मयूरपत्रवता, शरेण शक्रस्य महाशनिध्वजं महान्तम् अशनिरूपं ध्वजं, जहार चिच्छेद च, सः शक्रः सुरश्रियः प्रसह्य बलात्कृत्य, केशानां व्यपरोपणात् अवतारणात्, छेदनात् इव तस्मै रघवे भृशम् अत्यर्थं चुकोप तं हन्तुमिवेष इत्यर्थः ॥५६

কের তুল্য বলশালী রঘু স্বনামচিহ্নিত বাণ গাঢ়রূপে প্রবিষ্ট করিলেন ॥ ৫৫ ॥

এবং ময়ূরপক্ষ সমন্বিত অন্য বাণের দ্বারা ইন্দ্রের বজ্রধ্বজকে কাটিয়া ফেলিলেন; তাহাতে ইন্দ্র সাতিশয় কুপিত হইলেন, তাঁহার বোধ হইল যেন কেহ বলপূর্ব্বক সুরলক্ষ্মীর কেশাকর্ষণ পূর্ব্বক সেই কেশ ছেদন করিল ॥ ৫৬ ॥

of Indra, whose fingers were hardened by the constant goading of the elephant *Airabata* and on which Sachi, his wife, had cast many figures, in paint, as a token of her love.

56. And with another arrow, bearing peacock-plumes, he cut down the thunder-flag of Indra's chariot; whereupon Indra was highly incensed, as if it was the forcible lopping off of the hairs of the goddess of her heavenly fortunes.

तयोरुपान्तस्थितसिद्धसैनिकं
गरुत्मदाशीविषभीमदर्शनैः ।
बभूव युद्धं तुमुलं जयैषिणो-
रधोमुखैरूर्द्ध्वमुखैश्च पत्रिभिः ॥ ५७ ॥

अतिप्रबन्धप्रहितास्त्रवृष्टिभि-
स्तमाश्रयं दुष्प्रसहस्य तेजसः ।

तयोरिति। जयैषिणोः अन्योन्यजयाकाङ्क्षिणोः, तयोः इन्द्ररघ्वोः, गरुत्मन्तः पक्षवन्तः, आशीविषा आशिषि दंष्ट्रायां विषं येषां ते आशीविषाः सर्पाः, ते इव भीमदर्शनैः सपक्षाः सर्पाः इव भयावहाः इत्यर्थः, तैः अधोमुखैः ऊर्द्ध्वमुखैश्च धन्विनोरुपर्य्यधोदेशावस्थितत्वात् इति भावः, पत्रिभिः बाणैः उपान्तस्थिताः तटस्थाः सिद्धाः देवाः इन्द्रस्य सैनिकाश्च रघोः यस्मिन् तत् तथोक्तं, तुमुलं सङ्कुलं युद्धं बभूव ॥ ५७ ॥

अतीति। वासवः अतिप्रबन्धेन अतिसातत्येन, प्रहिताभिः प्रयुक्ताभिः, अस्त्रवृष्टिभिः दुष्प्रसहस्य दुःखेन प्रसह्यते इति दुष्प्रसहस्तस्य दुःखे-

---

আকাশমার্গে সিদ্ধগণ এবং ধরাপৃষ্ঠে রঘুর সৈনিক দল একপার্শ্বে দাঁড়াইয়া দেখিতে লাগিল; আর তাঁহাদের উভয়ের তুমুল যুদ্ধ চলিতে লাগিল; বাণ সকল যখন উর্দ্ধমুখে ও অধোমুখে ছুটিতে লাগিল, তখন তাহাদিগকে দেখিয়া পক্ষধারী সর্পের ন্যায় বোধ হইতে লাগিল ॥ ৫৭ ॥

মেঘ যেমন স্বচ্যুত বজ্রাগ্নিকে বৃষ্টিজলের দ্বারা নির্ব্বাণ করিতে পারে

---

57. The armies of both were standing aside as silent spectators, whilst the two combatants entered upon a mortal fight, their arrows flying upwards and downwards, like so many winged serpents.

58. Even with his ceaseless shower of missiles, Indra could

शशाक निर्वापयितुं न वासवः
स्वतश्च्युतं वह्निमिवाद्भिरम्बुदः ॥ ५८ ॥
ततः प्रकोष्ठे हरिचन्दनाङ्किते
प्रमथ्यमानार्णवधीरनादिनीम्
रघुः शशाङ्कार्द्धमुखेन पत्रिणा
शरासनज्यामलुनाद्विड़ौजसः ॥ ५९ ॥

नाप्यसह्यस्य इत्यर्थः. तेजसः प्रतापस्य, आश्रयं तं रघुम्, अम्बुदः अद्भिः स्वतः च्युतं निर्गतं वह्निम् इव, निर्वापयितुं न शशाक । रघोरपि लोकपालात्मकत्वेन्द्रांशसम्भवत्वात् इति भावः ॥ ५८ ॥

तत इति । ततः रघुः, हरिचन्दनाङ्किते प्रकोष्ठे मणिबन्धे, प्रमथ्यमानार्णवधीरनादिनीं प्रमथ्यमानार्णवः इव धीरं गम्भीरं नदतीति तां तथोक्तां, वेवेष्टि व्याप्नोतीति विट् व्यापकम् ओजः यस्य सः तस्य विड़ौजसः इन्द्रस्य, शरासनज्यां धनुर्मौर्वीं शशाङ्कस्य अर्द्धः खण्डः इव मुखं फलं यस्य तेन पत्रिणा अलुनात् अच्छिनत् ॥ ५९ ॥

না, সেইরূপ দেবরাজও অবিশ্রান্ত শরবৃষ্টি করিয়াও দুঃসহ তেজের আকর রঘুকে পরাভব করিতে পারিলেন না ॥ ৫৮ ॥

অনন্তর ইন্দ্রের যে শরাসন-জ্যা তাঁহার হরিচন্দনচর্চ্চিত মণিবন্ধে মন্থনকালীন সমুদ্রের ন্যায় ঘন ঘন ঘর্ঘরধ্বনি করিতেছিল, রঘু তাহা অর্দ্ধচন্দ্রাকৃতি বাণের দ্বারা ছিন্ন করিয়া ফেলিলেন ॥ ৫৯ ॥

---

not extinguish the fiery youth, just as the clouds fail to extinguish the fire of lightening, though emanating from themselves.

59. At last Raghu, with a crescent-shaped arrow, cut through the bow-string of Indra, which was roaring, at his wrist, be-decked with Harichandana, as roared the ocean during the churning process.

स चापमुत्सृज्य विवृद्धमत्सरः
प्रणाशनाय प्रबलस्य विद्विषः।
*महीध्रपक्षव्यपरोपणोचितं
स्फुरत्प्रभामण्डलमस्त्रमाददे ॥ ६० ॥
रघुर्भृशं वक्षसि तेन ताडितः
पपात भूमौ सह सैनिकाश्रुभिः।

स इति। विवृद्धमत्सरः प्रवृद्धवैरः, सः इन्द्रः, चापम् उत्सृज्य प्रबलस्य विद्विषः शत्रोः, प्रणाशनाय वधाय, महीं धारयन्तीति महीध्राः पर्वताः, तेषां पक्षव्यपरोपणे पक्षच्छेदे उचितं, स्फुरत्प्रभामण्डलम् अस्त्रं वज्रायुधम्, आददे जग्राह ॥ ६० ॥

रघुरिति। रघुः तेन वज्रेण, भृशम् अत्यर्थं, वक्षसि ताड़ितः सन् सैनिकानाम् अश्रुभिः सह भूमौ पपात, तस्मिन् पतिते ते रुरुदुः

দেবরাজ অতিশয় প্রকুপিত হইয়া শরাসন পরিত্যাগ পূর্ব্বক, প্রবল শত্রুর বিনাশোদ্দেশে, পর্ব্বতকুলের পক্ষচ্ছেদে চিরাভ্যস্ত, দীপ্তিশালী বজ্রাস্ত্র ধারণ করিলেন ॥ ৬০ ॥

রঘু সেই বজ্রাস্ত্র দ্বারা বক্ষঃস্থলে ভয়ানকরূপে আহত হইয়া ধরাতলে

60. Highly enraged, and resolved to destroy a powerful enemy, Indra laid aside his bow and took up the famous thunder-arm, encircled with rays of light, and long used in lopping off the wings of mountains.

61. Struck with that terrible weapon on his breast Raghu

---

* महीध्रपक्षव्यपरोपणोचितं—महीं पृथिवीं धारयन्ति (धृ+क) ये ते महीध्राः पर्व्वतास्तेषां पक्षाणां व्यपरोपणे छेदने उचितं अभ्यस्तं वज्रास्त्रमित्यर्थः।

निमेषमात्रादवधूय तद्व्यथां
सहोत्थितः सैनिकहर्षनिस्वनैः ॥ ६१ ॥

तथापि *शस्त्रव्यवहारनिष्ठुरे
विपक्षभावे चिरमस्य तस्थुषः ।
तुतोष वीर्य्यातिशयेन वृत्रहा
पदं हि सर्वत्र गुणैर्निधीयते ॥ ६२ ॥

इत्यर्थः, निमेषमात्रात् तद्व्यथां दुःखम्, अवधूय तिरस्कृत्य, सैनिकानां ये हर्षस्य निस्वनाः शब्दाः तैः सह उत्थितश्च ; तस्मिन् उत्थिते हर्षात् सिंहनादांश्चक्रुः इत्यर्थः ॥ ६१ ॥

तथापीति । तथापि वज्रपातेऽपि, शस्त्राणाम् आयुधानां व्यवहारेण व्यापारेण, निष्ठुरे क्रूरे, विपक्षभावे शात्रवे, चिरं तस्थुषः स्थितवतः अस्य रघोः वीर्य्यातिशयेन, हतं कृतवान् इति वृत्रहा

পতিত হইলেন ; অমনি সৈন্যদলের হাহাকার ধ্বনি উত্থিত হইল ; কিন্তু ক্ষণকালের মধ্যেই আবার সেই ব্যথাকে ঝাড়িয়া ফেলিয়া সৈনিকদিগের আনন্দধ্বনির সহিত উত্থিত হইলেন ॥ ৬১ ॥

বজ্রের আঘাত সহ্য করিয়াও সেই কঠোর সংগ্রামে রঘুকে পুনরায় বিপক্ষভাবে দণ্ডায়মান হইতে দেখিয়া, তাঁহার আশ্চর্য্য বলশালিতা অনু-

---

fell to the ground, along with the teares of his army ; but in a moment, shaking off the pain as it were, he once more stood up, amidst the shouts of his men.

62. When Indra saw him standing up once more, to carry

* शस्त्रव्यवहारनिष्ठुरे—शस्त्राणां आयुधानां व्यवहारेण पुनः पुनः प्रयोगेण निष्ठुरे क्रूरे ।

असङ्गमद्रिष्वपि सारवत्तया
न मे त्वदन्येन विसोढमायुधम् ।
अवेहि मां प्रीतमृते तुरङ्गमात्
किमिच्छसीति स्फुटमाह वासवः ॥६३॥

तुतोष ; स्वयं वीर एव वीरं जानाति इति भावः ; कथं शत्रोः सन्तोषोऽत आह, गुणैः सर्वत्र शत्रुमित्रोदासीनेषु पदम् अङ्घ्रिः निधीयते गुणैः सर्वत्र संक्रम्यते इत्यर्थः । गुणाः शत्रूनप्यावर्ज्जयन्ति इति भावः ॥ ६२ ॥

असङ्गमिति । सारवत्तया अद्रिषु अपि असङ्गम् अप्रतिबन्धं मे आयुधं वज्रं, त्वदन्येन न विसोढम् ; अतः मां प्रीतं सन्तुष्टम् अवेहि, तुरङ्गमात् ऋते, तुरङ्गं वर्ज्जयित्वा, किम् इच्छसि, इति, स्फुटं वासवः आह, तुरङ्गमात् अन्यददेयं नास्ति इति भावः ॥ ६३ ॥

ভব করিয়া দেবরাজ অতিশয় প্রীত হইলেন ;—গুণ থাকিলে, তাহা আপনার প্রাপ্য আদর সর্ব্বত্রই লাভ করে। ৬২ ।

আমার যে বজ্রাস্ত্র পর্ব্বতপৃষ্ঠেও বাধা পায় নাই, তোমা ভিন্ন কেহই সেই অস্ত্রকে সহ্য করিতে পারে নাই, আমি দেখিয়া বড়ই প্রীতি লাভ করিয়াছি, অতএব এই অশ্ব ভিন্ন আর কি প্রার্থনা কর বল ॥ ৬৩ ॥

on that terrible fight with murderous weapons, he was exceedingly pleased with his courage ; true merit seldom fails to find its appreciaton.

63. The power of my mighty weapon, which did not receive a check even from high mountains, has never been withstood by a second being but thyself. Know that I am much pleased with thy valour. Apart from this horse, ask of me any other favour.

ततो निषङ्गादसमग्रमुद्धृतं
*सुवर्णपुङ्खद्युतिरञ्जिताङ्गुलिम् ।
नरेन्द्रसूनुः प्रतिसंहरन्निषुं
प्रियंवदः प्रत्यवदत् सुरेश्वरम् ॥ ६४ ॥
अमोच्यमश्वं यदि मन्यसे प्रभो !
ततः समाप्ते विधिनैव कर्मणि ।

तत इति । ततः निषङ्गात् तूणीरात्, असमग्रं यथा तथा उद्धृतं, सुवर्णपुङ्खद्युतिभिः रञ्जिताः अङ्गुलयः येन तम्, इषुं प्रतिसंहरन् निवर्त्तयन्, नाप्रहरन्तं प्रहरेदिति निषेधात् इति भावः ; प्रियं वदतीति प्रियंवदः, नरेन्द्रसूनुः रघुः, सुरेश्वरं प्रत्यवदत् न तु प्राहरत् इति भावः ॥ ६४ ॥

अमोच्यमिति । हे प्रभो ! इन्द्र ! अश्वम् अमोच्यं मन्यसे यदि

ইত্যবসরে রঘু তূণীর হইতে সুবর্ণনির্ম্মিত পুঙ্খশালী দ্বিতীয় বাণ অর্দ্ধোদ্ধৃত করিতেছিলেন, এবং তাহার প্রভায় তদীয় অঙ্গুলিদ্বয় অনুরঞ্জিত হইতেছিল ; তিনি সেই বাণ পুনরায় তূণীরে রাখিয়া সুমিষ্ট বাক্যে ইন্দ্রের কথায় প্রত্যুত্তর দিলেন ॥ ৬৪ ॥

হে প্রভো ! যদি অশ্বকে মোচন করিতে আপনি নিতান্তই অসম্মত

64. Whereupon Raghu re-placed within its case the arrow, with golden wings, that he had half drawn, and whose reflections had began to adorn his fore-fingers with a golden hue ; and thus replied.

65. If the restoration of the horse be impossible according

*सुवर्णपुङ्खद्युतिरञ्जिताङ्गुलिं—सुवर्णनिर्म्मितः पुङ्खः (पुङ्खः बाणमूले)

अजस्रदीक्षाप्रयतः स मद्गुरुः
क्रतोरशेषेण फलेन युज्यताम् ॥ ६५ ॥
यथा च वृत्तान्तमिमं सदोगतः
त्रिलोचनैकांशतया दुरासदः ।
तवैव *सन्देशहराद्विशाम्पतिः
शृणोति लोकेश ! तथा विधीयताम्॥६६॥

ততঃ তর্হি অজস্রদীক্ষায়াং প্রযতঃ, সঃ মদ্গুরুঃ মম পিতা, বিধিনা এব কর্ম্মণি সমাপ্তে সতি, ক্রতোঃ যৎ ফলং তেন ফলেন অশেষেণ কৃৎস্নেন যুজ্যতাং যুক্তঃ অস্তু। অশ্বমেধফললাভে কিমশ্বেন ইতি ভাবঃ ॥ ৬৫ ॥

যথেতি। সদোগতঃ সদোমধ্যং গতঃ, ত্রিলোচনস্য ঈশ্বরস্য একাংশতয়া অষ্টানাম্ অন্যতমমূর্ত্তিত্বাৎ দুরাসদঃ, অন্যাদৃশৈঃ দুষ্প্রাপ্যঃ, বিশাম্পতিঃ

---

৬৫. তাহা হইলে, এই বর দিন যে নিরন্তর যজ্ঞনিরত আমার পিতা বিধিপূর্ব্বক বর্ত্তমান অনুষ্ঠান সমাপন করিয়া অশ্বমেধের সমগ্রফল লাভ করুন ॥ ৬৫ ॥

আর যাহাতে শঙ্করাংশজাত ও অপ্রতিমতেজা নরপতি সভামধ্যে

to your decision, please, my lord ! order it so, that after the completion of his present ceremony without the horse, my father may still enjoy the full benifit of his sacrificial ceremony.

66. Besides, arrange it so that the great king my father,

তস্য দ্যুতিভিঃ প্রতিফলিতাভিঃ প্রভাভিরিত্যর্থঃ, রঞ্জিতাঃ বিস্ফুরিতাঃ অঙ্গুলয়ঃ যেন তম্।

*সন্দেশহরাৎ—সন্দেশং বার্ত্তাং হরতি নয়তি বহতি বা যঃ সঃ সন্দেশহরস্তস্মাৎ।

तथेति कामं *प्रतिशुश्रुवान् रघोः
यथागतं मातलिसारथिर्ययौ ।
नृपस्य नातिप्रमनाः सदोगृहं
सुदक्षिणासूनुरपि न्यवर्त्तत ॥ ६७ ॥

यथा दूमं वृत्तान्तं तव सन्देशहरात् वार्त्ताहरात् स शृणोति च, हे लोकेश! इन्द्र! तथा विधीयताम् ॥ ६६ ॥

तथेति। मातलिसारथिः इन्द्रः, रघोः सम्बन्धिनं कामं मनोरथं तथेति तथास्त्विति प्रतिशुश्रुवान् यथागतं ययौ; सुदक्षिणासूनुः रघुः अपि नातिप्रमनाः विजयलाभेऽप्यश्वनाशान्नातीव हृष्टः सन् नृपस्य सदोगृहं प्रति न्यवर्त्तत ॥ ६७ ॥

বসিয়াই আপনার প্রেরিত লোকেমুখে এই বিবরণ শুনিতে পান এরূপ করুন ॥ ৬৬ ॥

তাহাই হইবে বলিয়া রঘুর নিকট প্রতিজ্ঞা করিয়া ইন্দ্র যে পথ দিয়া আসিয়াছিলেন সেই পথেই প্রস্থান করিলেন; সুদক্ষিণানন্দনও কিঞ্চিৎ বিমর্ষচিত্তে দিলীপের সভাগৃহের অভিমুখে যাত্রা করিলেন। ৬৭ ॥

may come to know of this incident, when seated in his council, from one of your own messengers.

67. "It shall be so,"—promised Indra and went his way; Raghu too, not quite happy for what had happened, returned towards the council, room of the king

* कामं प्रतिशुश्रुवान् रघोः—There is a rule in *Panini* प्रत्याङ्भ्यां श्रुवः पूर्व्वस्य कर्त्ता (१। ४। ४०), according to which, in every case of promise made by one man to another, he whose prayer extracts that promise, is to be accounted as सम्प्रदानं,

तमभ्यनन्दत् प्रथमं प्रबोधितः
प्रजेश्वरः शासनहारिणा हरेः ।
पराममृशन् हर्षजडेन पाणिना
तदीयमङ्गं कुलिशव्रणाङ्कितम् ॥ ६८ ॥
इति क्षितीशो नवतिं नवाधिकां
महाक्रतूनां महनीयशासनः ।

तमिति । हरेरिन्द्रस्य शासनहारिणा पुरुषेण, प्रथमं प्रबोधितः ज्ञापितः, वृत्तान्तम् इति शेषः, प्रजेश्वरः दिलीपः, हर्षजडेन हर्ष-शिशिरेण, पाणिना कुलिशव्रणाङ्कितं तस्य रघोः इदं तदीयम् अङ्गं शरीरं परामृशन् सन् तं रघुम् अभ्यनन्दत् ॥ ६८ ॥

इतीति । महनीयशासनः पूजनीयाज्ञः क्षितीशः इति अनेन

রঘুর পঁহুছিবার পূর্ব্বেই ইন্দ্রপ্রেরিত দূত আসিয়া দিলীপকে সমুদয় বৃত্তান্ত অবগত করিয়াছিল; সুতরাং তিনি রঘুকে আনন্দের সহিত অভ্যর্থনা করিয়া লইলেন এবং তদীয় বজ্রপাতের ক্ষত চিহ্ন বিশিষ্ট দেহে হস্ত বুলাইতে লাগিলেন ॥ ৬৮ ॥

এইরূপে নরপতি মরণান্তে স্বর্গারোহণ মানসে, স্বর্গের সোপান পর-

68. The king had been previously informed of every thing by the messenger of Indra, consequently when the young prince arrived he warmly received him, gently fuling with his hands the scars made by the weapons of Indra.

69. Thus king Dileep, completed ninetynine sacrificial

provided the verb भू is used with the उपसर्ग; प्रति or आङ्; hence, रमते would have been the most appro-

समारुरुक्षुर्दिवमायुषः
ततान सोपानपरम्परामिव ॥ ६९ ॥
अथ स विषयव्यावृत्तात्मा यथाविधि सूनवे
नृपतिककुदं दत्त्वा यूने सितातपवारणम् ।

प्रकारेण महाक्रतूनाम् अश्वमेधानां नवभिः अधिकां नवतिम् एकोनशतम्, आयुषः क्षये सति दिवं स्वर्गम् समारुरुक्षुः आरोढुमिच्छुः सोपानानां परम्परां पङ्क्तिम् इव ततान ॥ ६९ ॥

अथेति। अथ विषयेभ्यः व्यावृत्तात्मा विरक्तचित्तः सः दिलीपः यथाविधि यथाशास्त्रं यूने सूनवे नृपतिककुदं राजचिह्नम्, सितातपवारणं श्वेतच्छत्रं, दत्त्वा तया देव्या सुदक्षिणया सह मुनिवनतरोः छायां शिश्रिये श्रितवान् वानप्रस्थाश्रमं स्वीकृतवान् इत्यर्थः। तथाहि गलितवयसां वृद्धानाम् इक्ष्वाकूणाम् इक्ष्वाकोर्गोत्रापत्यानाम्, इदं वनगमनं कुलव्रतम्। देव्या सहेत्यनेन सपत्नीकवानप्रस्थाश्रमपक्ष उक्तः। तथाच याज्ञवल्क्यः, "सुतविन्यस्तपत्नीकः तया वानुगतो

ম্পরার ন্যায় নবাধিক নবতিসংখ্যক অশ্বমেধ যাগ সমাপন করিলেন॥ ৬৯॥

অনন্তর তিনি বিষয়ে বীতরাগ হইয়া পুত্রের হস্তে রাজচিহ্ন শ্বেতচ্ছত্র

ceremonies, like so many steps for his ascension to Heaven, after death.

70. In the end, disengaged from the world and its attractions, Dileep made over his white umbrella to his son, and took shelter with his queen, under the shade of the trees of a

priate form ; but the षष्ठी is to be explained by the general exception सम्बन्धविवक्षया षष्ठी ।

मुनिवनतरुच्छायां देव्या तया सह शिश्रिये
गलितवयसामिक्ष्वाकूणामिदं हि कुलव्रतम्॥ ७०॥

इति श्रीरघुवंशे महाकाव्ये कालिदास-
कृतौ रघुराज्याभिषेको नाम
तृतीयः सर्गः ।

वनम्। वानप्रस्थो ब्रह्मचारी साग्निः सोपासनो व्रजेत्॥" इति।
हरिणीवृत्तमेतत्॥ ७०॥

इति श्रीमहामहोपाध्यायकोलाचलमल्लिनाथसूरिविरचितायां
रघुवंशटीकायां सञ्जीवनीसमाख्यायां
तृतीयः सर्गः।

ন্যস্ত করিলেন, এবং মহিষীর সহিত তপোবনের তরুচ্ছায়াকে আশ্রয়
করিলেন, ইক্ষ্বাকুবংশীয় বৃদ্ধদিগের কৌলিক প্রথাই এই ছিল॥ ৭০॥

তৃতীয় সর্গ সমাপ্ত।

hermitage ; for such was the custom of the Ikshwaku princes, in the closing days of their lives.

चतुर्थः सर्गः ।

स राज्यं गुरुणा दत्तं प्रतिपद्याधिकं बभौ ।
दिनान्ते निहितं तेजः सवित्रेव हुताशनः ॥१॥
दिलीपानन्तरं राज्ये तं निशम्य प्रतिष्ठितम् ।
पूर्वं प्रधूमितो राज्ञां हृदयेऽग्निरिवोत्थितः ॥२॥

स इति। सः रघुः, गुरुणा पित्रा, दत्तं राज्यं राज्ञः कर्म प्रजापरिपालनात्मकम्, प्रतिपद्य प्राप्य, दिनान्ते सायंकाले, सवित्रा सूर्य्येण, निहितं तेजः प्रतिपद्य, हुताशनः अग्निः, इव अधिकं बभौ ॥ १ ॥

दिलीपेति। दिलीपानन्तरं राज्ये प्रतिष्ठितम् अवस्थितं तं रघुं निशम्य पूर्वं दिलीपकाले राज्ञां हृदये, प्रकर्षेण धूमोऽस्य सञ्जातः प्रधूमितः अग्निः, सन्तापाग्निः, उत्थितः प्रज्वलितः इव, पूर्वेभ्योऽधिकसन्तापोऽभूत इत्यर्थः ॥ २ ॥

দিবাশেষে অগ্নি যেমন সূর্য্য কর্ত্তৃক নিহিত তেজ প্রাপ্ত হইয়া দ্বিগুণ দীপ্তি ধারণ করে, সেইরূপ পিতৃদত্ত রাজ্য প্রাপ্ত হইয়া রঘু পূর্ব্বাপেক্ষা অধিক শোভা পাইতে লাগিলেন ॥ ১ ॥

দিলীপের পর তাঁহাকে রাজ্যে প্রতিষ্ঠিত শুনিয়া অপরাপর রাজা-

---

1. Having received the kingly office, delegated by his father, Raghu shone more brilliantly than ever before; as shines the evening fire with lustre bequeathed to it by the setting sun.

2. As the news of Raghu's ascension to the throne,

* पुरुहूतध्वजस्येव तस्योन्नयनपङ्क्तयः ।
नवाभ्युत्थानदर्शिन्यो ननन्दुः सप्रजाः प्रजाः ॥३॥
सममेव समाक्रान्तं द्वयं द्विरदगामिना ।

पुरुहूतेति । पुरुहूतध्वजः इन्द्रध्वजः, पुरुहूतध्वजस्य इव तस्य रघोः नवम् अभ्युत्थानम् अभ्युन्नतिम् अभ्युदयञ्च पश्यन्तीति नवाभ्युत्थानदर्शिन्यः, अत ऊर्द्धं प्रस्थिताः उन्नमिताश्च नयनपङ्क्तयः यासां ताः सप्रजाः ससन्तानाः प्रजाः जनाः ननन्दुः ॥ ३ ॥

सममिति । द्विरदः इव द्विरदैव गच्छतीति द्विरदगामिना, तेन

দিগের অন্তরে পূর্ব্ব হইতেই প্রধূমিত বিদ্বেষবহ্নি প্রজ্বলিত হইয়া উঠিল ॥ ২ ॥

ইন্দ্রধ্বজকে উত্থিত হইতে দেখিলে লোকে যেমন আনন্দের সহিত উন্মুখ হইয়া চায়, তেমনি তাঁহার নব অভ্যুদয় দর্শনে সসন্তান প্রজাগণ আনন্দ করিতে লাগিল ॥ ৩ ॥

spread the fire of jealousy, that was long smoking in the bosoms of rival princes, rose up in a flame.

3. His people with their children were pleased to see the rise of the young monarch, as men longingly look with up-turned eyes on the *indradhwaj*, literally the standard of Indra ;—meaning a long fole or flag staff raised as poit of a ceremony to avert the calamities of a long drought and consequent famine.

4 Raghu, whose movements were like those of an ele-

* पुरुहूतध्वजस्य—पुरुहूतस्य इन्द्रस्य ध्वजः इन्द्राराधनार्थमुत्थापितो वंशदण्ड इत्यर्थः ।— It was an ancient custom to worship a flag-staff for the propitiation of Indra, the god of rain, during a period of continued drought.

तेन सिंहासनं पित्र्यमखिलञ्चारिमण्डलम् ॥४॥

छायामण्डललक्ष्येण तमदृश्या किल स्वयम् ।

पद्मा पद्मातपत्रेण भेजे साम्राज्यदीक्षितम् ॥५॥

रघुणा समं युगपत् एव द्वयं समाक्रान्तम् अधिष्ठितम् । किं तत् द्वयम् ? पितुरागतं पित्र्यम् सिंहासनम्, अखिलम् अरेः मण्डलं चेति ॥ ४ ॥

"सिंहासनारोहणानन्तरं तस्य लक्ष्मीसन्निधानमाह" छायेति । अत्र रघोस्तेजोविशेषेण स्वयं सन्निहितया लक्ष्म्या छत्रधारणं कृतमित्युत्प्रेक्ष्यते । पद्मा लक्ष्मीः स्वयम् अदृश्या किल (किलेति सम्भावनायाम्) सती छायामण्डललक्ष्येण कान्तिपुञ्जानुमेयेन न तु स्वरूपतो दृश्येन पद्मातपत्रेण पद्ममेव आतपत्रं तेन करणभूतेन, साम्राज्ये साम्राज्यकर्म्मणि मण्डलाधिपत्ये दीक्षितम् अभिषिक्तं तं भेजे । अन्यथा कथमेतादृशी कान्तिसम्पत्तिः इति भावः ॥ ५ ॥

গজেন্দ্রগামী নবভূপতি পিতার সিংহাসন এবং শত্রুকুল উভয়কেই এক সঙ্গে আক্রমণ করিলেন ॥ ৪ ॥

তিনি সাম্রাজ্যে অভিষিক্ত হইলে, স্বয়ং লক্ষ্মী আসিয়া অলক্ষিতভাবে তাঁহার মস্তকে বোধ হয় ছত্র ধরিলেন ; কারণ এক আশ্চর্য্য ছায়ামণ্ডল তাঁহার দেহকে সর্ব্বদা ঘিরিয়া থাকিত ॥ ৫ ॥

phant, exercised his power over two things at the same time— first the throne bequeathed by his father ; secondly, all his enemies.

5. A peculiar halo of beauty always encircled him, methinks it was the goddess of fortune herself, who secretly served him by holding the umbrella over his imperial head.

*परिकल्पितसान्निध्या काले काले च बन्दिषु ।
स्तुत्यं स्तुतिभिरर्थ्याभिः †उपतस्थे सरस्वती ॥६॥
मनुप्रभृतिभिर्मान्यैर्भुक्ता यद्यपि राजभिः ।

सम्प्रति सरस्वतीसान्निध्यमाह, परिकल्पितेति। सरस्वती च काले काले, सर्वेषु अपि योग्यकालेषु, बन्दिषु परिकल्पितसान्निध्या कृतसन्निधाना, सती स्तुत्यं स्तोतार्हं तं रघुम् अर्थ्याभिः अर्थात् अनपेताभिः स्तुतिभिः स्तोत्रैः उपतस्थे, देवताबुद्ध्या पूजितवती इत्यर्थः। देवतात्वञ्च विष्णुः पृथिवीपतिरिति वा लोकपालात्मकत्वाद्वेत्यनुसन्धेयम् ॥ ६ ॥

मन्विति। वसुन्धरा, मनुप्रभृतिभिः मन्वादिभिः, मान्यैः पूज्यैः.

স্বয়ং সরস্বতী যথাকালে বন্দিগণের রসনাতে অধিষ্ঠান করিয়া স্তুতির যোগ্য রঘুকে অর্থপূর্ণ স্তুতি দ্বারা অর্চ্চনা করিতেন ॥ ৬ ॥

যদিও মনুপ্রভৃতি সর্ব্বলোকপূজিত রাজগণ ধরণীর অধিপতি ছিলেন,

6. The goddess of learning too, by her presence, in all appropriate seasons, in the tongues of the musical panegyrists attached to the palace, served him by inspring songs of deep meaning in his praise.

7. Though the soveriegnty of the earth, had been previ-

* परिकल्पितसान्निध्या—परिकल्पितं सम्पादितं सान्निध्यं नैकट्यं यया, सा, तथा।

† उपतस्थे—For explanation of the आत्मनेपद refer to वार्त्तिकसूत्रं—उपाद्देवपूजासङ्गतिकरणमित्रकरणपथिष्विति वाच्यं इत्यादि। According to the author of सिद्धान्तकौमुदी- देवतात्वारोपात् नृपस्य देवांशत्वाद्वा, अत्र देवपूजात्वारोपः तेन च आत्मनेपदं। Vide सिद्धान्तकौमुदी—Page 244. Taranath's edition 1863.

तथाप्यनन्यपूर्वेव तस्मिन् आसीद् वसुन्धरा ॥७॥

स हि सर्वस्य लोकस्य युक्तदण्डतया मनः।

आददे नातिशीतोष्णः नभस्वानिव दक्षिणः॥८॥

*मन्दोत्कण्ठाः कृतास्तेन गुणाधिकतया गुरौ।

राजभिर्भुक्ता यद्यपि, भुक्तेव इत्यर्थः, तथापि तस्मिन् रघौ, अन्यः पूर्वः यस्याः सा अन्यपूर्वा, अन्यपूर्वा न भवतीति अनन्यपूर्वा अनन्योपभुक्तेव, आसीत् तस्य प्रथमपतिकेवानुरक्तावती इत्यर्थः॥ ७॥

अत्र कारणमाह, स हीति। हि यस्मात् कारणात् सः रघुः, युक्तदण्डतया यथापराधदण्डतया, सर्वस्य लोकस्य, मनः आददे जहार। क इव? अतिशीतः अत्युष्णो वा न भवतीति नातिशीतोष्णः, दक्षिणः दक्षिणदिग्भवः, नभस्वान् वायुः इव मलयानिल इव इत्यर्थः। युक्तदण्डतयेत्यत्र कामन्दकः, "उद्वेजयति तीक्ष्णेन मृदुना परिभूयते। दण्डेन नृपतिस्तस्मात् युक्तदण्डः प्रशस्यते॥" इति॥ ८॥

मन्देति। तेन रघुणा, प्रजाः, गुरौ दिलीपविषये, सत्कारः

তথাপি পৃথিবী তদীয় হস্তে পড়িয়া অনন্যপূর্ব্বার ন্যায় হইলেন॥ ৭॥

নাতিশীতোষ্ণ মলয়বায়ু যেমন লোকের চিত্ত হরণ করে তেমনি তিনি ন্যায়ানুগত দণ্ডবিধান দ্বারা সকল শ্রেণীর মন আকর্ষণ করিলেন॥৮॥

চূত বৃক্ষে ফল ধরিলে আর তাহার ফুলের প্রতি লোকের যেমন

---

ously enjoyed by estimable princes, commencing from Manu, yet when it came to him, it seemed as if she had never known any other master.

8. On account of his wise and just punishments his rule was liked by all his subjects, just as the mild and equable southern breeze is liked by all.

9. He excelled even his father in point of many virtues,

---

* मन्दोत्कण्ठाः—मन्दा शिथिलीकृता उत्कण्ठा, राजवियोगजं दुःखं यासां ताः।

फलेन सहकारस्य पुष्पोद्गम इव प्रजाः ॥ ৯ ॥
* नयविद्भिर्नवे राज्ञि सदसच्चोपदर्शितम्।
पूर्व एवाभवत् पक्षः तस्मिन् नाभवदुत्तरः ॥১০॥

अतिसौरभः चूतः, तस्य फलेन पुष्पोद्गमे पुष्पोदये इव, ततोऽपि गुणाधिकतया हेतुना, मदोत्कण्ठाः अल्पोत्सुकाः जाताः। गुणोत्तरश्च उत्तरो विषयः पूर्वं विस्मारयति इति भावः ॥ ৯ ॥

नयेति। नयविद्भिः नीतिशास्त्रज्ञैः, नवे तस्मिन् राज्ञि विषये, तमधिकृत्य इत्यर्थः, सत् धर्मयुद्धादिकम् असत् कूटयुद्धादिकञ्च उपदर्शितं तस्मिन् राज्ञि पूर्वः पक्षः एव अभवत् संक्रान्तः इत्यर्थः; उत्तरः पक्षः न अभवत् न संक्रान्तः इत्यर्थः ॥ १० ॥

আস্থা থাকে না, তেমনি রঘুর গুণাবলীর অধিকতর শোভা দর্শনে প্রজাগণ দিলীপের বিয়োগের ক্ষোভ ভুলিতে লাগিল ॥ ৯ ॥

রাজনীতিজ্ঞ ব্যক্তিরা নবাভিষিক্ত ভূপতিকে সৎ ও অসৎ উভয়বিধ শাসন প্রণালী প্রদর্শন করিয়াছিলেন; কিন্তু রঘু সৎপক্ষই অবলম্বন করিলেন অসৎপক্ষ অবলম্বন করিলেন না ॥ ১০ ॥

so that the people ceased feeling keenly the old king's loss, as men naturally forget the flowery days of the sweet mango tree, when the latter begins to bear fruits.

10. Men skilled in state policy instructed the young king, in all the ways of government, both good and evil; but it was only the former that had any effect on him, and not the latter.

---

* नयविद्भिः—नयं राजनीतिं विदन्ति जानन्ति ये ते, नयविदस्तैः।

पञ्चानामपि भूतानामुत्कर्षं पुपुषुर्गुणाः ।
नवे तस्मिन् महीपाले सर्वं नवमिवाभवत् ॥११॥
यथा प्रह्लादनाच्चन्द्रः प्रतापात् तपनो यथा ।
तथैव सोऽभूदन्वर्थः राजा प्रकृतिरञ्जनात् ॥१२॥

पञ्चानामिति । पृथिव्यादीनां पञ्चानां भूतानाम् अपि गुणाः गन्धादयः उत्कर्षम् अतिशयं पुपुषुः । अन्योन्येषते, अस्मिन् रघौ नाम नवे महीपाले सति सर्वं वस्तुजातं नवम् इव अभवत् । तदेव भूतजातमिदानीमपूर्वगुणयोगादपूर्वमिवाभवत् इति भावः ॥ ११ ॥

यथेति । यथा चन्दति आह्लादयतीति चन्द्रः, चदि धातो-र्गौणादिको रप्रत्ययः । प्रह्लादनात् आह्लादकरणात् अन्वर्थः अनु-गतार्थनामकः अभूत्, यथा च तपतीति तपनः सूर्य्यः प्रतापात् सन्तापजननात् इत्यर्थः, तथा एव सः राजा प्रकृतिरञ्जनात् अन्वर्थः सार्थकराजशब्दः अभूत् । यद्यपि राजशब्दो राजतेर्दीप्त्यर्थात् कनिन्-

---

কি আশ্চর্য্য রঘু নবরাজ্যে প্রতিষ্ঠিত হইলে ক্ষিত্যপ্ তেজ মরু ব্যোম এই পঞ্চভূতের গুণ সকলও যেন বৃদ্ধি প্রাপ্ত হইল, সকলই যেন নবভাব ধারণ করিল ॥ ১১ ॥

আনন্দবিধান করাতে যেমন চন্দ্র নামের সার্থকতা, তাপ দেওয়াতে যেমন তপন নামের সার্থকতা, তেমনি প্রজারঞ্জন করাতে তাঁহার রাজা নামেরও সার্থকতা হইল ॥ ১২ ॥

---

11. When he became king everying had a renewed life as it were—even the properties of the five great elements, viz-earth, water, fire, air and ether received an unusual devolopment.

12. As the moon is called *chandra* on account of its power to please, and as the sun is called *tapana* on account of

कामं कर्णान्तविश्रान्ते विशाले तस्य लोचने।
चक्षुष्मत्ता तु शास्त्रेण सूक्ष्मकार्य्यार्थदर्शिना॥१३॥
लब्धप्रशमनस्वस्थम् अथैनं समुपस्थिता।
पार्थिवश्रीर्द्वितीयेव शरत् पङ्कजलक्षणा॥१४॥

प्रत्ययान्तो न तु रञ्जेः तथापि धातूनामनेकार्थत्वाद्रञ्जनाद्राजेत्युक्तं कविना॥ १२॥

काममिति। विशाले, तस्य रघोः लोचने, कामं, कर्णान्तयोः विश्रान्ते कर्णप्रान्तगते, चक्षुष्मत्ता तु चक्षुःफलं तु इत्यर्थः, सूक्ष्मान् कार्य्यार्थान् कर्त्तव्यार्थान् दर्शयति प्रकाशयतीति सूक्ष्मकार्य्यार्थदर्शिना शास्त्रेण एव। शास्त्रं दृष्टिर्विवेकिनाम् इति भावः॥ १३॥

लब्धेति। अथ लब्धस्य राज्यस्य प्रशमनेन, प्रतिपन्थिनाम् उद्धरण-प्रतीकाराभ्यां स्थिरीकरणेन, स्वस्थं समाहितचित्तम् एनं रघुं पङ्कज-

তাঁহার চক্ষুদ্বয় আকর্ণ বিশ্রান্ত ও বিশাল ছিল বটে, কিন্তু সে জন্য তাঁহাকে চক্ষুষ্মান বলা যাইত না; সূক্ষ্মার্থ দর্শনে ও শাস্ত্রে পটুতা ছিল বলিয়াই তাঁহার চক্ষুষ্মত্তা হইয়াছিল॥ ১৩॥

রঘু রাজ্যাভিষিক্ত হইয়া বিপক্ষকুলকে ভয় মৈত্রী প্রভৃতি দ্বারা শান্ত

its schorching rays, so in him the word Rajah found its truest application; in as much as he was truly the delight of his people.

13. Doubtless his two large eyes were drawn out up to his ears; but, his true eyesight lay in his penetrating intellect, rich with the knowledge of the *shastras*, and attentive to the minutest details of his daily duties.

14. By the time Raghu had fairly pracified his kingdom,

निर्वृष्टलघुभिर्मेघैः मुक्तवर्त्मा सुदुःसहः ।
प्रतापस्तस्य भानोश्च युगपद् व्यानशे दिशः॥१५॥
वार्षिकं संजहारेन्द्रः धनुर्जैत्रं रघुर्दधौ ।
प्रजार्थसाधने तौ हि पर्य्यायोद्यतकार्मुकौ ॥१६॥

[illegible] पद्मचिह्ना (श्रियोऽपि विशेषणमेतत्) शरत्, द्वितीया पार्थिवश्रीः राजलक्ष्मीः इव, समुपस्थिता प्राप्ता ॥ १४ ॥

निर्वृष्टेति । निःशेषं वृष्टाः निर्वृष्टाः कर्त्तरि क्तः, अतएव लघवः तैः मेघैः मुक्तवर्त्मा त्यक्तमार्गः, अतएव सुदुःसहः तस्य रघोः भानोश्च प्रतापः पौरुषम् आतपश्च, युगपत् दिशः व्यानशे व्याप ॥ १५ ॥

वार्षिकमिति । इन्द्रः वर्षासु भवं वार्षिकं वर्षानिमित्तम् इत्यर्थः, धनुः संजहार, रघुः जैत्रं जयशीलम् धनुः दधौ, हि यस्मात् तौ इन्द्ररघू प्रजानाम्, अर्थस्य प्रयोजनस्य वृष्टिविजयलक्षणस्य, साधनविषये

করিয়া সুস্থির হইয়া বসিলেন, ও দিকে পদ্মসমন্বিত শরৎ ঋতু দ্বিতীয় রাজ-লক্ষ্মীর ন্যায় উপস্থিত হইল ॥ ১৪ ॥

বৃষ্টিবিহীন স্বল্পভার মেঘ সকল আকাশ পরিত্যাগ করিয়া যাইতে লাগিল, এবং সূর্য্যের তেজ ও তাঁহার প্রতাপ উভয়ে দুঃসহ হইয়া সমুদায় জগতে ব্যাপ্ত হইল ॥ ১৫ ।

ইন্দ্র তাঁহার বর্ষাকালোচিত ধনু সংহার করিলেন ; রঘু দিগ্বিজয়ের

---

autumn, like a second goddess of kingly power, made her appearance,—heralded by the blooming lotus-flowers.

15. The rainless and light clouds rode away from the path of the sun's rays, and his intolerable heat, and also Raghu's conquering power, simultaneously spread themselves in all directions.

16. Indra removed from the sky his great annual bow,

पुण्डरीकातपत्रस्तं विकसत्काशचामरः।
ऋतुर्विडम्बयामास न पुनः प्राप तच्छ्रियम् ॥१७॥

पर्य्यायेण उद्यते कार्मुके याभ्यां तौ पर्य्यायोद्यतकार्मुकौ। पाठान्तरे पर्य्यायेण उद्यमः विक्रमस्य ययोः तौ पर्य्यायोद्यमविक्रमौ। द्वयोः पर्य्यायकरणादक्लेशः इति भावः ॥ १६ ॥

पुण्डरीकेति। पुण्डरीकं सिताम्भोजम् एव आतपत्रं यस्य सः तथोक्तः, विकसन्ति काशानि काशाख्यतृणकुसुमानि एव चामराणि यस्य सः तथोक्तः, ऋतुः शरदृतुः, पुण्डरीकनिभातपत्रं काशनिभचामरं तं रघुं विडम्बयामास अनुचकार, तस्य रघोः श्रियं पुनः शोभां तु न प्राप ॥ १७ ॥

জন্য ধনু ধারণ করিলেন; প্রজাকুলের প্রয়োজন সিদ্ধির জন্য তাঁহারা উভয়ে পর্য্যায়ক্রমে অস্ত্রধারণ করিতেন ॥ ১৬ ॥

প্রস্ফুটিত শ্বেতশতদল শরতের ছত্রের ন্যায় হইল, কাশকুসুম সকল চামরের শোভা ধারণ করিল; বোধ হইল শরৎ ঋতু যেন তাঁহার রাজসম্পদের অনুকরণে প্রবৃত্ত, কিন্তু তাঁহার রাজকীয় শোভা লাভ করিতে পারিল না ॥ ১৭ ॥

(viz. the rainbow, which generally makes its appearance in the rainy season) but Raghu took up his for the conquest of the earth,—thus they used tneir bows by turn for the good of the people.

17. The season of autumn faintly imitated his greatness by unfurling as umbrellas the lovely lotus flowers, and by using the blossoming Kusha grass as *chamar*, only imitated but could not approach it.

प्रसादसुमुखे तस्मिन् चन्द्रे च विशदप्रभे।
तदा चक्षुष्मतां प्रीतिः आसीत्*समरसा द्वयोः॥१८

†हंसश्रेणीषु तारासु कुमुद्वत्सु च वारिषु।
विभूतयस्तदीयानां पर्य्यस्ता यशसामिव॥१९॥

प्रसादेति। प्रसादेन सुमुखे तस्मिन् रघौ, विशदप्रभे निर्मलकान्तौ चन्द्रे च, द्वयोः विषये तदा चक्षुष्मतां प्रीतिः अनुरागः समरसा समस्वादा तुल्यभोगा इति यावत्, आसीत्॥ १८॥

हंसेति। हंसानां श्रेणीषु पङ्क्तिषु, तारासु नक्षत्रेषु, कुमुदानि

রঘুর মুখ যখন প্রসন্নতার হাস্যে পূর্ণ হইত এবং চন্দ্রের নির্ম্মল কান্তি যখন প্রকাশ পাইত, তখন চক্ষুষ্মান ব্যক্তিরা উভয়কে দেখিয়া সমান প্রীতি লাভ করিতেন॥ ১৮॥

শ্বেতবর্ণ হংসশ্রেণীতে, উজ্জ্বল নক্ষত্রপুঞ্জে, ও প্রস্ফুটিত কুমুদপূর্ণ

18. His loving and happy countenance and the unclouded moon—both equally became objects of pleasure to the eyes of all who beheld them.

19. In the white swans, in the bright stars, and also in

* समरसा—समः अभिन्नः रसः स्वादो यस्याः सा।

† हंसश्रेणीषु—It is customary with the Sanskrit poets to compare the good name of a man to white things. The student will meet with similar passages, in other poetical works. The following desoripion of poetical custom given by the author of साहित्यदर्पण will be found to be useful to him :—

मालिन्यं व्योम्नि पापे यशसि धवलता वर्ण्यते हासकीर्त्योः

इक्षुच्छायनिषादिन्यः तस्य गोप्तुर्गुणोदयम्।
आकुमारकथोद्घातं शालिगोप्यो जगुर्यशः॥२०॥

सन्ति येषु कुमुदन्ति तेषु कुमुदप्रायेषु इत्यर्थः, वारिषु च नदीयानां रघुसम्बन्धिनां यशसां विभूतयः सम्पदः प्रकीर्णाः इव प्रसारिताः किम्? इत्युत्प्रेक्षा। अन्यथा कथमेषां धवलिमा इति भावः॥ १९॥

इक्ष्विति। इक्षूणां छाया इक्षुच्छायम् तत्र निषण्णाः इक्षुच्छाय-

---

সরোবরে, রঘুর বিমল যশোরাশি যেন ছড়াইয়া পড়িল ॥ ১৯ ॥

যে রঘুর গুণাবলীসম্ভূত যশ শিশুগণ পর্য্যন্ত কীর্ত্তন করিত, তদীয় শস্য রক্ষণে নিযুক্ত কৃষকবালাগণ ইক্ষুবনের ছায়াতে বসিয়া সেই রঘুর যশোগীত গান করিতে লাগিল ॥ ২০ ॥

---

the waters covered with Kumud flower, lay scattered the properties of his spotless fame.

20. Women appointed to keep guard over growing corn.

रक्तौ च क्रोधरागौ सरिदुदधिगतं पङ्कजेन्दीवरादि।
तोयाधारेऽखिलेऽपि प्रसरति च मरालादिकः पक्षिसङ्घो
ज्योत्स्ना पेया चकोरैर्जलधरसमये मानसं यान्ति हंसाः॥
पादाघातादशोकं विकसति बकुलं योषितामास्यमद्यैः
यूनामङ्गेषु हाराः स्फुटति च हृदयं विप्रयोगस्य तापैः।
मौर्वी रोलम्बमाला धनुरथ विशिखाः कौसुमाः पुष्पकेतोः
भिन्नं स्यादस्य बाणैर्युवजनहृदयं स्त्रीकटाक्षेण तद्वत्॥
अह्न्यम्भोजं निशायां विकसति कुमुदं चन्द्रिका शुक्लपक्षे
मेघध्वानेषु नृत्यं भवति च शिखिनां नाप्यशोके फलं स्यात्।
न स्याज्जाती वसन्ते न च कुसुमफले गन्धसारद्रुमाणाम्
इत्याद्युन्नेयमन्यत् कविसमयगतं सत्कवीनां प्रबन्धे॥

कूलमुद्रुजाः—उदिकूले रुजिवहोः (३।२।२ *Panini*)

प्रससादोदयादम्भः कुम्भयोनेर्महौजसः ।
रघोरभिभवाशङ्कि चुक्षुभे द्विषतां मनः ॥ २१ ॥

निषादिन्यः, स्त्रीलिङ्गपाठे इक्षोः छाया इति विग्रहः, अन्यथा बहुत्वे नपुंसकत्वप्रसङ्गात्। शालीन् गोपायन्ति रक्षन्तीति शालिगोप्यः शस्यपालिकाः स्त्रियः, गोप्तुः रक्षकस्य, तस्य रघोः, गुणेभ्यः उदयः यस्य तत् गुणोदयं गुणोत्पन्नम्, आकुमारं कुमारात् आरभ्य कथोद्घातः कथारम्भः यस्य तत्, कुमारैरपि स्तूयमानम् इत्यर्थः, यशः जगुः गायन्ति स्म। अथवा कुमारस्य सतः रघोः याः कथाः इन्द्रविजयादयः ततः आरभ्य आकुमारकथम्, आकुमारकथम् उद्घातः यस्मिन् कर्म्मणि, गानक्रियाविशेषणमेतत्। आकुमारकथोद्भूतमिति पाठे कुमारस्य सतः तस्य कथाभिः चरितैः उद्भूतं यत् यशः तत् यशः आरभ्य यशः जगुः इति व्याख्येयम् ॥ २० ॥

प्रससादेति। महौजसः कुम्भयोनेः अगस्त्यस्य उदयात् अम्भः प्रससाद प्रसन्नं बभूव, महौजसः रघोः उदयात् अभिभवाशङ्कि द्विषतां मनः चुक्षुभे कालुष्यं प्राप। "अगस्त्योदये जलानि प्रसीदन्ति" इत्यागमः ॥२१॥

অগস্ত্যের উদয় হওয়াতে জল সকল প্রসন্নভাব ধারণ করিল, কিন্তু রঘুর অভ্যুদয়ে শত্রুকুলের মন ক্ষোভপ্রাপ্ত হইয়া কলুষিত হইল ॥ ২১ ॥

sheltering themselves under the shade of sugarcanes, sang sweet ballads recounting his several virtues, beginning with the period of his infancy.

21. The waters of rivers and tanks became pure, by reason of the appearance of the star called *Agastya*; but the hearts of his enemies became clouded with the apprehensions of approaching defeat.

मदोदग्राः ककुद्मन्तः सरितां कूलमुद्रुजाः।
लीलाखेलमनुप्रापुर्महोक्षास्तस्य विक्रमम्॥२२॥
प्रसवैः सप्तपर्णानां मदगन्धिभिराहताः।
असूययेव तन्नागाः सप्तधैव प्रसुस्रुवुः ॥ २३ ॥

मदेति। मदोदग्राः मदोद्धताः ककुदेषामस्तीति ककुद्मन्तः महाककुदः इत्यर्थः। यवादित्वात् मकारस्य वत्वाभावः। सरितां कूलानि उद्रुजन्तीति कूलमुद्रुजाः। महान्तः उक्षाणः महोक्षाः। लीलाखेलं विलासलुभगं तस्य रघोः उक्षाहवतः वपुष्मतः परभञ्जकस्य विक्रमं शौर्य्यम् अनुप्रापुः अनुचक्रुः ॥ २२ ॥

प्रसवैरिति। मदस्य इव गन्धः येषां तैः मदगन्धिभिः, उपमानान्तेतोकारः समासान्तः, सप्तपर्णानां वृक्षविशेषाणाम्, प्रसवैः पुष्पैः, आहताः तस्य रघोः नागाः गजाः, असूयया इव आहतिनिमित्तया स्पर्द्धया इव सप्तधा एव प्रसुस्रुवुः मदं ववृषुः। "करात् कटाभ्यां मेढ्राच्च नेत्राभ्याञ्च मदस्रुतिः" इति पालकाव्ये। करात् नासारन्ध्राभ्याम् इत्यर्थः ॥ २३ ॥

মদোদ্ধত বিপুল ককুদশালী ষণ্ডগণ শৃঙ্গের দ্বারা নদী সকলের তীরদেশ ভগ্ন করিয়া ক্রীড়াপরায়ণ রঘুর বিক্রমের অনুকরণ করিতে লাগিল ॥ ২২ ॥

প্রস্ফুটিত ছাতিম পুষ্পের মদগন্ধানুকারী গন্ধের দ্বারা যেন অপমানিত হইয়াই রঘুর হস্তিগণ সপ্তধারে মদজল বর্ষণ করিতে লাগিল ॥ ২৩ ॥

---

22. Bulls of ample humps, maddened with excess of strength, began to beat against the banks of rivers with their horns, as if in that they imitated the strange and playful doings of his valour.

23. Wounded in their vanity by the flowers of the "tree

सरितः कुर्वती गाधाः पथश्चाश्यानकर्द्दमान्।
यात्रायै चोदयामास तं शक्तेः प्रथमं शरत्॥२४॥
तस्मै सम्यक् हुतो वह्निः वाजिनीराजनाविधौ।
प्रदक्षिणार्च्चिर्व्याजेन हस्तेनेव जयं ददौ ॥ २५ ॥

सरित इति। सरितः गाधाः सुप्रतराः, कुर्वती, पथः मार्गान् च आश्यानकर्द्दमान् शुष्कपङ्कान् कुर्वती शरत् शरदृतुः। तं रघुं शक्तेः उत्साहशक्तेः प्रथमं प्राक् यात्रायै दण्डयात्रायै चोदयामास प्रेरयामास। प्रभावमन्त्रशक्तिसम्पन्नस्य शरत् स्वयमुत्साहमुत्पादयामास इत्यर्थः ॥२४॥

तस्मा इति। वाजिनाम् अश्वानां, नीराजनाविधौ नीराजनाख्ये शान्तिकर्म्मणि, सम्यक् विधिवत्, हुतः होमसमिद्धः वह्निः, प्रगता दक्षिणं प्रदक्षिणम्, प्रदक्षिणं या अर्चिः ज्वाला तस्याः व्याजेन हस्तेन

শরতের সমাগমে নদী সকলের জল হ্রাস হইয়া তরণযোগ্য হইল, পথের কর্দ্দম শুষ্ক হইয়া আসিল, শরৎ যেন রঘুকে দিগ্বিজয়যাত্রার নিমিত্ত প্রেরণা করিতে লাগিল ॥ ২৪ ॥

যুদ্ধার্থ মনোনীত গজবাজি প্রভৃতির নীরাজনানামক সংস্কারার্থ উদ্দীপিত অগ্নি দক্ষিণগামী জ্বালারাশিরূপ হস্ত দ্বারাই যেন সাক্ষাৎ-ভাবে তাঁহাকে জয়লক্ষ্মী প্রদান করিল ॥ ২৫ ॥

---

of seven leaves", (called Chhatim in Bengali) that resembled in their smell the temporal juice, the elephants of Raghu, streamed out from seven different parts of the body their temporal juice.

24. The rivers became fordable, and the roads became dry; thus at the very commencement of his rule the season of autumn incited him to start on a career of conquest.

25. On the occasion of the protective ceremony for horses,

स गुप्तमूलप्रत्यन्तः शुद्धपार्ष्णिरयान्वितः ।
षड्विधं बलमादाय प्रतस्थे दिग्जिगीषया ॥२६॥

इव तस्मै जयं ददौ। उक्तमाहवयात्रायाम्, "दक्षः प्रदक्षिणगतो हुत-भुक् स्वपक्ष धात्रीं ससमुद्ररशनां वशगां करोति" इति। वाजिग्रहणं गजादीनामप्युपलक्षणं तेषामपि नीराजनाविधानात् ॥ २५॥

स इति। गुप्तौ मूलं स्वनिवासस्थानं, प्रत्यन्तः प्रान्तदुर्गञ्च येन सः गुप्तमूलप्रत्यन्तः शुद्धपार्ष्णिः उद्धृतपृष्ठशत्रुः, सेनया रक्षितपृष्ठदेशो वा, अयान्वितः शुभदैवान्वितः, रघुः, षड्विधं मौलभृत्यादिरूपं बलं सैन्यम्, 'मौलं भृत्यः सुहृच्छ्रेणी द्विषदाटविकं बलम्" इति कोषः। आदाय दिशां जिगीषया जेतुमिच्छया प्रतस्थे प्रयात ॥ २६ ॥

সেই রঘু আপনার নিবাসস্থান ও প্রান্তস্থিত দুর্গকে সর্ব্বদা প্রচ্ছন্ন রাখিয়া, পশ্চাতের সমুদায় শত্রুকে উন্মুলিত করিয়া, এবং নানাপ্রকার মঙ্গলকর দেবক্রিয়া দ্বারা আপনাকে সুরক্ষিত করিয়া ষড়্বিধ বল সমভি-ব্যাহারে দিগ্বিজয়ার্থ নির্গত হইলেন ॥ ২৬ ॥

previous to marching, the kindled fire spread such a beautiful flame, and it rose in such circling volumes, that led one to think as if the fire gave the laurel of victory with his own hand.

26. Keeping his private quarters in the camp, as well as the defences of frontier, always strictly concealed, and also detaching at every step strong contingents for keeping guard on the vanquished realms in the rear, he marched on in his career of conquest, with an army consisting of seven kinds of soldiers.

অবাকিরন্ বয়োবৃদ্ধাস্তং লাজৈঃ পৌরযোষিতঃ।
পৃষতৈর্মন্দরোদ্ধূতৈঃ ক্ষীরোর্ম্ময় ইবাচ্যুতম্ ॥ ২৭ ॥
স যযৌ প্রথমং প্রাচীং তুল্যঃ প্রাচীনবর্হিষা।
অহিতাননিলোদ্ধূতৈস্তর্জয়ন্নিব কেতুভিঃ ॥২৮॥

অবাকিরন্নিতি। বয়োবৃদ্ধাঃ পৌরযোষিতঃ, তং রঘুং, প্রযান্তং, লাজৈঃ আচারলাজৈঃ, মন্দরোদ্ধূতৈঃ, পৃষতৈঃ বিন্দুভিঃ, ক্ষীরোর্ম্ময়ঃ ক্ষীরসমুদ্রোর্ম্ময়ঃ, অচ্যুতং বিষ্ণুম্ ইব, অবাকিরন্ পর্য্যক্ষিপন্ ॥ ২৭ ॥

স ইতি। প্রাচীনবর্হির্নাম কশ্চিন্মহারাজঃ ইতি কেচিৎ, প্রাচীনবর্হিঃ ইন্দ্রঃ, "পর্য্যন্যো মঘবা বৃষা হরিহয়ঃ প্রাচীনবর্হিস্তথা" ইতি ইন্দ্রপর্য্যায়েষু হলায়ুধাভিধানাৎ। তেন তুল্যঃ সঃ রঘুঃ অনিলেন অনুকূলবাতেন, উদ্ধূতৈঃ, কেতুভিঃ ধ্বজৈঃ, অহিতান্ রিপূন্, তর্জয়ন্ ইব ভর্ৎসয়ন্ ইব, প্রথমং প্রাচীং দিশং যযৌ ॥ ২৮ ॥

মন্থনকালে মন্দরের দ্বারা উত্থাপিত ক্ষীরসাগরের জলকণিকা সকল যেমন বিষ্ণুর মস্তকে বর্ষিত হইয়াছিল, সেইরূপ বয়োবৃদ্ধা পুরনারীগণ যাত্রাকালে রঘুর শিরে লাজাঞ্জলি বর্ষণ করিতে লাগিলেন ॥ ২৭ ॥

ইন্দ্রতুল্য পরাক্রমশালী রঘু অনুকূল বায়ু-তাড়িত নিজ রথধ্বজের দ্বারা শত্রুদিগকে ভর্জ্জন করিতে করিতে সর্ব্বপ্রথমে পূর্ব্বদিকের অভিমুখে ধাবিত হইলেন ॥ ২৮ ॥

---

27. The elderly women of the city showered fried paddies on his head, as a mark of benediction, as the waves of the milky ocean did once sprinkle on the body of Vishnu with their soft particles.

28. Raghu, who resembled Indra in his valour, marched first towards the East, holding out a warning as it were to his enemies with his flags unfurled in the air.

रजोभिः स्यन्दनोद्धूतैः गजैश्च घनसन्निभैः।
भुवस्तलमिव व्योम कुर्वन् व्योमेव भूतलम्॥२९॥
प्रतापोऽग्रे ततः शब्दः परागस्तदनन्तरम्।
ययौ पश्चाद्रथादीति चतुःस्कन्धेव सा चमूः॥३०॥

रजोभिरिति। किं कुर्वन्? स्यन्दनोद्धूतैः रजोभिः, घनसन्निभैः वर्णतः क्रियातः परिमाणतश्च मेघतुल्यैः, गजैश्च यथाक्रमं, व्योम आकाशं, भुवः तलम् इव भूतलञ्च, व्योम इव कुर्वन्, ययौ इति पूर्वेण सम्बन्धः॥ २९॥

प्रताप इति। अग्रे प्रतापः तेजोविशेषः, ततः शब्दः सैन्यकलकलः, तदनन्तरं परागः धूलिः, पश्चात् रथादि चतुरङ्गबलम् इति इत्थं चतुःस्कन्धा इव चतुर्व्यूहा इव सा चमूः ययौ। रथानीकमिति पाठे इतिशब्दाध्याहारेण बोध्यम्॥ ३०॥

রথচক্রোত্থিত ধূলি সকলের দ্বারা গগনকে আচ্ছাদন করিয়া ও মেঘসদৃশ গজ সকলের দ্বারা ধরাকে আচ্ছাদন করিয়া তিনি আকাশকে ধরণী ও ধরণীকে আকাশ করিয়া ফেলিলেন॥ ২৯॥

সর্ব্বাগ্রে প্রতাপ, তৎপশ্চাৎ মহাকোলাহল, তৎপশ্চাৎ ধূলিরাশি, তৎপশ্চাৎ রথ অশ্ব গজ প্রভৃতি, এইরূপে তাঁহার বিপুল সৈন্য চারি-ভাগে বিভক্ত হইয়া চলিল॥ ৩০॥

---

29. Covering the sky with the dust thrown up by the chariots, and the earth with dark cloud-like elephants, Raghu changed the sky into the earth, and the earth into the sky.

30. That vast army moved in four parts ;—first the terror of his name, then the great noise, then clouds of dust, and lastly the chariots, and other things.

मरुपृष्ठान्युदम्भांसि नाव्याः सुप्रतरा नदीः ।
विपिनानि प्रकाशानि शक्तिमत्त्वाच्चकार सः ॥३१॥
स सेनां महतीं कर्षन् पूर्वसागरगामिनीम् ।
बभौ हरजटाभ्रष्टां गङ्गामिव भगीरथः ॥ ३२ ॥

মর্বিতি। স রঘুঃ, শক্তিমত্ত্বাৎ সমর্থত্বাৎ, মরুপৃষ্ঠানি নির্জলস্থানানি, উদম্ভাংসি উদ্ভূতজলানি, চকার, নাব্যাঃ নৌভিঃ তার্য্যাঃ নদীঃ সুপ্রতরাঃ সুখেন তার্য্যাঃ চকার, বিপিনানি অরণ্যানি, প্রকাশানি নির্বৃক্ষাণি চকার। শক্ত্যুৎকর্ষাৎ তস্যাগম্যং কিমপি নাসীদ ইতি ভাবঃ ॥ ৩১ ॥

স ইতি। মহতীং সেনাং পূর্বসাগরগামিনীং কর্ষন্, সঃ রঘুঃ হরস্য জটাভ্যঃ ভ্রষ্টাং গঙ্গাং কর্ষন্ ভগীরথঃ ইব বভৌ। ভগীরথো নাম কশ্চিৎ কপিলদগ্ধানাং সাগরাণাং নপ্তা তৎপাবনায় হরকিরীটাৎ গঙ্গাপ্রবর্ত্তয়িতা রাজা যৎসম্বন্ধাদ্গঙ্গা চ ভাগীরথীতি গীয়তে ॥ ৩২ ॥

সেই রঘু বিপুল বিক্রমে মরু সকলকে জলাশয়পূর্ণ করিয়া, নৌসাধ্য নদী সকলকে সেতু প্রভৃতির দ্বারা অনায়াসে তরণীয় করিয়া, ও বন সকল পরিষ্কার করিয়া চলিলেন ॥ ৩১ ॥

ভগীরথ পুরাকালে হরজটাভ্রষ্টা গঙ্গাকে সঙ্গে করিয়া পূর্ব্বাভিমুখে যখন গিয়াছিলেন তখন তাঁহার যেরূপ শোভা হইয়াছিল, সেই বিপুল সৈন্য পশ্চাতে লইয়া পূর্ব্বসাগরাভিমুখী হওয়াতে রঘুরও সেই প্রকার শোভা হইল ॥ ৩২ ॥

---

31. Ho dug tanks in the midst of deserts, made rivers, that were difficult of crossing easily crossable, and cleared up largo forests, all this be made by the dint of his power.

32. As Bhagirath did once lead out the great Ganges, from

ত্যাজিতৈঃ ফলমুৎখাতৈর্ভগ্নৈশ্চ বহুধা নৃপৈঃ।
তস্যাসীদুল্বণো মার্গঃ পাদপৈরিব দন্তিনঃ ॥৩৩॥
পৌরস্ত্যানেবমাক্রামন্ তাংস্তান্ জনপদান্ জয়ী।
প্রাপ তালীবনশ্যামম্ উপকণ্ঠং মহোদধেঃ ॥৩৪॥

ত্যাজিতৈরিতি। ফলং, লাভং বৃক্ষপক্ষে প্রসবঞ্চ, ত্যাজিতৈঃ, উৎখাতৈঃ স্বপদাৎ ত্যাজিতৈঃ, অন্যত্র উৎপাটিতৈঃ, বহুধা ভগ্নৈঃ রণে জিতৈঃ, অন্যত্র ছিন্নৈঃ, নৃপৈঃ পাদপৈঃ, দন্তিনঃ গজস্য ইব তস্য রঘোঃ মার্গঃ উল্বণঃ প্রকাশঃ আসীৎ ॥ ৩৩ ॥

পৌরস্ত্যানিতি। জয়ী জয়নশীলঃ, সঃ রঘুঃ এবং পুরঃ ভবান্ পৌরস্ত্যান্ প্রাচ্যান্, তান্ তান্ সর্বান্ ইত্যর্থঃ, জনপদান্ দেশান্, আক্রামন্ তালীবনৈঃ শ্যামং মহোদধেঃ উপকণ্ঠম্ অন্তিকং প্রাপ ॥ ৩৪ ॥

ফলবিহীন, বা উন্মূলিত, বা ভগ্ন বৃক্ষ সকল যেমন গজরাজের গমনপথের পরিচায়কস্বরূপ থাকে, সেইরূপ রঘু যে যে পথ দিয়া যাইতে লাগিলেন, কোন রাজাকে বা হৃতসর্ব্বস্ব করিয়া, কাহাকেও বা স্বস্থানচ্যুত করিয়া, কাহাকেও বা যুদ্ধে পরাজিত ও হতশ্রী করিয়া দেদীপ্যমান প্রমাণস্বরূপ রাখিয়া যাইতে লাগিলেন ॥ ৩৩ ॥

জয়শালী রঘু এইরূপে পূর্ব্বদেশীয় সমুদায় দেশ ও জনপদ আক্রমণ

---

amongst the matted locks of Siva, so he led after him that vast army towards the Eastern sea.

33. As the condition of the trees on both sides of a road best indicate that an elephant had passed by that way, so the princes, some of whom were robbed of their wealth, others dethroned, others broken and destroyed, carried the marks of the progress of his army.

34. Conquering the Eastern countries in this manner, the

অনম্রাণাং সমুদ্ধর্তুস্তস্মাৎ সিন্ধুরযাদিব।
আত্মা সংরক্ষিতঃ সুহ্মৈর্বৃত্তিমাশ্রিত্য বৈতসীম্॥৩৫॥
বঙ্গানুৎখায় তরসা নেতা নৌসাধনোদ্যতান্।
নিচখান জয়স্তম্ভান্ গঙ্গাস্রোতোঽন্তরেষু সঃ॥৩৬॥

অনম্রাণামিতি। অনম্রাণাম্ সমুদ্ধর্তুঃ উন্মূলয়িতুঃ তস্মাৎ রঘোঃ সকাশাৎ, সিন্ধুরযাৎ নদীবেগাৎ ইব, সুহ্মৈঃ সুহ্মদেশীয়ৈঃ বৈতসী বেতসঃ সম্বন্ধিনী বৃত্তিং প্রবৃত্তিম্ ইত্যর্থঃ, আশ্রিত্য আত্মা সংরক্ষিতঃ. অত্র কৌটিল্যঃ "বলীয়সাভিযুক্তো দুর্বলঃ সর্বত্রানুপ্রণতো বৈতসধর্মমাতিষ্ঠেৎ" ইতি॥৩৫॥

বঙ্গানিতি। নেতা নায়কঃ, সঃ রঘুঃ, নৌভিঃ সাধনৈঃ, উদ্যতান্ সন্নদ্ধান্ বঙ্গান্, রাজ্ঞঃ তরসা বলেন, উৎখায় উন্মূল্য, গঙ্গায়াঃ স্রোতসাং

ও পরাজয় করিয়া অবশেষে সমুদ্রতীরবর্ত্তী তালবনপূর্ণ প্রদেশে গিয়া উপনীত হইলেন॥ ৩৪॥

নদীর স্রোত যেমন নমনশীল তরুলতাকে ভগ্ন করে না, কিন্তু কঠিন ও উন্নত মস্তক বৃক্ষকেই ভগ্ন করে সেইরূপ রঘুও গর্ব্বিত এবং উন্নত-মস্তক বৃক্ষদিগকে ভগ্ন করিতেন; সুহ্মদেশীয়গণ বেত্রের ন্যায় তাঁহার চরণে নত হইয়া আত্মরক্ষা করিল॥ ৩৫॥

বঙ্গদেশীয়গণ সেই যুদ্ধে প্রবৃত্ত হইলে রঘু নিজবলে তাহাদিগকে

---

hero at last reached the shores of the sea, covered with forests of palm trees.

35. The stiff-necked and proud he loved to destroy: consequently as his vast army approached like a storm-wave, the sumha princes sarved themselves only by bending their necks, in imitation of the cane plant.

36. He vanquished with his power the princes of Bengal,

আপাদপদ্মপ্রণতাঃ কলমা ইব তে রঘুম্।
ফলৈঃ সংবর্দ্ধয়ামাসুঃ উৎখাতপ্রতিরোপিতাঃ ॥৩৭॥
স তীর্ত্বা কপিশাং সৈন্যৈঃ বদ্ধদ্বিরদসেতুভিঃ।

প্রবাহান্তরালেষু, অন্তরীপে দ্বীপেষু, জয়স্তম্ভান্ নিচখান স্থাপিতবান্ ইত্যর্থঃ ॥ ৩৬ ॥

আপাদেতি। আপাদপদ্মম্ অঙ্ঘ্রিপদ্মপর্য্যন্তং, প্রণতাঃ অতএব উৎখাতাঃ পূর্ব্বমুদ্ধৃতাঃ অপি প্রতিরোপিতাঃ পশ্চাৎ স্থাপিতাঃ তে বঙ্গাঃ, কলমাঃ ইব শালিবিশেষাঃ ইব, তেঽপি আপাদপদ্মং পাদপদ্মমূলপর্য্যন্তং, প্রণতাঃ উৎখাতপ্রতিরোপিতাশ্চ, রঘুং ফলৈঃ, ধনৈঃ অন্যত্র শস্যৈঃ, সংবর্দ্ধয়ামাসুঃ ॥ ৩৭ ॥

স ইতি। স রঘুঃ বদ্ধাঃ দ্বিরদাঃ এব সেতবঃ যৈঃ তৈঃ সৈন্যৈঃ, কপিশাং

পরাজয় করিয়া গঙ্গার স্রোতের মধ্যে জয়সূচক স্তম্ভ নির্ম্মাণ করাইলেন। ৩৬ ॥

তাহাদিগকে জয় করিয়া যখন আবার স্বস্থানে প্রতিষ্ঠিত করিলেন, তখন তাহারা ধান্যের ন্যায় মস্তক অবনত করিয়া ধনদান দ্বারা তাঁহার সন্তোষ সাধন করিল। ৩৭ ॥

সেই রঘু হস্তিদিগের দ্বারা সেতু রচনা করিয়া সসৈন্যে কপিশা

who had marshalled together a strong naval force, and as monuments of his victory got pillars to be erected within the stream of the Ganges.

37. He re-instated many of the princes on their thrones and as a mark of their gratitude they bowed themselves to the dust at his feet, like unto the pliable paddy and made presents of fruits.

38. He crossed the river Kapisha with his army on an

उत्कलादर्शितपथः कलिङ्गाभिमुखो ययौ ॥ ३८ ॥

स प्रतापं महेन्द्रस्य मूर्ध्नि तीक्ष्णं न्यवेशयत् ।

अङ्कुशं द्विरदस्येव यन्ता गम्भीरवेदिनः ॥ ३९ ॥

नाम नदीम्, करभाम् इति केचित् पठन्ति । तीर्णा उत्कलैः राजभिः, आदर्शितपथः सन्दर्शितमार्गः सन्, कलिङ्गाभिमुखः ययौ ॥ ३८ ॥

स इति । सः रघुः, महेन्द्रस्य कुलपर्वतविशेषस्य, "महेन्द्रो मलयः सह्यः शक्तिमानृक्षपर्वतः । विन्ध्यश्च पारियात्रश्च सप्तैते कुलपर्वताः ॥" इति विष्णुपुराणात् । मूर्ध्नि तीक्ष्णं दुःसहं प्रतापं, यन्ता सारथिः गम्भीरवेदिनः द्विरदस्य गजविशेषस्य, मूर्ध्नि तीक्ष्णं निशितम् अङ्कुशम् इव न्यवेशयत् निक्षिप्तवान् । "त्वग्भेदाच्छोणितस्रावात् मांसस्य क्रथनादपि । आत्मानं यो न जानाति स स्याद्गम्भीरवेदिता ॥" इति राजपुत्रीये । "चिरकालेन यो वेत्ति शिक्षां परिचितामपि । गम्भीरवेदी विज्ञेयः स गजो गजवेदिभिः" इति मृगचर्मीये ॥ ३९ ॥

নদী উত্তীর্ণ হইয়া উৎকল-দেশীয় রাজগণের প্রদর্শিত পথে কলিঙ্গাভিমুখে যাত্রা করিলেন ॥ ৩৮ ॥

মাহুত যেমন গজরাজের শিরে অঙ্কুশ প্রোথিত করে সেইরূপ রঘু মহেন্দ্র পর্ব্বতের শিখরে আপনার দুঃসহ প্রতাপকে নিখাত করিলেন ॥৩৯॥

elephant bridge, and being led by the princes of Orissa, bent his course towards Kalinga.

39. He encamped with all the influence of his military glory, on the Mahendra Hill, like into the elephant driver, who plunges deep his goading rod, on the head of an elephant made restless with the pain.

প্রতিজগ্রাহ কালিঙ্গঃ তমস্ত্রৈর্গজসাধনঃ* ।
পক্ষচ্ছেদোদ্যতং শক্রং শিলাবর্ষীব পর্ব্বতঃ ॥ ৪০ ॥
দ্বিষাং বিষহ্য কাকুৎস্থঃ তত্র নারাচদুর্দ্দিনম্ ।
সন্মঙ্গলস্নাত ইব প্রতিপেদে জয়শ্রিয়ম্ ॥ ৪১ ॥

প্রতীতি। গজসাধনঃ সন্ কালিঙ্গঃ কলিঙ্গানাং রাজা অস্ত্রৈঃ আয়ুধৈঃ, তং রঘুং পক্ষাণাং ছেদে উদ্যতম্ উদ্যুক্তং, শক্রং শিলাবর্ষী পর্ব্বতঃ ইব প্রতিজগ্রাহ প্রত্যভিযুক্তবান্ ॥ ৪০ ॥

দ্বিষামিতি। কাকুৎস্থঃ রঘুঃ, তত্র মহেন্দ্রাদ্রৌ দ্বিষাং নারাচদুর্দ্দিনং নারাচানাং বাণবিশেষাণাং দুর্দ্দিনং, তদ্বারা বর্ষমুচ্যতে, বিষহ্য

ইন্দ্র পক্ষচ্ছেদে উদ্যত হইলে পর্ব্বত সকল যেমন তাঁহার উপর শিলাবৃষ্টি করিয়াছিল, সেইরূপ কলিঙ্গ নরপতি গজসৈন্য লইয়া অস্ত্র বৃষ্টি পূর্ব্বক রঘুকে গ্রহণ করিলেন ॥ ৪০ ॥

রঘু শত্রুগণের বাণবৃষ্টি সহ্য করিয়া, যেন মঙ্গল স্নান করিয়া উঠিলেন ; ও জয়শ্রী লাভ করিলেন ॥ ৪১ ॥

---

40. The prince of Kalinga, who came to the fight with a large number of elephants recieved Raghu with a shower of missiles ; as the mountain did once receive Indra with a shower of stones, when the latter made an attempt to cut down their wings.

41. Raghu came out victorious from their shower of

গজসাধনঃ—গজাঃ করিণ এব সাধনং প্রধানং যুদ্ধোপকরণং যস্য স গজসাধনঃ গজবলসমন্বিত ইত্যর্থঃ ।—attended by an elephant army.

ताम्बूलीनां दलैस्तत्र रचितापानभूमयः ।
नारिकेलासवं योधाः शात्रवञ्च पपुर्यशः ॥४२॥
गृहीतप्रतिमुक्तस्य स धर्मविजयी नृपः ।
श्रियं महेन्द्रनाथस्य जहार न तु मेदिनीम् ॥४३॥

वहिला, तत् यथायाक्यं मङ्गलस्नातः इव विजयमङ्गलार्थे अभिषिक्तः इव जयश्रियं प्रतिपेदे प्राप ॥ ४१ ॥

ताम्बूलीनामिति । तत्र महेन्द्राद्रौ, युध्यन्ते इति योधाः, रचिताः कल्पिताः, आपानभूमय पानयोग्यप्रदेशा, यैः ते तथोक्ताः सन्तः, नारिकेलासवं नारिकेलमद्यं ताम्बूलीनां नागवल्लीनां दलैः पपुः तत्र पिजह्रुः इत्यर्थः ; शात्रवं यशश्च पपुः जह्रुः इत्यर्थः ॥ ४२ ॥

गृहीतेति । धर्म्मविजयी धर्म्मार्थं विजयशीलः स नृपः रघुः गृहीतश्चासौ प्रतिमुक्तः तस्य महेन्द्रनाथस्य, कालिङ्गस्य श्रियं जहार ।

রঘুর সৈনিকগণ সেখানে সুরাপানোচিত স্থান প্রস্তুত করিয়া তাম্বূল পত্রের পাত্র দ্বারা নারিকেলজাত এক প্রকার মদ্যপান করিল ; সেই সঙ্গে সঙ্গে শত্রুদিগের যশও পান করিল ॥ ৪২ ॥

ধর্ম্মবিজয়ী রঘু মহেন্দ্রাধিপতিকে বন্দী করিয়া আবার ছাড়িয়া দিলেন, তাঁহার রাজলক্ষ্মীকেই হরণ করিলেন, রাজ্য হরণ করিলেন না ॥ ৪৩ ॥

---

arrows, and shone in his glory, as if fresh from an ablution, preparatory to some holy ceremony

42. His soldiers made little drinking-grounds in the forest of those hills, and drank the cocoanut-wine from vessels made of the betel-leaves, the wine resembling the good name of their enemies.

43. Raghu, who always adhered to the rules of righteous

ततो वेलातटेनैव *फलवत्पूगमालिना ।
†अगस्त्याचरितामाशाम् अनाशास्यजयो ययौ॥४४

धर्म्मार्थिम् इति भावः, मेदिनीं तु न जहार शरणागतवात्सल्यात् इति भावः ॥ ४३ ॥

तत इति। ततः प्राचीविजयानन्तरं, फलवत्पूगमालिना फलितक्रमुकश्रेणीमता वेलायाः समुद्रकूलस्य तटेन उपान्तेनैव अगस्त्येन आचरिताम् आशां दक्षिणां दिशम् अनाशास्यजयः अयत्नसिद्धत्वात् अप्रार्थनीयजयः सन् ययौ। "अगस्त्यो दक्षिणामाशाम् आश्रित्य नभसि स्थितः। वरुणस्यात्मजो योगी विन्ध्यवातापिमर्दनः॥" इति ब्रह्मपुराणे ॥ ४४ ॥

এইরূপে অতি সহজে পূর্ব্বদেশ জয় করিয়া রঘু গুবাকবৃক্ষসমাকীর্ণ সমুদ্রের উপকূলভাগ দিয়া দাক্ষিণাত্যাভিমুখে অগ্রসর হইলেন ॥ ৪৪ ॥

warfare, liberated the prince of Mahendra, whom he had taken captive; and robbed him of his glory and not of his lands.

44. They moved towards the south along the sea shore covered with forests of fruit-bearing *pugu* tree, scarcely obstructed in his course.

* फलवत्पूगमालिना—फलवतां फलशालिनां पूगानां गुवाकवृक्षाणां माला श्रेणिर्विद्यते यत्र, तेन फलवत्पूगमालिना ।

† अगस्त्याचरितां—अगस्त्येन तन्नाम्ना ग्रहविशेषेण ऋषिविशेषेण वा ।—The direction indicated by the star Agastya.

स *सैन्यपरिभोगेण गजदानसुगन्धिना ।
कावेरीं सरितां पत्युः शङ्कनीयामिवाकरोत् ॥४५॥
बलैरध्युषितास्तस्य विजिगीषोर्गताध्वनः ।

स इति । सः रघुः गजानां दानेन मदेन सुगन्धिना सुरभिगन्धिना (गन्धस्येत्यादिना इकारादेशः समासान्तः यद्यपि गन्धस्येत्वे तदेकान्तग्रहणं कर्त्तव्यमिति नैसर्गिकगन्धविवक्षायामेवेकारादेशस्तथापि निरङ्कुशाः कवयः। तथा माघकाव्ये "ववुरयुक्छदसुगन्धयः सततगास्ततगानगिरोऽलिभिः।" नैषधे च "अपां हि तृप्ताय न वारिधारा स्वादुः सुगन्धिः स्वदते तुषारा" इति। न कर्मधारयान्मत्वर्थीय इति निषेधादिनिप्रत्ययपक्षोऽपि जघन्य एव।) सेनायां समवेताः सैन्याः तेषां परिभोगेण कावेरीं नाम सरितं सरितां पत्युः समुद्रस्य शङ्कनीयां न विश्वसनीयामिव अकरोत् ॥ ४५ ॥

बलैरिति । विजिगीषोः विजेतुमिच्छोः, गताध्वनः तस्य रघोः बलैः

তাহার সৈন্যগণ কাবেরী নদীর জল সেবা করাতে জলমগ্ন করিগণের মদজল গন্ধে তাহার বারি মদ-গন্ধ-বিশিষ্ট হইল, সুতরাং কাবেরী যেন, সরিৎপতি সমুদ্রের আশঙ্কার কারণ হইল ॥ ৪৫ ॥

দিগ্বিজয়ী সেই দিকের সৈন্যগণ বহু পথ অতিক্রম করিয়া অবশেষে

45. His soldiers enjoyed a hearty bath in the waters of the river Kaveri, fragrant with the smell of elephant sweat, thus making that river an object of jealousy to her Lord the ocean.

46. Tired by their long journey, his soldiers rested them

* सैन्यपरिभोगः—सैन्यानां सैनिकपुरुषाणां यः परिभोगः विहारः जलक्रीडादिरित्यर्थः तेन ।

मारीचोद्भ्रान्तहारीता मलयाद्रेरुपत्यकाः ॥४६॥

ससञ्जुरश्वक्षुण्णानाम्* एलानामुत्पतिष्णवः ।
तुल्यगन्धिषु मत्तेभकटेषु फलरेणवः ॥ ४७ ॥

सैन्यैः मारीचेषु मारीचवनेषु उद्भ्रान्ताः परिभ्रान्ताः हारीताः पक्षिविशेषाः यासु ताः मलयाद्रेः उपत्यकाः आसन्नभूमयः अध्युषिताः उपत्यकाद्रेरासन्ना भूमिरूर्ध्वमधित्यकेत्यमरः । उपान्वध्याङ्वसः इति कर्म्मत्वम ॥ ४६ ॥

ससञ्जुरिति । अश्वैः क्षुण्णानाम् एलानाम् उत्पतिष्णवः उत्पतनशीलाः, फलरेणवः फलरजांसि, तुल्यगन्धिषु समानगन्धिषु मत्तेभानां कटेषु, ससञ्जुः सक्ताः ॥ ४७ ॥

মলয় পর্ব্বতের উপত্যকাতে গিয়া শিবির সন্নিবিষ্ট করিল, যেথানে মারীচবনে হারীত পক্ষী সকল উড়িয়া বেড়াইতেছে ॥ ৪৬ ॥

সেই স্থানে অশ্বের খুর-পিষ্ট, এলাইচ দলের রেণু সকল উড়িয়া সমগন্ধী মত্তগজ সমূহের গণ্ডপ্রদেশে লগ্ন হইতে লাগিল ॥ ৪৭ ॥

---

selves, in the valley of the Malaya mountains covered with *Maricha* forests, where flock of *Harita* birds were flying about at their ease.

47. Beaten by hoofs of horses, the dust of *elachi* fruits stick on the sweating temples of the elephants, having a similar smell.

*अश्वक्षुण्णानां—अश्वैः सेनाङ्गभूतैः वाजिभिः क्षुण्णानां पाददलितानां । एतेन दिशि तस्यां एलालताबाहुल्यं ध्वन्यते ।—The implied sense—There was such a plenty of एलालता in those parts of the country, that the horses trampled any number of them under foot as they passed.

*भोगिवेष्टनमार्गेषु चन्दनानां समर्पितम्।
नास्रसत् करिणां ग्रैवं त्रिपदीच्छेदिनामपि॥४८॥
दिशि मन्दायते तेजः दक्षिणस्यां रवेरपि।
तस्यामेव रघोः पाण्ड्याः प्रतापं न विषेहिरे॥४९॥

भोगीति। चन्दनानां चन्दनद्रुमाणां, भोगिवेष्टनमार्गेषु सर्पवेष्टनात् निम्नेषु, समर्पितं सक्तिं त्रिपदीच्छेदिनां पादशृङ्खलच्छेदकानाम् अपि करिणां ग्रीवासु भवं ग्रैवं कण्ठबन्धनम् नास्रसत् न स्खलन्मुक्त॥ ४८॥

दिशीति। दक्षिणस्यां दिशि रवेः अपि तेजः मन्दायते मन्दं

সর্পগণ চন্দন বৃক্ষকে নিরন্তর বেষ্টন করিয়া থাকাতে সেই সকল বৃক্ষদেহের যে যে ভাগ নত হইয়া গিয়াছে, সেই খাঁজে খাঁজে হস্তীর গ্রীবার বন্ধন রজ্জু লগ্ন করাতে করিগণ পদশৃঙ্খল ভগ্ন করিয়াও সেই বন্ধন ছাড়াইতে পারিল না॥ ৪৮॥

যে দাক্ষিণাত্য প্রদেশে সূর্য্যের কিরণেরও উগ্রতা হ্রাস হইয়া

48. The long chains of the elephants stuck so fitly in the grooves, made on the barks of *chandana* trees by serpents twisting round them, that such of the animals as had broken the chains of their necks, were held in their places, by the chains sticking in the bark-grooves.

49. In the south, even the scorching rays of the sun are

* भोगिवेष्टनमार्गेषु—भोगः फणा विद्यते एषां भोगिनः सर्पास्तेषां वेष्टनानि तैः कृतान्यावेष्टनानीत्यर्थः तानि भोगिवेष्टनानि तेषां ये मार्गाः पन्थानः पुनःपुनरावेष्टनजाताः खातविशेषाः तेषु।

ताम्रपर्णीसमेतस्य मुक्तासारं महोदधेः ।
ते निपत्य ददुस्तस्मै यशः स्वमिव सञ्चितम् ॥५०॥
स निर्विश्य यथाकामं तटेष्वालीनचन्दनौ ।
स्तनाविव दिशस्तस्याः शैलौ मलयदर्दुरौ ॥५१॥

भवति। दक्षिणायने तेजोमान्द्यात् इति भावः, तस्याम् एव दिशि पाण्ड्याः पाण्ड्यानां जनपदानां राजानः पाण्ड्याः, रघोः प्रतापं न विषेहिरे न सोढवन्तः। सूर्यविजयिनोऽपि विजितवानिति नायकस्य महानुत्कर्षो गम्यते ॥ ४९ ॥

ताम्रपर्णीति। ते पाण्ड्याः ताम्रपर्ण्या नद्या समेतस्य सङ्गतस्य महोदधेः सम्बन्धि सञ्चितं मुक्तासारं मौक्तिकवरम्, स्वं स्वकीयं सञ्चितं यशः इव, तस्मै रघवे निपत्य प्रणिपत्य ददुः। यशसः शुभ्रत्वादौपम्यम्। ताम्रपर्णीसङ्गमे मौक्तिकोत्पत्तिरिति प्रसिद्धम् ॥ ५० ॥

स इति। असह्येति च। युग्ममेतत्। असह्यविक्रमः सः रघुः,

থাকে, সেই থানেই পাণ্ড্যগণ রঘুর প্রতাপ সহ্য করিতে পারিল না ॥৪৯॥

সেই পাণ্ড্যগণ তাঁহার চরণে প্রণত হইয়া তাম্রপর্ণী নদীর সাগর-সঙ্গম-স্থল-জাত, উৎকৃষ্ট মুক্তা সকল, স্বীয় যশের ন্যায় তাঁহাকে উপহার দিল ॥ ৫০ ॥

অসহ্যবিক্রম রঘু দক্ষিণ ভূমির স্তনস্বরূপ চন্দনবৃক্ষ সমন্বিত মলয় ও

---

of no effect, on the inhabitants ; even there the Pandya princes could not bear the great prowess of Raghu.

50. Those princes offered large presents of pearls, collected from that part of the sea, where the river *Tamraparni* falls into it.

51. 52. Having enjoyed to his heart's content, the two

असह्यविक्रमः सह्यं दूरान्मुक्तमुदन्वता ।
नितम्बमिव मेदिन्याः स्रस्तांशुकमलङ्घयत् ॥५२॥
तस्यानीकैर्विसर्पद्भिः अपरान्तजयोद्यतैः ।
रामास्त्रोत्सारितोऽप्यासीत् सह्यलग्न् इवार्णवः ५३

तटेषु सानुषु, आलीनचन्दनौ व्याप्तचन्दनद्रुमौ, पक्षे प्रान्तेषु व्याप्तचन्दनानुलेपौ, तस्याः दक्षिणस्याः दिशः, स्तनौ इव स्थितौ मलयदर्दुरौ नाम शैलौ, यथाकामं यथेच्छं, निर्विश्य उपभुज्य, उदकानि अस्य सन्तीति उदन्वान् उदधिः, उदन्वता दूरात् मुक्तं दूरतः त्यक्तम्, स्रस्तांशुकं मेदिन्याः नितम्बम् इव स्थितं, सह्यं सह्याद्रिम्, अलङ्घयत् प्राप्तः अतिक्रान्तो वा ॥ ५१ ॥ ५२ ॥

सम्प्रति प्रतीचीं दिशमभियायादित्याह, तस्येति । अपरान्तानां पाश्चात्यानां, जये उद्यतैः उद्युक्तैः विसर्पद्भिः गच्छद्भिः, तस्य रघोः

দর্দ্দুর নামক পর্ব্বত দ্বয়কে উপভোগ করিয়া, তৎপরে সমুদ্রের জলরাশি কর্ত্তৃক পরিত্যক্ত সুতরাং মেদিনীর বিবস্ত্র নিতম্বের ন্যায় শোভমান সহ্যাদ্রিকে উল্লঙ্ঘন করিলেন ॥ ৫১ ॥ ৫২ ॥

পূর্ব্বকালে পরশুরামের অস্ত্রপ্রভাবে সাগর বহুদূরে পড়িয়াছিল. কিন্তু এক্ষণে রঘুর বিপুল সৈন্যদল যখন পাশ্চাত্যদিগের জয়োদ্দেশে

hills Malaya and Dardura, both of which were girdled by the chandana forest, and looked by reason like two rising breasts of the earth, he, of irresistible valour crossed the Sahya mountains from which the sea retreating gave it the appearance of the uncovered button of the earth.

53. Long before had the sea been obliged to retreat from the Sahya Mountain, by the might of the arms of *Parasuram*,

भयोत्सृष्टविभूषाणां तेन केरलयोषिताम् ।
अलकेषु चमूरेणुः *चूर्णप्रतिनिधीकृतः ॥ ५४ ॥

अनीकैः सैन्यैः । अर्णवः रामस्य जामदग्न्यस्य अस्त्रैः उत्सारितः परिहारितः अपि सह्यलग्नः इव आसीत् । सैन्यं द्वितीयोऽर्णव इव दृश्यते इति भावः ॥ ५३ ॥

भयेति । तेन रघुणा भयेन उत्सृष्टविभूषाणां परिहृतभूषणानां, केरलयोषितां केरलाङ्गनानाम्, अलकेषु, चमूरेणुः सेनारजः, चूर्णस्य कुङ्कुमादिरजसः प्रतिनिधीकृतः, एतेन योषितां पलायनं चमूनाञ्च तदनुधावनं ध्वन्यते ॥ ५४ ॥

অগ্রসর হইল, তখন বোধ হইতে লাগিল, যেন সাগর বিস্তৃত হইয়া সহ্যাদ্রিতে লাগিয়াছে ॥ ৫৩ ॥

কেরল নারীগণ ভয়ে ভূষণাদি পরিত্যাগ করিয়া পলায়নপরায়ণ হইলে, সৈন্যের পদোত্থিত ধূলিপটল কুঙ্কুমাদি রেণুর ন্যায় তাহাদের কুন্তল জালে পতিত হইতে লাগিল ॥ ৫৪ ॥

---

but now when Raghu's army marched towards the west in battle array, for the conquest of the kings of the western coast, they looked like an extended arm of the sea, and the distance between the Sahya and the sea was thus annihilated.

54. The women of the Kerala country fled before him and the clouds of dust raised by his army settled down upon their locks, thus representing ladie's powders, as it were.

* चूर्णप्रतिनिधीकृतः—चूर्णानां सुवासितरजसां प्रतिनिधिः अनुकल्पः कृतः । कामिनीनां रीतिरियं यत्ताः कुङ्कुमादिरजोभिः कबरीं सुवासितां कुर्वन्ति, समायाते तु रघुसैन्ये केरलनार्यो

मुरलामारुतोद्धूतम् अगमत् कैतकं रजः।
तद्योधवारबाणानाम् * अयत्नपटवासताम् ॥५५॥
अभ्यभूयत वाहानां चरतां गात्रशिञ्जितैः।
वर्मभिः पवनोद्धूत-राजतालीवन-ध्वनिः ॥ ५६ ॥

मुरलेति। मुरला नाम केरलदेशेषु काचित् नदी। मरलीति केचित् पठन्ति। तस्याः मारुतेन, उद्धूतम् उत्थापितं, कैतकं केतकीसम्बन्धि, रजः तद्योधवारबाणानां रघुभटकञ्चुकानाम् अयत्नपटवासताम् अयत्नसिद्धवस्त्रवासनाद्रव्यत्वम् अगमत् ॥ ५५ ॥

अभ्यभूयतेति। चरतां गच्छतां वाहानां वाजिनाम्, गात्रशिञ्जितैः गात्रेषु शब्दायमानैः, सञ्जितैरिति वा पाठः। वर्म्मभिः कवचैः, पवनेन

মুরলা নদীর বায়ুতাড়িত কেতকীপুষ্পের রেণু সকল, রঘুর যোদ্ধৃগণের কঞ্চুকোপরি অযত্নসিদ্ধ বস্ত্রাবরণের ন্যায় পড়িতে লাগিল ॥ ৫৫ ॥

ধাবমান অশ্বদলের গাত্রস্থিত বর্ম্ম সকলের ঝন্ ঝন্ ধ্বনিতে পবন-

55 The dust of Ketaki flowers wafted by the breezes of the river Murala, settled down upon the armour of his soldiers, and served the purpose of dress-perfuming powders, as it were.

56. The noises by the Rajtalee trees beaten by the breeze

भयात् पलायनपरायणाः नाङ्गरागादिकरणे अवसरं प्रापुः, पुनस्तु रघोश्चमूरेणुस्तासां कबरीषु, कुङ्कुमादिरजसामनुकल्पो बभूवेति भावः।

अयत्नपटवासतां—पटं वस्त्रं वासयन्ति ये ते पटवासाः वस्त्रादौ सुगन्धोत्पादकाः द्रव्यविशेषाः अयत्नसिद्धाः अनायासलब्धा इत्यर्थः पटवासास्तेषां भावः अयत्नपटवासता ताम्।

19

খর্জ্জূরীস্কন্ধনদ্ধানাং মদোদ্গারসুগন্ধিষু।
কটেষু করিণাং পেতুঃ পুন্নাগেভ্যঃ শিলীমুখাঃ ॥৫৭॥
অবকাশং কিলোদন্বান্ রামায়াভ্যর্থিতো দদৌ।

উদ্ধূতানাং কম্পিতানাং রাজতালীবনানাং ধ্বনিঃ অভ্যভূয়ত তিরস্কৃতঃ। মর্ম্মরঃ ইতি পাঠে বাহানাং গাত্রশিঞ্জিতৈঃ গাত্রধ্বনিভিঃ ভূষণৈঃ। মর্ম্মরঃ মর্ম্মরাত্মনাথাঃ ইতি ধ্বনেবিশেষণম্ ॥ ৫৬ ॥

খর্জ্জূরীতি। খর্জ্জূরীণাং বৃক্ষবিশেষাণাম্ স্কন্ধেষু প্রকাণ্ডেষু নদ্ধানাং করিণাং মদোদ্গারেণ মদস্রাবেণ, সুগন্ধিষু কটেষু গণ্ডেষু পুন্নাগেভ্যঃ নাগকেশরেভ্যঃ, পুন্নাগপুষ্পাণি বিহায়, শিলীমুখাঃ অলয়ঃ পেতুঃ ততোঽপি সৌগন্ধ্যাতিশয়াৎ ইতি ভাবঃ ॥ ৫৭ ॥

অবকাশমিতি। উদন্বান্ উদধিঃ, রামায় জামদগ্ন্যায়, অভ্যর্থিতঃ যাচিতঃ, সন্, অবকাশং স্থানং, দদৌ, কিলেতি প্রসিদ্ধৌ, রঘবেতু অপরান্তমহীপালব্যাজেন করং বলিং দদৌ, অপরান্তানাং সমুদ্রমধ্য-

তাড়িত রাজতালীবনের শব্দকে পরাভূত করিয়া ফেলিল ॥ ৫৬ ॥

ভ্রমর সকল পুন্নাগ বৃক্ষ হইতে উড়িয়া উড়িয়া খর্জ্জুর বৃক্ষে বদ্ধ করিগণের মদগন্ধ-বিশিষ্ট গণ্ডস্থলে পড়িতে লাগিল ॥ ৫৭ ॥

পরশুরামের প্রার্থনানুসারে পুরাকালে সমুদ্র সরিয়া গিয়া তাঁহাকে

were quite drowned by the jinglings of the armours, which were on the bodies of his horses.

57. His elephants were tied to the trunks of *Kharjur* trees, and as the animals stood there, flights of bees fell, from the *Punnaga* flowers, upon their temples fragrant with the temporal juice.

58. The ocean gave a pass to Rama, only when the latter

***अपरान्तमहीपाल-व्याजेन रघवे करम् ॥५८॥**
मत्तेभ-रदनोत्कीर्ण-व्यक्त-विक्रम-लक्षणम् ।
त्रिकूटमेव तत्रोच्चैः जयस्तम्भं चकार सः ॥५९॥

देशवर्त्तित्वात् तैर्दत्ते करे समुद्रदत्तत्वोपचारः । कदाचित्तु भीत्या न तु याच्ञयेति रामाद्रघोरुत्कर्षः ॥ ५८ ॥

मत्तेति । तत्र स रघुः मत्तानाम् इभानां, रदनोत्कीर्णानि दन्तक्षतानि, एव व्यक्तानि, स्फुटानि विक्रमलक्षणानि पराक्रमचिह्नानि, विजयवर्णावलिस्थानानि यस्मिन् तं तथोक्तं त्रिकूटम् एव उच्चैः जयस्तम्भं चकार । गाढ़प्रकाशस्त्रिकूटोऽद्रिरेवोत्कीर्णवर्णास्तम्भ इव रघोर्जयस्तम्भोऽभूत् इत्यर्थः ॥ ५९ ॥

স্বয়ং দিয়াছিলেন, এক্ষণে প্রতিনিধি-স্বরূপ পাশ্চাত্য রাজগণের হস্ত দ্বারা রঘুকে উপহার দিলেন ॥ ৫৮ ॥

রঘুর মত্ত গজ সকল দন্ত দ্বারা ত্রিকূট পর্ব্বতকে ক্ষত বিক্ষত করিয়া ফেলিল, সুতরাং সেই ত্রিকূট পর্ব্বতই যেন রঘুর বিজয়সূচক স্তম্ভ-স্বরূপ হইল ॥ ৫৯ ॥

had besought for it, but to Raghu it gave its tribute through the princes of the western coast.

59. In those parts of the country Raghu made the mountain Trikuta, bearing many marks of his valour, in the shape of deep scars made by the tusks of his infuriated elephants, the best trophy of his conquest.

* अपरान्तमहीपालव्याजेन—अपरान्ते पाश्चात्यप्रदेशे ये महीपालाः राजानः, त एव व्याजः अपदेशस्तेन ; स्वयं न दत्त्वा तेषामेव छलेन ददौ इत्यर्थः ।

पारसीकांस्ततो जेतुं प्रतस्थे स्थलवर्त्मना ।
इन्द्रियाख्यानिव रिपून् तत्त्वज्ञानेन संयमी ॥६०॥
यवनीमुखपद्मानां सेहे मधुमदं न सः ।
बालातपमिवाब्जानाम् अकालजलदोदयः ॥६१॥

पारसीकानिति। ततः सः रघुः, संयमी योगी, तत्त्वज्ञानेन, इन्द्रियाख्यान् इन्द्रियनामकान्, रिपून् इव, पारसीकान् राज्ञः, जेतुं स्थलवर्त्मना प्रतस्थे न तु निर्दिष्टेनापि जलपथेन समुद्रयानस्य निषिद्धत्वात् इति भावः ॥ ६० ॥

यवनीति। सः रघुः यवनीनां यवनस्त्रीणाम्, मुखानि पद्मानि इव मुखपद्मानि (उपमितसमासः) तेषां मधुना मद्येन यः मदः मदरागः तं न सेहे। कमिव? अकाले प्रावृड्व्यतिरिक्ते काले जलदोदयः प्रायेण प्रावृषि पद्मविकाशस्याप्रसक्तत्वात् अब्जानां सम्बन्धिनं बालातपम् इव। अब्जाहितत्वादसम्बन्धित्वं सौरातपस्य ॥ ६१ ॥

তদনন্তর, সংযমী যেমন তত্ত্বজ্ঞানকে অবলম্বন করিয়া ইন্দ্রিয় সকলকে জয় করিতে অগ্রসর হন, সেই রূপ রঘু স্থলপথ অবলম্বন করিয়া পারসী-দিগকে জয় করিতে অগ্রসর হইলেন ॥ ৬০ ॥

অকালে মেঘ-সঞ্চার হইয়া পদ্ম সকলের বিকাশকারী বালারুণের কিরণজালকে অস্তমিত করে, সেই রূপ যবননারীগণের মুখের মদজনিত আরক্ত প্রভাকে হরণ করিলেন ॥ ৬১ ॥

60. Then he proceeded on by land to conquer the Parsees, as proceeds a saint to conquer his internal enemies—his passions.

61. He could not bear the flush caused by wine in the faces of the *Jabana* women, as an untimely gathering of clouds

संग्रामस्तुमुलस्तस्य पाश्चात्यैरश्वसाधनैः ।
शार्ङ्गकूजितविज्ञेयप्रतियोधे रजस्यभूत् ॥ ६२ ॥

भल्लापवर्जितैस्तेषां शिरोभिः श्मश्रुलैर्महीम् ।
तस्तार सरघाव्याप्तैः स क्षौद्रपटलैरिव ॥ ६३ ॥

संग्राम इति । तस्य रघोः अश्वसाधनैः वाजिसैन्यैः । पाश्चात्यैः यवनैः सह । दक्षिणापश्चात्पुरस्तस्त्यक् । इत्यन्नायां विकाराः शार्ङ्गाणि धनूंषि तेषां कूजितैः शब्दैः, अथवा शार्ङ्गैः इत्यन्नसम्बन्धिभिः कूजितैः विज्ञेयाः अनुमेयाः प्रतियोधाः प्रतिभटाः यस्मिन् तस्मिन् रजसि तुमुलः संग्रामः सङ्कुलं युद्धम् अभूत ॥ ६२ ॥

भल्लेति । सः रघुः भल्लापवर्जितैः बाणविशेषच्छिन्नैः श्मश्रुलैः प्रवृद्ध-श्मश्रुरोमवद्भिः, सिध्मादिभ्यश्चेति लच्प्रत्ययः, तेषां पाश्चात्यानां शिरोभिः, सरघाभिः मधुमक्षिकाभिः व्याप्तैः क्षुद्राः सरघाः । क्षुद्राभिः कृतानि

অশ্বারোহিসৈন্যসমন্বিত পশ্চিমদেশবাসী যবনদিগের সহিত তাঁহার তুমুল যুদ্ধ হইল; যুদ্ধ স্থলে এত ধূলি উৎক্ষিপ্ত হইয়াছিল, যে শৃঙ্গ-ধ্বনি ভিন্ন পক্ষ প্রতিপক্ষ জানিবার অন্য উপায় ছিল না ॥ ৬২ ॥

যবনদিগের শ্মশ্রুপূর্ণ মস্তক সকল রঘুর ভল্লাস্ত্র দ্বারা দ্বিখণ্ডিত

---

bears not beauty of the lotus flower, lit up by the morning sun.

62. Fierce was the battle that took place between him and the inhabitants of the western coast; so thick were the volumes of dust raised by the contending armies, that the horns alone indicated the opposing ranks.

63. Till he filled up the whole field, with their bearded heads, severed from their bodies, looking like bee-hives covered with the bees.

*अपनीतशिरस्त्राणाः शेषास्तं शरणं ययुः।
प्रणिपातप्रतीकारः संरम्भो हि महात्मनाम् ॥६४॥
विनयन्ते स्म तद्योधा मधुभिर्विजयश्रमम्।

क्षौद्राणि मधूनि तैषां पटलैः सञ्चयैः इव महीं तस्तार आच्छादयामास ॥ ६३ ॥

अपनीतेति। शेषाः हतावशिष्टाः, अपनीतशिरस्त्राणाः अपसारितशीर्षण्याः सन्तः। शरणागतलक्षणमेतत्। तं रघुं शरणं ययुः। तथाहि महात्मनां संरम्भः कोपः, प्रणिपातः प्रणतिरेव प्रतीकारः यस्य सः। महतां परकीयमौद्धत्यमेवासह्यं न तु जीवितम् इति भावः ॥ ६४ ॥

विनयन्त इति। तस्य रघोः, योधाः भटाः, आस्तीर्णानि अजिन-

হইয়া রণভূমির চতুর্দ্দিকে ছড়াইয়া পড়িল; মুখগুলি মধুমক্ষিকা পূর্ণ মধুচক্রের ন্যায় দেখাইতে লাগিল॥ ৬৩॥

যাহারা অবশিষ্ট রহিল তাহারা মস্তকের উষ্ণীষ উন্মোচন করিয়া তাঁহার শরণাপন্ন হইল; মহামনা ব্যক্তিদিগের ক্রোধ প্রণিপাত করিলেই বিদূরিত হয়॥ ৬৪॥

তাঁহার সৈনিকগণ দ্রাক্ষাক্ষেত্রে উৎকৃষ্ট চর্ম্মাসন বিস্তার করিয়া

64. Those that escaped death, uncovered their heads and sought refuge under him; the great ones of the earth always give way to leniency, when one bows before them.

65. Squatting upon their precious deer-skins in the vine

* अपनीतशिरस्त्राणाः—शिरसः त्राणं रक्षणं येन तत्, उष्णीषमित्यर्थः, अपनीतं सम्मानप्रदर्शनार्थमुन्मोचितं शिरस्त्राणं यैः ते; प्रणतिपरायणा इत्यर्थः।

आस्तीर्णाजिनरत्नासु द्राक्षावलयभूमिषु ॥ ६५ ॥

ततः प्रतस्थे कौवेरीं *भास्वानिव रघुर्दिशम्।
शरैरुस्रैरिवोदीच्यान् उद्धरिष्यन् रसानिव ॥ ६६ ॥

विनीताध्वश्रमास्तस्य *सिन्धुतीरविचेष्टनैः।

रत्नानि चर्म्मश्रेष्ठानि यासु तासु, द्राक्षावलयानां भूमिषु, मधुभिः द्राक्षाफलप्रकृतिकैर्मद्यैः विजयश्रमं युद्धखेदं विनयन्तोऽपनीतवन्तः। कर्त्तृस्थे चाशरीरे कर्म्मणीत्यात्मनेपदं लट् स्म इति भूतार्थे लट् ॥ ६५ ॥

तत इति। ततः रघुः भास्वान् सूर्य्यः इव शरैः वाणैः उस्रैः किरणैः इव, उदीच्यान् उदग्भवान् नृपान्, रसान् उदकानि इव, उद्धरिष्यन् कौवेरीं कुवेरसम्बन्धिनीं दिशम् उदीचीं प्रतस्थे ॥ ६६ ॥

विनीतेति। सिन्धुनाम काश्मीरदेशेषु कश्चिन्नदविशेषः, सिन्धोः

বসিয়া, দ্রাক্ষারস-সম্ভূত সুরা পান দ্বারা শ্রম দূর করিতে লাগিল ॥ ৬৫ ॥

সূর্য্য যেমন কিরণজাল দ্বারা রসাকর্ষণের নিমিত্ত উত্তর পথাবলম্বী হয়, সেইরূপ রঘু শরবর্ষণের দ্বারা উত্তরদেশবাসিদিগকে বিনাশ করিবার নিমিত্ত উত্তরাভিমুখে অগ্রসর হইলেন ॥ ৬৬ ॥

তাঁহার অশ্বগণ সিন্ধুনদের কূলে পার্শ্বপরিবর্ত্তন পূর্ব্বক, পথশ্রম

---

grounds, his soldiers refreshed themselves by wine.

66. Then Raghu careered towards the north to conquer the Northerners, with his arrows, as careers the sun also towards the north to draw the sap of the earth by his rays.

67. By turning from side to side, on the banks of the

---

*भास्वानिव—भाः दीप्तिः किरणा वा विद्यते अस्य इति भास्वान् सूर्य्यः।

* सिन्धुतीरविचेष्टनैः—सिन्धोः तन्नामकस्य नदस्य तीरे यानि विचेष्टनानि अङ्गपरिवर्त्तनानि (श्रमान्ते अश्वानां रीतिरियम्) तैः।

दुधुवुर्वाजिनः स्कन्धांल्लग्नकुङ्कुमकेसरान् ॥६७॥
तत्र हूणावरोधानां भर्तृषु व्यक्तविक्रमम्।
*कपोलपाटलादेशि बभूव रघुचेष्टितम् ॥६८॥

तीरे विचेष्टनैः अङ्गपरिवर्त्तनैः, विनीताध्वश्रमाः, तस्य रघोः, वाजिनः अश्वाः, लग्नाः कुङ्कुमकेसराः कुङ्कुमकुसुमकिञ्जल्काः येषां तान्, यद्वा लग्नकुङ्कुमाः केसराः सटाः येषां तान्, "केसरो नागकेसरे, तुरङ्गसिंहयोः स्कन्धकेशेषु वकुलद्रुमे। पुन्नागवृक्षे किञ्जल्के स्यात्" इति हैमः, स्कन्धान् कायान्, दुधुवुः कम्पयन्ति स्म ॥६७॥

तत्रेति। तत्र उदीच्यां दिशि, भर्तृषु व्यक्तविक्रमं भर्तृवधेन स्फुटपराक्रमम् इत्यर्थः, रघुचेष्टितं रघुव्यापारः, हूणाः जनपदाख्याः, क्षत्रियाः, तेषाम् अवरोधाः अन्तःपुरस्त्रियः, तासां कपोलेषु पाटलस्य पाटलिम्नः, ताड़नादिकृतारुण्यस्य आदेशि उपदेशकं बभूव, अथवा पाटलः आदेशी आदेष्टा यस्य तत् बभूव ; स्वयं व्याख्यास्यते इत्यर्थः ॥६८॥

দূর করিয়া কুঙ্কুম-রেণুময়-কেশরজাল ঝাড়িতে লাগিল ॥ ৬৭ ॥

সেই দেশে রঘু হূণ জাতীয় পুরুষদিগকে হত্যা করিয়া তাহাদের অন্তঃপুরবাসিনী নারীদিগের কপোল যুগল পাটল বর্ণ করিলেন ॥ ৬৮ ॥

river Indus. his horses lessened their fatigue, and shook off from their manes, the sweat- scented dust of *Kum-kum*.

68. The doings of Raghu in those regions had the effect of making the cheeks of *Hun*-women pale, on account of the fate that their husbands met with at his hands.

कपोलपाटलादेशि—कपोलयोः पाटलवर्णस्य आदेशि, पाण्डुतापादकमित्यर्थः ; भर्तृवियोगात् हूणरमणीनां मुखमण्डलं म्लानमासीदित्यर्थः।

কাম্বোজাঃ সমরে সোঢ়ুং তস্য বীর্য্যমনীশ্বরাঃ।
গজালানপরিক্লিষ্টৈরক্ষোটৈঃ সার্দ্ধমানতাঃ ॥৬৯॥
তেষাং সদশ্বভূয়িষ্ঠাস্তুঙ্গা দ্রবিণরাশয়ঃ।
উপদা বিবিশুঃ শশ্বৎ নোৎসেকাঃ কোশলেশ্বরম্॥৭০॥

কাম্বোজা ইতি। কাম্বোজাঃ রাজানঃ, সমরে তস্য রঘোঃ, বীর্য্যং প্রভাবম্, সোঢুম্ অনীশ্বরাঃ অসমর্থাঃ সন্তঃ গজানাম্ আলানং বন্ধনম্ ভাবে ল্যুটি বিভাষা লীয়তেরিত্যাত্বম্, তেন পরিক্লিষ্টৈঃ পরিক্ষতৈঃ অক্ষোটৈঃ বৃক্ষবিশেষৈঃ সার্দ্ধম্ আনতাঃ ॥ ৬৯ ॥

তেষামিতি। তেষাং কাম্বোজানাং, সদ্ভিঃ অশ্বৈঃ ভূয়িষ্ঠাঃ বহুলাঃ তুঙ্গাঃ দ্রবিণানাং হিরণ্যানাম্, রাশয়ঃ এব উপদাঃ উপায়নানি, কোশলেশ্বরং কোশলদেশাধিপতিং তং রঘুং শশ্বৎ অসকৃৎ বিবিশুঃ, তথাপি উৎসেকাঃ গর্ব্বাস্তু ন বিবিশুঃ, সত্যপি গর্ব্বকারণে ন অগর্ব্ব ইত্যর্থঃ ॥ ৭০ ॥

কাম্বোজদেশীয় রাজগণ যুদ্ধে তাঁহার বিক্রম সহ্য করিতে পারিল না; সুতরাং গজ সকল বাঁধিয়া রাখাতে তাহাদের অক্ষোট বৃক্ষ সকল যেমন নত হইতে লাগিল, তাহারাও রঘুর সমীপে তেমনি নত হইল ॥৬৯॥

কাম্বোজবাসিগণ উৎকৃষ্ট উৎকৃষ্ট অশ্ব ও রাশি রাশি ধন রত্ন বার বার রঘুকে উপহার দিতে লাগিল, কিন্তু তথাপি তাঁহার গর্ব্ব জন্মিল না ॥ ৭০ ॥

---

69. The *Kamboja* princes unable to withstand his valour, bent down, along with *akshota* trees, with which the elephants were tied.

70. These princes presented to him beautiful horses, and also hoards of gold, yet pride never entered his soul.

ततो गौरीगुरुं शैलम् आरुरोहाश्वसाधनः।
वर्द्धयन्निव तत्कूटान् उद्धूतैर्धातुरेणुभिः॥ ৭১ ॥

शशंस *तुल्यसत्त्वानां सैन्यघोषेऽप्यसम्भ्रमम्।
गुहाशयानां सिंहानां परिवृत्यावलोकितम्॥৭২॥

तत इति। ततः अनन्तरम्, अश्वसाधनः सन्, गौर्याः गुरुं पितरं शैलं हिमवन्तम्, उद्धूतैः अश्वखुरोद्धूतैः, धातूनां गैरिकादीनां रेणुभिः, तत्कूटान् तस्य शृङ्गाणि, वर्द्धयन् इव आरुरोह। उद्धूतधूलिदर्शनाद्गिरिशिखरवृद्धिभ्रमो जायते इति भावः॥ ৭১॥

शशंसेति। तुल्यसत्त्वानां सैन्यैः समानबलानां, गुहासु शेरते इति गुहाशयाः तेषाम्, सिंहानां हरीणाम् सम्बन्धि, परिवृत्य परावृत्य,

অনন্তর অশ্বারোহী সৈন্য সমভিব্যাহারে তিনি হিমালয় শিখরে আরোহণ করিলেন; অশ্বখুরাঘাতে ধাতুময় ধূলিপটল উত্থিত হওয়াতে এরূপ বোধ হইতে লাগিল, যেন ঐ গিরির শিখর-শ্রেণী আরও উচ্চ হইয়া উঠিল॥ ৭১॥

গুহাশায়ী ও তুল্যবলশালী সিংহগণ সৈন্যদলের কল কল ধ্বনি শ্রবণ করিয়াও বিন্দুমাত্র ভীত হইল না, কেবল মাত্র গ্রীবা ফিরাইয়া একবার দৃষ্টিপাত করিল; ইহা দেখিয়া তিনি তাহাদের সাহসের প্রশংসা করিলেন॥ ৭২॥

71. Then he mounted the Himalayas, increasing the height of their peaks, as it were, by the hill-dust raised by his army.

72. The lions simply turned their necks and looked without the least fear, on his noisy army, thus betokening the equal might that lay in them.

*तुल्यसत्त्वानां—समानबलशालिनाम्।

भूर्जेषु मर्मरीभूताः कीचकध्वनिहेतवः ।
गङ्गाशीकरिणो मार्गे मरुतस्तं सिषेविरे ॥७३॥
विशश्रमुर्नमेरूणां छायास्वध्यास्य सैनिकाः ।

अवलोकितं शयित्वैव क्षोभभङ्गेनावलोकनं, कर्त्तृ सैन्यक्षोभे सेनाकलकले सञ्जनकारणे सत्यपि असञ्जनम् अन्तःक्षोभविरहितम्, शशंस कथयामास। सैन्येभ्य इत्यर्थाल्लभ्यते। बाह्यचेष्टितमेव मनोवृत्तेरनुमापकम् इति भावः। असञ्जनान्तत्वे हेतुः सुखसञ्जातमिति। न हि ममबलः स्वबलाद्बिभेति इति भावः॥ ७२॥

भूर्जेष्विति। भूर्जेषु भूर्जपत्रेषु, मर्मरः शुष्कपर्णध्वनिः, अयञ्च शुक्लादिशब्दवद्गुणिनि वर्त्तते यथोच्यते च मर्मरैरगुरुधूपगन्धिभिरिति अतः मर्मरीभूताः मर्मरशब्दवन्तो भूताः इत्यर्थः, कीचकानां वेणुविशेषाणां ध्वनिहेतवः, शीतलत्वाश्च इति भावः, गङ्गाशीकरिणः शीतलाः इत्यर्थः, मरुतः वाताः मार्गे तं सिषेविरे॥ ७२॥

विशश्रमुरिति। सैनिकाः सेनायां समवेताः, नमेरूणां सुरपुन्ना-

গঙ্গাতরঙ্গের কণাবাহী বায়ু প্রবাহিত হওয়াতে কোথাও বা ভূর্জ্জ-পত্রের বনে মর্ম্মর শব্দ হইতে লাগিল, কোথাও বা বংশ-রন্ধ্রে প্রবিষ্ট হইয়া বংশীর ধ্বনি উৎপাদন করিতে লাগিল ; সেই বায়ু তাঁহাকে সেবা করিতে লাগিল ॥ ৭৩ ॥

সৈনিকগণ নমেরু বৃক্ষের ছায়াতে কস্তুরী মৃগের নাভিগন্ধদ্বারা

---

73. The soft breezes of the river Ganges rustled on among the dry leaves of the *bhurja* trees making the wild bamboo resound and refreshed him on the way.

74. Seated in the shades of *nameru* trees, on pieces of

दृषदो *वासितोत्सङ्गा निषण्णमृगनाभिभिः ॥৭৪॥

सरलासक्तमातङ्गग्रैवेयस्फुरितत्विषः ।
आसन्नोषधयो नेतुः नक्तमस्नेहदीपिकाः ॥৭৫॥

गानां छायासु निषण्णानां दृषदुपविष्टानां मृगाणां कस्तूरीमृगाणां नाभिभिः वासितोत्सङ्गाः, सुरभिततलाः, दृषदः शिलाः अध्यास्य अधिष्ठाय दृषत्सु अधिरुह्य इत्यर्थः, विशश्रमुः विश्रान्ताः ॥ ৭৪ ॥

सरलेति । सरलेषु देवदारुविशेषेषु आसक्तानि यानि मातङ्गानां गजानां ग्रीवासु भवानि ग्रैवेयाणि कण्ठशृङ्खलानि, तेषु स्फुरितत्विषः प्रतिफलितभासः, ओषधयः ज्वलन्त्यो ज्योतिर्लताविशेषाः नक्तं रात्रौ, नेतुः नायकस्य रघोः अस्नेहदीपिकाः तैलनिरपेक्षाः प्रदीपाः आसन् ॥ ৭৫ ॥

সুরভীকৃত প্রস্তরের উপরে বসিয়া বিশ্রাম লাভ করিতে লাগিল ॥ ৭৪ ॥

সরল বৃক্ষের শাখাতে হস্তিগণের শৃঙ্খল বাঁধা ছিল ; রাত্রিকালে প্রজ্বলিত ওষধিগণের দীপ্তিমালা ঐ সকল শৃঙ্খলে প্রতিফলিত হইয়া তাঁহার প্রদীপের কার্য্য করিতে লাগিল ॥ ৭৫ ॥

stone, made fragrant by the musk-deer, his soldiers took their rest.

75. His elephants were tied by chains to the *sarala* trees, and a peculiar glow came out of them and of similar plants during the night, all of which served the purpose of lamps without oil.

* वासितोत्सङ्गाः — वासितः सुरभीकृतः उत्सङ्गः क्रोडो येषां ते ।

तस्योत्सृष्टनिवासेषु कण्ठरज्जुक्षतत्वचः ।
गजवर्ष्म किरातेभ्यः शशंसुर्देवदारवः ॥ ७६ ॥
तत्र जन्यं रघोर्घोरं पर्वतीयैर्गणैरभूत् ।
नाराचक्षेपणीयाश्म-निष्पेषोत्पतितानलम् ॥ ७७ ॥

तस्येति । तस्य रघोः, उत्सृष्टेषु उज्झितेषु, निवासेषु सेनानिवेशेषु, कण्ठरज्जुभिः गजग्रैवैः क्षताः निघृष्टाः त्वचः येषां ते देवदारवः, किरातेभ्यः वनचरेभ्यः, गजानां वर्ष्म प्रमाणम्, शशंसुः कथितवन्तः, देवदारुस्कन्धलग्नकक्षतैर्गजानामौन्नत्यमनुमीयते इत्यर्थः ॥ ७६ ॥

तत्रेति । तत्र हिमाद्रौ, रघोः पर्वते भवैः पर्वतीयैः, गणैः, उत्सवसङ्केताख्यैः सप्तभिः ("गणानुत्सवसङ्केतान् अजयत् सप्त पाण्डवः" इति महाभारते,) नाराचानां वाणविशेषाणां क्षेपणीयानां भिन्दिपालानाम्, अश्मनाञ्च निष्पेषेण सङ्घर्षेण उत्पतिताः अनलाः यस्मिन् तत् तथोक्तम्, घोरं भीमं जन्यं युद्धम्, अभूत् ॥ ७७ ॥

তিনি কোন সেনা-নিবেশ-স্থান পরিত্যাগ করিয়া গেলে পর, ব্যাধেরা বৃক্ষদেহে গজ-বন্ধনের রজ্জুর দাগ দেখিয়া তাঁহার গজ সকলের উচ্চতার অনুমান করিতে লাগিল ॥ ৭৬ ॥

সেখানে পার্ব্বতীয় জাতিগণের সহিত রঘুর ঘোর যুদ্ধ হইল। তাঁহার বাণে ও পার্ব্বতীয়গণ কর্ত্তৃক প্রক্ষিপ্ত পাষাণময় অস্ত্রে সংঘর্ষণ হইয়া অগ্ন্যুৎপাত হইতে লাগিল ॥ ৭৭ ॥

---

76. After he had left a place of encampment, by the scars on their barks made by the tying chains of the elephants, the fir trees indicated to the foresters the height of those animals.

77. His battle with the hill-tribes was a terrible one, throwing off sparks of fire as the arrows and the swords clashed vehemently against the stones.

शरैरुत्सवसङ्केतान् स कृत्वा *विरतोत्सवान्।
जयोदाहरणं बाह्वोः गापयामास किन्नरान्॥৭৮॥
परस्परेण विज्ञातस्तेषूपायनपाणिषु।
राज्ञा हिमवतः सारः राज्ञः सारो हिमाद्रिणा॥৭৯

शरैरिति। सः रघुः शरैः बाणैः, उत्सवसङ्केतान् नाम गणान्, विरतोत्सवान् कृत्वा जित्वा इत्यर्थः किन्नरान् बाह्वोः स्वभुजयोः जयोदाहरणं, जयख्यापकं प्रबन्धविशेषं गापयामास ॥ ৭৮ ॥

परस्परेणेति। तेषु गणेषु, उपायनयुक्ताः पाणयः येषां तेषु सत्सु, परस्परेण अन्योन्यं, राज्ञा हिमवतः सारः धनरूपः विज्ञातः; हिमाद्रिणा अपि राज्ञः सारः बलरूपः विज्ञातः, एतेन तत्रत्य-वस्तूनामनर्घत्वं गणानामभूतपूर्वस्य पराजय इति ध्वन्यते ॥ ৭৯ ॥

রঘু বাণ দ্বারা উৎসব-সংকেত নামক জাতিকে উৎসব-হীন করিয়া কিন্নরগণের দ্বারা নিজ বাহুর জয়-গান করাইলেন ॥ ৭৮ ॥

সেই পার্ব্বতীয় জাতি সকল যখন উপঢৌকন হস্তে লইয়া আসিতে লাগিল, তখন রঘু হিমালয়ে যে পদার্থ আছে তাহা বুঝিতে পারিলেন, হিমালয়ও তাঁহার সারবত্তা বিশেষ রূপে অনুভব করিল ॥ ৭৯ ॥

78. After having made cheerless the tribe of *utsavsanketas*, by his arrows, he caused the *Kinnaras* to sing his glory.

79. When the *utsavasanketa* princes brought their presents to him, his prowess became known to the great mountain, and its wealth became known to him.

*विरतोत्सवान्—विरताः प्रशमिताः उत्सवाः आनन्दजनकव्यापाराः नृत्यगीतादयः येषां ते विरतोत्सवास्तान्; पराभवपीड़या विपन्नान् इत्यर्थः।

तत्राक्षोभ्यं यशोराशिं निवेश्यावरुरोह सः ।
*पौलस्त्यतुलितस्याद्रेः आदधान इव ह्रियम् ॥८०॥
चकम्पे तीर्णलौहित्ये तस्मिन् प्राग्ज्योतिषेश्वरः ।
तद्गजालानतां प्राप्तैः सह कालागुरुद्रुमैः ॥८१॥

तत्रेति । सः रघुः तत्र हिमाद्रौ अक्षोभ्यम् अक्षुण्णं, यशोराशिं निवेश्य निधाय पौलस्त्येन रावणेन तुलितस्य, चालितस्य, अद्रेः कैलासस्य, ह्रियम् आदधानः जनयन् इव अवरुरोह अवततार ; कैलासमगत्वैव प्रतिनिवृत्तः इत्यर्थः । न हि शूराः परेण पराजितमभियुञ्जन्ते इति भावः ॥ ८० ॥

चकम्प इति । तस्मिन् रघौ तीर्णा लौहित्या नाम नदी, येन तस्मिन् तीर्णलौहित्ये सति प्राग्ज्योतिषाणां जनपदानाम् ईश्वरः.

রঘু সেই হিমাদ্রিশিখরে চিরস্থায়ী কীর্ত্তি স্থাপন পূর্ব্বক কৈলাস পর্ব্বতে না গিয়া অবতরণ করিলেন ॥ ৮০ ॥

লৌহিত্যা নামক নদী পার হইয়া তিনি প্রাগ্জ্যোতিষ প্রদেশে গিয়া কালাগুরু ক্রমে যখন গজ সকল বন্ধন করিতে লাগিলেন, তখন সেই প্রদেশের রাজা ঐ সকল কালাগুরু বৃক্ষের ন্যায় কাঁপিতে লাগিলেন ॥৮১॥

80. He descended from the mountains after having established his spotless fame, causing the rival mountain of *Kailasa* to blush, as it were.

81. When he crossed the river *Lohitya*, the King of Pragjyotish began to quake with fear along with Kalaguru trees to which his elephants were tied.

*पौलस्त्यतुलितस्य—पुरा किल कैलासो रावणेन चालित आसीत् इति रामायणे द्रष्टव्यम् ।

न प्रसेहे स रुद्धार्कम् अधारावर्षदुर्दिनम् ।
रथवर्त्मरजोऽप्यस्य कुत एव पताकिनीम् ॥८२॥

तस्य रघोः गजानाम् आलानतां प्राप्तैः कालागुरुद्रुमैः कृष्णागुरुवृक्षैः, सह चकम्पे कम्पितवान् ॥ ८१ ॥

नेति । सः प्राग्ज्योतिषेश्वरः रुद्धार्कम् आवृतसूर्य्यम्, अधारावर्षञ्च तत् दुर्दिनञ्च धारावर्षं विना दुर्दिनभूतम्, अस्य रघोः रथवर्त्मरजः, अपि न प्रसेहे पताकिनीं सेनां कुत एव प्रसेहे न कुतोऽपि इत्यर्थः ॥ ८२ ॥

প্রাগ্‌জ্যোতিষ দেশের রাজা, সূর্য্যমণ্ডলের আবরণকারী, বৃষ্টিবিহীন দুর্দ্দিনের ন্যায় প্রতীয়মান, রঘুর রথবর্ত্মের ধূলিও সহ্য করিতে পারিলেন না, তাঁহার সেনার পরাক্রম কি করিয়া সহ্য করিবেন? ॥ ৮২ ॥

82. He could not bear even the dust raised by his chariots which spread over the sky like thick showerless clouds, far less his invading army.

---

* अधारावर्ष-दुर्दिनं—धारायाः वृष्टिधारायाः वर्षः वर्षणं न विद्यते यत्र अधारावर्षं, अधारावर्षं दुर्दिनं—अधारावर्ष-दुर्दिनम् । Generally a दुर्दिनं is characterized by costant down pour of rain; but as Raghu advanced with his vast army, the clouds of dust completely covered the sun, so that there were all the signs of a day of weather with the exception of a downpour.

तमीशः कामरूपाणाम् *अत्याखण्डलविक्रमम् ।
भेजे भिन्नकटैर्नागैरन्यानुपरुरोध यैः ॥ ८३ ॥
कामरूपेश्वरस्तस्य हेमपीठाधिदेवताम् ।
रत्नपुष्पोपहारेण छायामानर्च पादयोः ॥ ८४ ॥

तमिति । कामरूपाणां नाम देशानाम् ईशः अत्याखण्डलविक्रमम्, अतीन्द्रपराक्रमं तं रघुं, भिन्नाः स्रवन्मदाः कटाः गण्डाः येषां तैः, नागैः गजैः, साधनैः भेजे, नागान् दत्त्वा शरणं गतः इत्यर्थः । कीदृशैर्नागैः ? यैः अन्यान् रघुव्यतिरिक्तान् नृपान् उपरुरोध । शूराणामपि शूरो रघुः इति भावः ॥ ८३ ॥

कामरूपेश्वर इति । कामरूपेश्वरः हेमपीठस्य अधिदेवतां तस्य

কামরূপেশ্বর যে সকল প্রবল হস্তিকুলের দ্বারা অন্যান্য রাজাকে পরাভব করিয়াছিলেন, সেই সকল মদমত্ত হস্তী উপহার লইয়া রঘুর নিকট উপস্থিত হইলেন ॥ ৮৩ ॥

কামরূপেশ্বর রঘুর স্বর্ণ নির্ম্মিত পীঠস্থিত পদ ছায়াতে রত্নাদি অর্পণ দ্বারা পূজা করিলেন ॥ ৮৪ ॥

83. The king of *Kamrupa*, who had successfully withstood other conquerors with his elephants paid homage to Raghu with those elephants of streaming temples,—Raghu, who was greater in valour than Indra himself.

84. The king of *Kamrupa* worshipped the shadow of his feet placed on golden foot-stool, with the offering of flowers and precious stones.

* अत्याखण्डलविक्रमम्—अतिक्रान्तः आखण्डलस्य इन्द्रस्य विक्रमो येन, स अत्याखण्डल-विक्रमः तम् । इन्द्रबलातीतबलमित्यर्थः ।

इति जित्वा दिशो जिष्णुर्न्यवर्त्तत रथोद्धतम् ।
रजो विश्रामयन् राज्ञां छत्रशून्येषु मौलिषु ॥८५॥
स विश्वजितमाजह्रे यज्ञं सर्वस्वदक्षिणम् ।
*आदानं हि विसर्गाय सतां वारिमुचामिव ॥८६॥

रघोः पादयोः छायां कनकमयपादपीठव्यापिनीं कान्तिं रत्नानि एव पुष्पाणि तेषाम् उपहारेण समर्पणेन आनर्च अर्चयामास ॥ ८४ ॥

इतीति। जिष्णुः जयशीलः सः रघुः, इति इत्थं, दिशः जित्वा, रथैः उद्धतं रजः, छत्रशून्येषु रघोरेकच्छत्रकत्वात् इति भावः, राज्ञां मौलिषु किरीटेषु, विश्रामयन् संक्रामयन् इत्यर्थः, न्यवर्त्तत निवृत्तः॥८५॥

स इति। सः रघुः सर्व्वस्वं दक्षिणा यस्य तं सर्वस्वदक्षिणम्, विश्वजित् नाम यज्ञम् आजह्रे कृतवान् इत्यर्थः। युक्तञ्चैतदित्याह,

এইরূপে রঘু সমুদয় দেশ জয় করিয়া নিজ রথ হইতে উৎক্ষিপ্ত ধূলি পটলকে রাজাদিগের ছত্রবিহীন মস্তকে স্থাপন পূর্ব্বক প্রতিনিবৃত্ত হইলেন ॥ ৮৫ ॥

সেই রঘু বিশ্বজিৎ নামে যজ্ঞ সমাপন করিলেন ; ঐ যজ্ঞের দক্ষিণা-

85. Thus having finished his conquest the conqueror returned home making the dust of his chariots on the uncovered heads of princes.

86. He performed Biswajit sacrifice, of which the gifts were all that a man might possess ; good men collect taxes only to give away in charity in copious showers like clouds.

---

* आदानं हि विसर्गाय—विसर्गाय दानाय, आदानं ग्रहणं—Compare this passage, सहस्रगुणमुत्स्रष्टुमादत्ते हि रसं रविरिति, 18th, श्लोक, 1St सर्गः ।

सत्रान्ते सचिवसखः पुरस्क्रियाभिः
गुर्वीभिः शमितपराजयव्यलीकान् ।
काकुत्स्थश्चिरविरहोत्सुकावरोधान्
राजन्यान् स्वपुरनिवृत्तयेऽनुमेने ॥८७॥

सतां साधूनां, वारिमुचां मेघानाम् इव, आदानम् अर्जनं विसर्गाय त्यागाय हि पात्रविनियोगाय इत्यर्थः ॥ ८६ ॥

सत्रान्त इति । काकुत्स्थः रघुः, सत्रान्ते यज्ञान्ते सचिवानाम अमात्यानां सखा इति सचिवसखः सन्, तेषामत्यन्तानुसरणद्योतनार्थं, राज्ञः सचिवत्वव्यपदेशः । गुर्वीभिः महतीभिः, पुरस्क्रियाभिः पूजाभिः, शमितं पराजयेन व्यलीकं दुःखं वैलक्ष्यं वा येषां तान्, चिरविरहेण उत्सुकाः उत्कण्ठिताः, अवरोधाः अन्तःपुराङ्गनाः, येषां तान्, राज्ञः अपत्यानि राजन्याः क्षत्रियाः तान्, स्वपुरं प्रति निवृत्तये प्रति गमनाय अनुमेने अनुज्ञातवान् ॥ ८७ ॥

সৎপাত্রে সর্ব্বস্ব দান করিলেন, মেঘ যেমন বর্ষণ করিবার জন্যই শোষণ করে, সেইরূপ সাধুগণ দান করিবার জন্যই গ্রহণ করেন ॥ ৮৬ ॥

যজ্ঞ শেষ হইলে রঘু মন্ত্রী সমভিব্যাহারে নানা প্রকারের সম্মান ও সন্তোষের চিহ্ন সকল প্রদান পূর্ব্বক রাজগণের পরাজয় ক্ষোভ দূর করিয়া, তাঁহাদের পত্নীগণের বিরহোৎকণ্ঠা নিবারণের নিমিত্ত তাঁহাদিগকে স্বদেশে প্রত্যাবৃত্ত হইবার জন্য অনুমতি করিলেন ॥ ৮৭ ॥

87. After the sacrifice Raghu, with his ministers, honoured the princes with substantial tokens of respect which mitigated to a large extent their sense of defeat, and he ordered them to return to their wives who were anxiously longing for them after long and painful separation.

ते रेखाध्वजकुलिशातपत्रचिह्नं
सम्राजश्चरणयुगं प्रसादलभ्यम् ।
प्रस्थानप्रणतिभिरङ्गुलीषु चक्रुः
मौलिस्रक्च्युतमकरन्दरेणुगौरम् ॥ ८८ ॥

इति श्रीरघुवंशे महाकाव्ये कालिदासकृतौ
रघुदिग्विजयो नाम चतुर्थः सर्गः ।

त इति । ते राजानः रेखाः एव ध्वजाश्च कुलिशानि च आतपत्राणि च ध्वजाद्याकाररेखाः इत्यर्थः, तानि चिह्नानि यस्य तत् तथोक्तं, प्रसादेन एव लभ्यं प्रसादलभ्यं, सम्राजः सार्वभौमस्य रघोः चरणयुगं, प्रस्थाने प्रयाणसमये याः प्रणतयः नमस्काराः ताभिः, करणैः, अङ्गुलीषु मौलिषु केशबन्धनेषु याः स्रजः, माल्यानि, ताभ्यः च्युतैः मकरन्दैः पुष्परसैः, रेणुभिः परागैश्च, गौरं गौरवर्णं चक्रुः ॥ ८८ ॥

इति श्रीमहामहोपाध्याय कोलाचलमल्लिनाथ-सूरिविरचितायां
रघुवंशटीकायां सञ्जीवनीसमाख्यायां चतुर्थः सर्गः ।

তাহারা সম্রাটের ধ্বজ বজ্রাঙ্কুশ চিহ্ন শোভিত চরণ-যুগলে প্রণত হইয়া শিরঃস্থিত মালার পরাগরেণুর দ্বারা তাঁহার চরণাঙ্গুলিকে গৌর বর্ণ করিতে লাগিলেন ॥ ৮৮ ॥

88. Those princes when bowing at his feet bearing the marks of flag, thunder and umbrella at the time of their departure made his toes covered with the dust of the flowers of their crowns.

FINIS.